MW01470719

Christian Theology of Public Policy

Highlighting the American Experience

For Duane Lindsey
Soldier for liberty & Truth —
Prov. 23:23

John M. Cobin, Ph.D.
4-8-06

Alertness Books
Greenville, South Carolina

Copyright © John M. Cobin 2006

All rights reserved. No part of this publication may be re-produced, stored in a retrieval system, or transmitted in any form or by any means, electronic, mechanical, photocopying, digital, recording or otherwise without the prior written permission of the author.

Published by
Alertness Ltd.
P.O. Box 25686
Greenville, SC 29616 USA
phone: +1-866-492-2137
fax: +1-413-622-9441
email: alertness@policyofliberty.net

Library of Congress Control Number: 2005910661
Publisher's Cataloging-in-Publication Data
Cobin John M., 1963-
Christian Theology of Public Policy: Highlighting the American Experience / by John M. Cobin
Includes bibliography, footnotes and index.
ISBN 0-9729754-9-7 (hardback)
ISBN 0-9729754-0-3 (electronic book/CD)
ISBN 0-9729754-1-1 (Spanish electronic book/CD)
1. Theology—Practical. 2. Bible—Civil Government. 3. Economic policy. 4. Public Policy. 5. Political Oppression. 6. Civil Government—History. 7. Torture. 8. Apostle Paul—Teachings. 9. Apostle Peter—Teachings. 10. Welfare State. 11. Nationalism. 12. Revolution. 13. Second Amendment. 14. Slavery I. Title II. Cobin, John M. HD87.C632 2006

Contents

iv

Acknowledgments

I wish to thank the chief editors of this work: my assiduous wife Lesle Long Cobin, M.D. and my reliable friend Chuck Fields for proofreading drafts. They made excellent observations about the organization, readability, and logic of the text, as well as helping with the subject index and the cover design. I would also like to thank my good friend Gregg Farrier for helping to compile the bibliography and the subject index, as well as reviewing the text and finding useful sources for some longer quotations. My children Grace Cobin and Matthew Cobin helped me compile the Scripture and subject indices. Seth Farrier was responsible for the initial mapping out the inspiring cover design. Mark Cochran, another pre-publication reader, did the lion's share of the cove's preparation and mixed the audio files associated with the main portions of this book (recording most of the content of chapters 1 through 15).

Several other folks also did a great service to me by reading drafts of the text, looking for grammatical errors and challenging me on the logic of certain arguments, making the final result far better: Dr. Dan Olinger, Professor of Theology and Bible at Bob Jones University; Dr. Paul Dean, Jr., radio talk show host of "Calling for Truth" (Providence Ministries) and Pastor of Providence Baptist

Church in Greer, South Carolina; Dr. Steven Yates, adjunct Professor of Philosophy in upstate South Carolina; Dr. Michael Hill, adjunct Professor of History and President of the League of the South; Dr. D. Eric Schansberg, Professor of Economics at Indiana University (New Albany) School of Business; Dr. Laurence M. Vance, Director of the Francis Wayland Institute; Robert Hayes, Director of the South Carolina League of the South; and Jeff Petric, a deacon at Woodruff Road Presbyterian Church in Simpsonville, South Carolina. Joyce Worthington and Mark Molinari did some minor proofreading too and helped check through the subject index.

Other interested pre-publication readers appreciated by the author (many of whom will likely be writing reviews of the book) included: Dr. David Black, professor of New Testament and Greek at Southeastern Baptist Theological Seminary; Dr. Tim Terrell, Professor of Economics at Wofford College; Dr. Nick Wilburn, Professor at Greenville Presbyterian Theological Seminary; and Carl D. Robbins, Pastor of Woodruff Road Presbyterian Church in Simpsonville, South Carolina.

Editor's Foreword

Should you read this book? Perhaps you are a Christian who believes or suspects that today's public policies are wrong, or at least harmful to Christians. You would like to understand better what the Bible, informed by logic, history, economics, and political science, teaches about citizenship and what kind of society is best for Christians. If so you will find this book interesting and useful.

You might first ask yourself, as I have, if public policy is a proper pursuit for a Christian. D. Martyn Lloyd-Jones, in his early preaching at Sandfields, said "Many churches these days make a new member sign a pledge of total abstinence from alcoholic liquors. Now I do not believe in pledges of any sort..., but there are times when I almost feel like advocating that all members should sign another pledge, and that is, 'a pledge of total abstinence from politics', for I believe that is causing greater harm in our churches these days than almost anything else."[1] Let us consider some reasons this champion of our faith would say such a thing, for the study of public policy is a path to be walked with care.

---

[1] Iain H. Murray (1982), *David Martyn Lloyd-Jones: The First Forty Years*, Carlisle, Pennsylvania: The Banner of Truth Trust, p. 143.

Politics Many Christians find politics dirty, and filled with men of low character. The American founding fathers saw what today passes for politics as the evil of faction. This book agrees with both positions. We must be about truth, not faction, and while this book should cause you to question your favorite political party, it is not intended to steer you toward any particular party. Lloyd-Jones objected to his parishioners' pursuit of socialism as a way to achieve the social aims of the Bible. Many Christians today want to use the state to enforce godliness among all citizens. This book will show that Christians are mistaken to seek alliance with the state, as it is not to be trusted. A state powerful enough to enforce godliness is also able to forbid it.

Distraction While the church must live in the world, we are warned against being of the world. Our primary concern must be to glorify God and to spread the gospel. Nevertheless, the body of Christ consists of many parts.[2] While many will teach, serve the body, and minister to the unfortunate, there is a role to be played by *some* Christians in fending off the enemies of God, chiefly the state.

Resistance to tyrants may seem a distraction. What about working long hours to be able to pay for necessities when up to half of that work is lost to onerous taxes, and made less efficient by heavy regulation? What if a child who was raised with care in the admonition of God's Word is lost in a senseless war? Are these any less distracting? Please consider that while we obviously may not all spend time resisting tyrants, the efforts of a few may profit us all. We should at least be aware of who our friends and our enemies are in the public sector.

We are blessed by God with the means of defense—and at least a few members willing to take an interest in this subject. If you have this interest, consider that it may

---

[2] 1 Corinthians 12:12-31

be a gift from God for use in defending his church but beware making an idol of earthly power.

Bitterness This book may open your eyes to the evils that form much of public policy. You risk bitterness toward those in authority, but please keep in mind that they are ordained by God for his purposes, and in God's economy their sins are no worse than our own. We all need God's grace every day and should be grateful that he supplies it.

So should you read this book? By all means! But pray first for deliverance from three snares: politics, distraction from first things, and bitterness towards authority.

—Charles Fields, Greenville, SC

Economist's Foreword

Have you ever played the game Taboo? It's a great party game. One person has to get his group of people to say words, but he's not allowed to say certain "taboo" words. Of course, the forbidden words are typically the words one would most likely use for such a task. The funniest part is when the person blurts out a forbidden word and then catches himself a moment too late. One of the lessons of Taboo: "think before you talk".

Have you ever known someone who is impulsive? They often make trivial and critical decisions without thinking through the ramifications. They don't seem to do any sort of conscious or unconscious cost-benefit analysis. And they consistently regret their decisions, bemoaning consequences that they fail to anticipate but most others foresee. They are a living, breathing example of a famous dictum: "think before you act".

Have you ever heard a pastor describe sex as a wonderful God-given gift before exhorting his congregation to avoid sexual immorality by comparing sex to dynamite? He'll note that both are powerful, but outside of their proper use and context, they will both cause incredible damage.

Think before you talk. Think before you act. Embrace powerful means but use them properly. All of these are great lessons for life. Sadly, these great lessons have not yet been learned by most Christians in their approach to government. Too little thought has preceded ill-informed action. Christians embrace government even when it is inconsistent with the ministry model of Christ and other Biblical principles. Christians advocate government when it is an impractical means to the desired ends, often because of unintended consequences they fail to anticipate. Worst of all, some Christians unknowingly fall into idolatry of the State—imagining that we should look to the State first for sustenance, security, and solutions.

In evangelical circles, a range of errors emerge—sins of omission and commission. Some believers are apathetic, with little concern for the most pressing problems of our world. As a bumper sticker reminds us, "If you're not angry, you're not paying attention". There are gross injustices in our world that are ignored by the vast majority of Christians—from the atrocities of Darfur to our own government's redistribution from the poor to the non-poor. In other circles, zeal and passion are not at all lacking. But the focus is too limited, emphasizing certain important issues while ignoring or downplaying others of equivalent significance. Sins of commission abound as well. Again, zeal is no problem, but government activism turns out to be an unbiblical and otherwise impractical means to the ends desired.

There are two primary matters at the heart of this sad state of affairs. First, there is a theological failure—incoherency in terms of one's approach to Scripture in general or what the Bible says about government in particular. On the latter, it is quite common for Christians to believe that their political beliefs emanate from Scripture. Instead, they are engaged in an implied eisegesis, deriving their politics from their culture, background, and other secular influences—and then dressing their views up in pseudo-biblical clothing. Second, there is a technical ignorance of political economy—a failure to understand basic economics, basic political theory, and the historical practice of government activism in the economic and social realms.

Of course, at some level, ignorance here is quite excusable. Christians, like virtually everyone else, are busy mowing their lawns and raising their kids. Most people don't want to invest the relevant energy to have an informed view. That's fine. But given the power of government and the warnings throughout Scripture about government, wisdom demands ample doses of humility and caution in embracing government as a prospective tool. For those who want to move beyond ignorance, Alertness Books stands at the ready, hoping to inform believers about government with the goal of forming a consistent Christian philosophy of government. We hope that you'll join us for the ride.

—D. Eric Schansberg, Ph.D.[3] (January 2006)

---

[3] Professor of Economics, Indiana University Southeast; Visiting Professor of Economics, The King's College; Author of *Turn Neither to the Right nor to the Left: A Thinking Christian's Guide to Politics and Public Policy* (Alertness Books, 2003).

Pastor's Foreword

A special word to Baptists and other Christians

In this bold work, Baptists will find their nationalistic ideas counted treasonous to Christ by their forefathers in the faith. Neoconservatives will find their blind commitment to contemporary Republicanism to be liberal in the eyes of the American Founding Fathers. Christians in general will find that much of what they embrace runs counter to the biblical and foundational concepts of justice and liberty for all.

Long held notions concerning war, torture, capital punishment, and more will no doubt be challenged, if not reformed. Pastors, theologians, and church leaders will hopefully have coddled errors eviscerated from their teaching ministries and expunged from their Christian practice.

Regrettably, Baptists along with other Evangelicals today have succumbed to statist ideologies that do not glorify Jesus Christ. These ideologies have caused them to unduly rely upon, and confide in, the delinquent state and its proactive public policies (1) to change people's bad behavior and (2) to provide for their material welfare. Statism has so undermined the church's role in civil society and crippled its ability to engage its culture that the modern church can hardly be viewed as "a city that is set on a hill" (Matthew 5:14) any longer.

Pastors and church leaders, Baptists in particular, would do well to digest the contents of this important book and apply it to their work for Christ. Otherwise Christians will continue to be duped by the charlatans that persist in preying upon their well-meaning motives and using them for the cause of evil instead of the cause of the truth.

—Paul J. Dean, D.Min.[4] (January 2006)

Addendum from a liberty-loving biblical scholar...

This is an outstanding book that I could not have written if I tried. It is a thoroughly-biblical and much-needed remedy to Christian apologists for the state and its wars. Dr. Cobin hits the proverbial nail on the head when he describes states as "parasites and predators that dole out privileges and siphon off prosperity through taxes and regulation." I highly recommend this book to all Christians, and especially those Christians who blindly follow the conservative movement and the Republican Party while repeating their "obey the powers that be" mantra.

—Laurence M. Vance, Ph.D.[5] (December 2005)

---

[4] Pastor of Providence Baptist Church in Greer, South Carolina, biblical counselor with Providence Ministries, and co-host of the "Calling for Truth" talk radio program in Greenville, South Carolina (AM 660).

[5] Author of *Christianity and War and Other Essays Against the Warfare State* (2005), Director of the Francis Wayland Institute, freelance writer on theological and libertarian issues, including regular columns at www.LewRockwell.com, and an adjunct instructor in accounting and economics at Pensacola Junior College in Pensacola, Florida.

Philosopher's Foreword

How should Christians view the institution of government? Are Christians obligated on Scriptural grounds to obey those with political power or authority, because of Romans 13:1-7 (for example)? In answering the latter question in the negative, this book fills a significant gap in Christian scholarship about public policy. No longer need Christians interpret Romans as calling for automatic subservience to the state, or blind obedience to worldly authority without qualification or consideration of context. If we consider the "whole counsel of God," we recognize that such passages must be considered in light of a multiplicity of others. In fact, Scripture discloses many cases where what we today call *civil disobedience* occurred, as in Daniel. It follows that, under the right circumstances, civil disobedience by Christians is not only justified, but even required.

Dr. Cobin integrates both economic theory and rights theory into his Biblical analysis of a Christian view of government. He also substantiates how negative rights—rights not to be interfered with—are both Scriptural as well as in accordance with America's founding principles establishing constitutionally limited government. The latter does not create rights; only God can do that. It encodes and protects them. Positive rights—rights to specific goods and services—can only be administered by an expansive state, a mutation of government that has fallen into the hands of secular power brokers. The latter bring out the worst sins in human nature, inclining a population to rely on secular authority (a welfare state, or Marxian or UN doctrine, and so tend to elevate the very sort of plunder that Scripture condemns into a secular moral principle. Dr. Cobin refreshes our memory how strict adherence to negative rights within the confines of limited government tends to bring about genuinely prosperous societies by encouraging wholesome values, both economic and otherwise. Positive rights, however, expand government into a Leviathan state, thus sabotaging both prosperity and morality. Since this is out of accord with what God has willed for us, it should not surprise us that the latter fail in the economic realm as well.

There is a great deal more worth saying about this book, Dr. Cobin's second one integrating public policy and theology (his first was *Bible and Government: Public Policy from a Christian Perspective*). There is a chapter, for example, on the dangers of a divine ordination of rulers, one on slavery and why slavery is bad news both economically and biblically, and one on just war theory. Dr. Cobin's critical analysis of the "four Christian views of the State" is especially lucid, and I learned—am still learning—a lot from studying it. In short, this book belongs in a prominent place on the bookshelf of every thinking Christian who wishes the soundest biblical perspective on American heritage and American public policy today.

—Steven Yates, Ph.D.[6] (January 2006)

---

[6] Author of *Civil Wrongs: What Went Wrong with Affirmative Action* (1994), *Worldviews: Christian Theism versus Modern Materialism* (2005); columnist for LewRockwell.com, NewsWithViews.com, and *The Times Examiner* (a Greenville, South Carolina weekly newspaper).

And from the desk of an admirer of the esteemed political philosopher John C. Calhoun...

It has often been written that such and such a book is a must read for this or that group, that it has become a cliché. However, as that may be, I truly believe that this book is a must read for all Christians in general, but most certainly is a must read for all Christian ministers and anyone else in Christian leadership. Faithfully using Scripture, Dr. Cobin clearly lays out the problems Christians face today in dealing with ever increasing anti-Christian states and, more importantly, presents said Christians with a biblical course of action. He clearly delineates the true role of government and states how all states have overstepped their given authority with proactive policies.

Dr. Cobin explains how states are tools of Satan and again, using Scripture, informs Christians how to understand and deal with this evil. Dr. Cobin clearly shows in his work why it is not sinful to pick up, figuratively, the sword of God in order to resist satanic states. Much, if not most, of the problems Christians face in dealing with public policy could be alleviated if every Christian minister understood this book's teachings and began to preach them from their pulpits.

Yes, for freedom-loving Christians, a must read.

—Robert B. Hayes[7] (December 2005)

---

[7] Director of the South Carolina League of the South.

Historian's Foreword

John Cobin's *Christian Theology of Public Policy: Highlighting the American Experience* ought to be read by every Christian and indeed by everyone who wishes to understand the role of God's word vis-à-vis the American polity in the 21st century. Lucidly written, Cobin's work integrates Biblical passages (often misunderstood) that deal with public policies (e.g. the role of government, economics, military and foreign policy, etc.) into their historical context.

Cobin's conclusions likely will shock the average, historically-challenged, Evangelical. Many of the sacred cows of both the Left and Right are spared no criticism, among whom are Lincoln, FDR, and the current occupant of the White House.

But Cobin's most shocking conclusions (at least to those who do not know their American and Southern history) regard the South and her bid for independence. He understands that antebellum Southerners were the direct philosophical and theological descendants of the Founders. As such, they were right to pursue their independence in 1860-61. And their offspring are still right today in seeking independence for the South from a godless American Empire.

Though readers may disagree with elements of Cobin's theology, they have much to gain from his historical insight and his solutions for a people and nation rapidly descending into chaos. John Cobin's book deserves a serious audience in these perilous times.

—Michael J. Hill, Ph.D.[8] (January 2006)

---

[8] Dr. Michael J. Hill is President of the League of the South; formerly Professor of History at the University of Alabama.

Preface

The intended audience for this book is *thinking Christians*: theologians, pastors, seminary students, economists and scholars from public policy and other related fields looking to integrate their disciplines with Christian theology. This book is about what the Bible says about the state and its public policies.[9] Its chief appeal will likely be to academics and theologians, and I anticipate that they will assimilate its contents and spread its ideas to those over whom they have influence. I also hope to convince thinking Christians of (1) the veracity of the liberty of conscience perspective, or (2) to at least encourage them to be more active in engaging their culture.

Perhaps this book will be useful to a wider audience of serious students of the Bible and public policy too: (a) Christian college students, (b) homeschoolers studying government, economics, theology, history, or political philosophy, and (c) adult Sunday school teachers who are willing to challenge conventional wisdom regarding politics and public policy by taking on topics in American culture or practical theology pertaining to the Christian worldview.

---

[9] Unless otherwise noted, all Scripture quotations in this book are taken from the *New King James Version* of the Bible.

I have presumed upon my reader some considerable background knowledge of the Scriptures. Thus, for many people, completing these pages will require a substantial commitment of time for reflection and analysis—not only on account of the economic and public policy theory but also because of the requisite level of Bible knowledge.

Nevertheless, my target of a more academic audience is deliberate, and I trust prudent, since in the "intellectual pyramid of society" scholars (or other idea generators) are rightly recognized as having the greatest influence on the "climate of opinion" over time. Correspondingly, along with my previous works, I hope this book will play at least a small role in reversing what Mark Noll bemoans as the scandalous modern "Evangelical inattention to intellectual life" and "anti-intellectual attitude". He warns Christians of the perils of this disposition: "If the history of Christianity shows how fruitful it can be to cultivate the mind for Christ, it also indicates how dangerous it can be to neglect such activity."[10]

---

[10] Mark A. Noll (1995), *The Scandal of the Evangelical Mind*, Grand Rapids, Michigan: W. B. Eerdmans & Co., pp. 4, 12, 46).

If the foundations are destroyed,
what can the righteous do?
—Psalm 11:3

The essence of Government is power; and power, lodged as it must be in human hands, will ever be liable to abuse.
— President James Madison (1829)

Under democracy, one party always devotes its chief energies to trying to prove that the other party is unfit to rule—and both commonly succeed, and are right.
—H.L. Mencken (1880-1956)

For the law of Nature would, as all other laws that concern men in this world, be in vain if there were nobody that in the state of Nature had a power to execute that law, and thereby preserve the innocent and restrain offenders...
—John Locke (1690)

I am desirous of discrediting the whole system of corruption, and of rendering all civil government fair, just, open, and honourable. All government, founded on insincerity and injustice, debases the morals and injures the happiness, while it infringes on the civil rights of the people.
—Vicesimus Knox (c. 1795)

1

Introduction

The exegetical problem: Romans 13:1-6 (annotated)

Let us begin with some interpretive exegesis that is probably nothing short of shocking to the contemporary Evangelical mindset. One of the most important Bible passages dealing with the civil authority and the Christian's relationship to it is Romans 13:1-7. Yet this passage is seldom read in light of its historical context. Assuming that the Apostle Paul had in view the Roman regime circa AD55, if we substitute the names of the then current Caesar (i.e., Nero) and a particular local king (e.g., Herod, Felix or Agrippa) in place of the words "governing authorities", "God's minister", and corresponding pronouns, the passage comes across in a strikingly different manner. Consider how a first century Christian in Rome (or elsewhere in the Empire) would have heard Paul's teaching in Romans 13:1-6.

> *1* Let every soul be subject to Nero and Herod. For there is no authority except from God, and Nero and Herod are appointed by God. *2* Therefore whoever resists Nero or Herod resists the ordinance of God, and those who resist will bring judgment on themselves. *3* For neither

2

Nero nor Herod is a terror to good works, but to evil. Do you want to be unafraid of Nero and Herod? Do what is good, and you will have praise from Nero and/or Herod. *4* For Nero and Herod are God's ministers to you for good. But if you do evil, be afraid; for Nero and Herod do not bear the sword in vain; for Nero and Herod are God's ministers, avengers to execute wrath on him who practices evil. *5* Therefore you must be subject, not only because of wrath but also for conscience' sake. *6* For because of this you also pay taxes, for Nero and Herod are God's ministers attending continually to this very thing.

Does reading this annotation surprise you? Does the words substitution change your conceptions (i.e., affect your interpretative premonitions) or give the passage new devotional meaning for you? How should Christians reconcile the fact that the evil Caesar Nero was ruling at the time the Apostles Paul and Peter wrote to Roman Christians regarding submission to the civil authorities? How can Christians resolve the ensuing theological quandary that comes from knowing that Nero killed and punished good people (i.e., Christians) when the passage plainly says that civil government rewards those who do well? As well, the character and sordid actions of lower rulers such as Herod were little different than Nero's.

How then may the timeless injunctions of the Scriptures be reconciled with the fact that the state has been the greatest earthly disseminator of evil and oppression in the history of man? Regrettably, the public polices of Hitler and Stalin's Europe, Mao Tse-tung's China, Lincoln's brutal war and Grant's dreadful Reconstruction program, Pol Pot's Cambodia, Idi Amin's Uganda, Salvadore Allende's socialist Chile, Bloody Mary's cruel England, Domitian's Rome, and so forth are not so very rare. How may we reconcile the Bible with public policy's checkered and often brutal history? Indeed, every decade seems to spawn a new generation of dictators and repressive regimes. Peaceful times are short-lived for most people. America has been largely anomalous and its public policies better than those of most other countries (at least for Americans), but ultimately America is not immune to the same political maladies that plague other parts of the world.

Without a doubt, a more profound understanding of historical and cultural elements is necessary for good interpretation of these passages—even though such elements may not be apparent to the casual reader or preacher. The historical context of these passages is crucial to properly interpreting the text. Paul was writing to Christians in the church situated in the imperial capital city of Rome. As well, Peter was writing to Roman Christians who were suffering, after having been banished from Rome and other parts of the empire to regions on the southern end of the Black Sea (what is modern north-central Turkey).

Consider again the pertinent part of the Romans 13 passage without the annotation, along with the pertinent part of 1 Peter 2. Does the apostolic language regarding the purpose of rulers and their public policies still seem plain?

Romans 13:3-4

> *3* For rulers are not a terror to good works, but to evil. Do you want to be unafraid of the authority? Do what is good, and you will have praise from the same. *4* For he is God's minister to you for good. But if you do evil, be afraid; for he does not bear the sword in vain; for he is God's minister, an avenger to execute wrath on him who practices evil.

1 Peter 2:13-14

> *13* Therefore submit yourselves to every ordinance of man for the Lord's sake, whether to

4

the king as supreme, *14* or to governors, as to those who are sent by him for the punishment of evildoers and for the praise of those who do good.

After a cursory reading of these texts, and without much reflection, the plain meaning of the passages might lead one to conclude that civil government or the state serves to uphold the Law of God in the world, killing or punishing those who do evil in the sight of the Lord. Nevertheless, this view is lacking.

Apostolic admonitions regarding civil government cannot easily be reconciled with modern public policy by employing a casual, plain reading of the New Testament texts. Without careful analysis, an objective reader would tend to think—along with a host of gainsayers outside the faith—that the Apostles were (1) wrong, (2) conditioned by a now irrelevant cultural context, (3) merely speaking about civil government in the abstract (without direct relevance to the first century Christians), or (4) simply out of their minds. Some more liberal Bible scholars have gone so far as to argue that certain texts relevant to public policy, such the first few verses of Romans 13, are uninspired, defective, or later additions to the canon of Scripture.

Conservative Christian scholars would like to avoid holding to one of these rather radical conclusions. Yet they encounter a rather intractable or awkward interpretive problem. How can the plain meaning of Paul and Peter's words make sense given the political and cultural setting in which they wrote? The fact is that Nero, renowned for his calloused cruelty and repressive policies, was Caesar when the Apostles wrote!

To begin with, no Bible-believing Christian considers the commands in Romans 13:1-7, 1 Peter 2:13-17, and Titus 3:1 to be *absolute*. Indeed, considering the "whole counsel of God", it is clear that God's people have *not* submitted (and should *not* submit) to "*every* ordinance of man" (1 Peter 2:13). As John McGarvey and Philip Pendleton note:

> The government [or state] must exact nothing contrary to or inconsistent with Christian duty. If it does, we must obey God rather than men (Acts 4:18-20; 5:28, 29); for under no circumstance can God's children be justified in doing wrong (Matt. 10:28; Rom. 3:8). Allegiance ceases when the law of the land seeks to subvert the law of God; and Paul teaches nothing to the contrary. As the martyr Polycarp said to the governor who bade him denounce Christ, and swear by the fortunes of Cæsar: "We are taught to give honor to princes and potentates, but such honor as is not contrary to God's religion."[11]

The Hebrew midwives in Egypt defied Pharaoh's decree to murder infants (Exodus 1:15-21). Ehud acted against public policy by deceiving the king's ministers and then slew the king (Judges 3:15-26). Daniel, Shadrach, Meshach, and Abed-Nego refused to comply with public policies that mandated religious rituals contrary to proper worship (Daniel 3:8-18; 6:6-10). The wise men from the East (Magi) disobeyed Herod's direct order to disclose Jesus' whereabouts (Matthew 2:7-12). Peter and John forthrightly disobeyed the "ordinance of man" that mandated that they desist from preaching (Acts 5:28-29). So then, the foremost doctrinal issue revolves around *when* or *why* Christians may or must disobey, rather than *if* Christians may ever disobey at all.

---

[11] John W. McGarvey and Philip Y. Pendleton (1916), *Thessalonians, Corinthians, Galatians and Romans*, vol. 3, ch. IV, "The faith-life discharging civil duties, and recognizing the divine ordination of governments", Cincinnati: The Standard Publishing Company, p. 509.

Still, Evangelicals disagree about the extent to which a Christian may disobey. For example, not every Christian view would permit disobedience to public policies that provide for preferential hiring of homosexuals, prohibition of spanking, mandatory attendance in public schools, mandatory working on Sunday, poaching, hiring of illegal aliens (even if Christians), speeding (e.g., driving 67mph in a posted 65mph zone), minimum drinking ages for wine in one's own home, and mandatory purchase of automobile insurance. It is not certain how many Christians would deal with many actual policies, such as the prohibition of throwing stones at birds in Dublin, Georgia, the prohibition of playing pinball for those under 18 in South Carolina and Nashville, Tennessee, or the prohibition of spitting on the street in Dunn, North Carolina. Again, the reason *why* Christians must obey, or may disobey, is important. And one's point of view will largely stem from his presuppositions about the nature and role of the state and public policy that have been delineated, resulting in one of the four views outlined in chapter 3: theonomy, revitalized divine right of kings, pacifist, or liberty of conscience.

Consequently, a consistent and cogent paradigm for interpreting texts that deal with public policy must be developed and applied to create a biblical theology of public policy. While this book elaborates on the hermeneutic set forth in *Bible and Government: Public Policy from a Christian Perspective* (2003),[12] known as the liberty of conscience perspective, the crux of the three alternative (competing) views is also developed in chapters 7 and 8. In the final analysis, the expedient paradigm of the liberty of conscience view is applied in order to exegete Romans 13:1-7 (along with its counterpart in Titus 3:1) and

---

[12] The book is available in paperback and in e-book (PDF) format from Alertness Books at http://policyofliberty.net/checkout/products.php.

1 Peter 2:13-17,[13] thus developing a proper framework for establishing a biblical public policy theology.

Public policy theology is important!

Public policy theology has far-reaching and important practical applications in daily life. One useful extrapolation is to consider the theoretical and theological motivations of Christians for supporting or rejecting the rightness of the American Revolution. Professor Mark Noll's work *Christians and the American Revolution* (1977) is especially helpful in forming a historical perspective on this point. Not surprisingly, the instigators of the American Revolution were largely theonomic Presbyterians and Congregationalists, along with liberty of conscience Baptists.

These groups took an active role in transforming their world, albeit for very distinct reasons. The theonomists wanted to overthrow the evil state, by means of a "lower magistrate", in order to replace it with a godly one. The Baptists wanted freedom in order to be able to serve God better. They often cited Galatians 5:1 in their cry for being free from bondage to the state, pursuing freedom as the opportunity arose (cf. 1 Corinthians 7:21). Unlike the theonomists, their comrades in arms, they did not primarily want to install a "better" state or civil government. That is why they became ardent supporters of a Bill of Rights to ensure that their civil rights were protected against government intrusion, despite the fact that the Constitution was based on a Presbyterian framework.

It should also come as little surprise that the Anglicans and most Methodists of the day turned out to be Tories, critical of other Christians who did not "submit" as they should. Many Tories, passive and non-confrontational

---

[13] The first *Merriam-Webster* definition of *expedient* is being "suitable for achieving a particular end in a given circumstance." Accordingly, the word expedient is used in the sense of what is practical, prudent, or advantageous for a believer living in his culture.

divine right of kings adherents, thus returned to England or went to Canada. Similarly, the Anabaptists, being pacifists, did not participate in the American Revolution, although they did tend to revolt against paying any taxes that would go to finance the conflict. Obviously, one's public policy theology makes a difference indeed, as evidenced by the American Revolution.

It seems that many thinking Christians today are quick to charge the Christian activists who revolted against Great Britain in the 1770s with sin. Much of this thinking is based on naiveté and ignorance of both Christian theology and public policy—not to mention the impact of the First Great Awakening and the War for American Independence that flowed from its principles.

Thus, Christians ought to think about public policy more seriously and develop their view in a manner that coincides with sound biblical principles that take cultural context seriously. Remember that Jesus commanded His disciples, "occupy till I come" (Luke 19:13 *KJV*). Christians are to carry on the "business" of life until He returns, including all aspects of social life: work, politics, cultural dynamics, church, etc. that they encounter. Nothing should stand in the way of a Christian in fulfilling this mission. Thus, if common, popular views of public policy are found wanting, then they should be replaced by better ones.

Accordingly, this book provides both a challenge to prevailing attitudes among Evangelicals and a framework whereby Christians can appreciate the rightness of individual and collective self-defense—including resisting tyrants and evil public policies at opportune moments in history.

Organization and contents of the book

This book is laid out in such a way to help the reader systematize the theology of public policy and think through the tougher issues. **Part I** deals with fundamental knowledge and paradigms. Chapter 1 identifies key economic and public policy tools to establish the three types of public policies: reactive, proactive, and inefficient provision of goods and services, along with the key theories of perverse economic incentives, the knowledge problem, and the public choice problems facing political actors.

In chapter 2 the historical context of political life under rulers Nero and Herod is reviewed. This context formed the backdrop for apostolic writings regarding the civil authorities. The concept of the welfare state and legalized plunder are also reviewed in historical context with application to the present day. Chapter 3 describes the two schools of Christian thought regarding public policy and the nature of the state, viz. the integrated authority school and the competing kingdom school, along with the four views that devolve from them: (1) theonomy, (2) revitalized or reshaped divine right of kings, (3) pacifism, and (4) liberty of conscience. These views are discussed in some detail. (Appendix 1 provides responses to aberrant views of submission to the state stemming from the divine right perspective.)

Part II covers the particulars of the liberty of conscience perspective. In chapter 4 the distinction between limited government and the state is pointed out (along with the distinction between law and legislation in Appendix 1). A fundamental feature developed is the satanic nature of the state. Indeed, the state is shown to be the enemy of God's people. Chapter 5 covers the theology of God's ordination or appointment of all things, including criminals, evil rulers, and the devil himself. God uses such "calamity" (cf. Isaiah 45:7) to further His purposes in this world and to glorify His name. Christians must work within this providential agenda to fulfill the dominion mandate. Chapter 6 provides a concise commentary on Romans 12–14 and 1 Peter 2 highlighting the liberty of conscience framework.

Part III develops the key issues in the theology of public policy. Chapter 7 develops the biblical doctrine of self-defense: its rightness and necessity in a fallen world. Christians may use lethal force to defend themselves against predators, even if those predators are elected or appointed to political office. If self-defense were not justifiable then there could be no justification for collective self-defense through a limited government.

Chapter 8 outlines the importance of viewing God as the source of law, and the principles upon which fundamental rights are established, with the state being merely the progenitor of proactive legislation. The nature and validity of natural, political and civil rights are expounded. The crucial question of whether or not Christians have rights is considered too. The appropriateness of self-defense individually and just wars of defense collectively is shown—as opposed to aggression and empire-building. Plus, the virtues of assassination policy over full-scale war against a state predator are accredited. In addition, cruel practices like torture are excoriated as being anti-biblical, and the wholesale acceptance of policies of capital punishment carried out by wayward states is questioned.

Chapter 9 discusses the theology of slavery, involuntary slavery in particular (even in its part-time form in America), identifying it as a horrible institution that should be avoided by Christians and opposed in policy when possible. A comprehensive look at the Scriptures is undertaken to show what the mind of God is regarding different types of slavery and the Christians obligation to escape from it by any means available.

Recounting some of the key events of the American Revolution, chapter 10 certifies the rightness of rebellion or resistance against state tyrants and oppressors as justifiable Christian action under the appropriate circumstances. Chapters 11 and 12 explain that Christians must, paradoxically, fight for peace. American Christians may rightly

11

make use of the Second Amendment in their favor. Not doing so is to defy God's provision in their lives and to disobey the intentions of the Founders codified in the highest legal authorities: the Constitution and the Declaration of Independence.

Part IV deals with the application of public policy, including some further fundamental themes in public policy theology, and the Christian's duty as he engages his culture. Chapter 13 explains that the word "nation" in the Bible refers to an ethnic aggregate rather than territory demarcated by the arbitrary and capricious political boundaries of men. Moreover, the word nation in the Bible cannot be properly applied to America or any other political organization, even though several pet verses are popularly used by preachers today to do just that. Furthermore, Christians must not be nationalists in their policy advocacy or local church organization, but instead should prefer Christians of any nationality or citizenship above all other men—even if their brethren must flee persecution and thus enter America as "illegal aliens".

Chapter 14 advocates the use of state lotteries as the best means to finance public expenditure. They represent voluntary taxation and allow the wealth of the wicked to be stored up for the righteous. Finally, in chapter 15, proper Christian civic duty is shown to be marked by activism: in voting and attending local meetings or reading contemplative materials, as well as in sitting on juries and writing to politicians to ask them to uphold the principles of liberty. Chapter 16 provides a summary of the book's key motifs, as well as lists the policies that should be promoted or assailed by activist Christians. A call for Christian civic duty is given along with encouraging the moral character of tolerance for Christians with different points of view.

PART I

FUNDAMENTAL KNOWLEDGE AND PARADIGMS

The inherent vice of capitalism is the unequal sharing of the blessings. The inherent blessing of socialism is the equal sharing of misery.
        —*Pr. Minister Winston Churchill (1874-1965)*

The first lesson of economics is scarcity: there is never enough of anything to fully satisfy all those who want it. The first lesson of politics is to disregard the first lesson of economics.
        —*Thomas Sowell (1930-)*

Elections are decided by the votes of the uneducated many for the corrupt few.
        —*George Bernard Shaw (1856-1950)*

Democracy was the right of the people to choose their own tyrants.
        — *President James Madison (1751-1836)*

1 Basic Economics and Public Policy Theory for the Theology of Public Policy

Self-interested action vs. selfishness

Economic theory tells us a lot about the nature of political actors along with the inadequacy of their knowledge in regulating society to bring about the common good. All rational men act purposefully to remove uneasiness from their lives. They try to maximize those things in life that give them the greatest satisfaction (e.g., money, love, power, influence, charity, altruism, holiness, etc.). However, they also act in such a way that engenders cooperation with others, facilitating and exploiting mutually beneficial gains from trade. Peaceful cooperation is the result of the operation of the market economy. People pursuing their own self-interest voluntarily cooperate to provide the needs and wants demanded in society.

We must be careful to not equate self-interested motives with selfish ones. The former describes one's economic motivation while the latter deals with one's character. For example, a person might have altruism or to "shepherd the flock of God" (1 Peter 5:2) as his highest goal. He would thus pursue the self-interested agenda that he believes has the highest probability of attaining that goal. He might also pursue other things along with this objective, such as owning his home debt-free, raising four children, and taking his wife on an annual skiing trip. But all these elements (and others we might think of) mix together into concerted, purposeful, self-interested action to attain the conglomerate goal.

As economist Ludwig von Mises states in the opening chapter of *Human Action: A Treatise on Economics* (1966), men aim purposefully at ends. "Human action is purposeful behavior...aiming at ends and goals...[and is] a person's conscious adjustment to the state of the universe that determines his life." Sane people do not act without reason, and they do not act unless they believe that their action will remove some uneasiness. This axiom can and must be squared with the Word of God. The Bible states: "the righteous God tests the hearts and minds" (Psalm 7:9; cf. Proverbs 15:11; 17:3; 24:12), noting that "Every way of a man is right in his own eyes, but the Lord weighs the hearts" (Proverbs 21:2). Moreover, the fact that human action is purposeful and aims at ends does not mean that such action is always righteous. Indeed the opposite may be true.

The Scriptures indicate that *all* men are flawed in their judgments and choices. The ends that men aim at are marred by sin, just as the Bible exclaims: "All we like sheep have gone astray; we have turned, every one, to his own way" (Isaiah 53:6). While God has "put eternity in their hearts" still "the hearts of the sons of men are full of evil; madness is in their hearts while they live, and after that they go to the dead" (Ecclesiastes 3:11; 9:3).[14] Consequently, men's economic choices—like spiritual ones—are

---

[14] As a result, "There is none righteous, no, not one; There is none who understands; There is none who seeks after God. They have all turned aside; They have together become unprofitable; There is none who does good, no, not one...Destruction and misery are in their ways; and the way of peace they have not known" (Romans 3:10-12, 16-17). The natural man in his sin "devises wickedness on his bed; he sets himself in a way that is not good; he does not abhor evil" (Psalm 36:4). "Perversity is in his heart, He devises evil continually, He sows discord...A heart that devises wicked plans...For their heart devises violence" (Proverbs 6:14, 18; 24:2). Even sinful rulers "devise evil by law" (Psalm 94:20).

tainted, marred, and corrupted by sin. Men may think that they are doing justice and pursuing righteousness but instead actually be doing what is wrong. Certainly, while self-interest is not necessarily selfish, its objective is always tainted by sin to some extent. Therefore, ends may be righteous or unrighteous.

We are left only to marvel when we think that under God's common grace men of such character, pursuing their own self-interests, can produce peaceful social cooperation. Capitalism and private property,[15] especially when coupled with thrift, industry, and entrepreneurship, must be viewed as facets of God's common grace that allow civilizations to rise and survive within a fallen world. Accordingly, the self-interest motivation is helpful and good, and wrongly demonized by some journalists and academics that have confused self-interest with selfishness.

A selfish person is one who is absorbed in himself to the exclusion of others. He is self-interested too but his motivation is hamstrung by a character flaw. The theory of self-interest is born out in the Scriptures, often evincing the selfish foibles of human nature. We are told twice for instance that: "There is a way that seems right to a man, but its end is the way of death" (Proverbs 14:12; 16:25). Young men are admonished to not pursue their unbridled thoughts and desires: "Rejoice, O young man, in your youth, and let your heart cheer you in the days of your youth; walk in the ways of your heart, and in the sight of your eyes; but know that for all these God will bring you into judgment" (Ecclesiastes 11:9)—just as erring Lot did: "Then Lot chose for himself all the plain of Jordan, and Lot journeyed east" (Genesis 13:11)[16] as well as the foolish man in Christ's par-

---

[15] For an excellent basic book on the virtues of capitalism, see Thomas J. DiLorenzo (2004), *How Capitalism Saved America*, New York: Crown Forum.

[16] God can and does turn the bad actions of men into blessing at times. For instance, Joseph told his brothers "you meant evil against me; but God meant it for good" (Genesis 50:20). Paul "was consenting" to the death of Stephen (Acts 8:1) but God likewise turned his foul play into great benefit for His people.

17

able who shortly after being satisfied with this world's goods went to meet his frowning Maker.[17]

Nonetheless, not all of the self-interested purposes of men are bad or selfish. The Bible speaks of godly men purposing to do things too. For instance, "Paul purposed in the Spirit, when he had passed through Macedonia and Achaia, to go to Jerusalem" (Acts 19:21). The Bible also contrasts the vain purposes of "those who desire to be rich" (1 Timothy 6:9)—noting that "the schemes of the schemer are evil; he devises wicked plans to destroy the poor with lying words"—with the good purposes of "a generous man [who] devises generous things" (Isaiah 32:7-8).

Furthermore, there are many biblical encouragements to pursue righteous ends: "Commit your works to the Lord, and your thoughts will be established" (Proverbs 16:33).[18] Therefore, Christians ought to seek to align their self-interested purposes with the principles of the Word of God. Likewise, Christians should advocate and support collective actions through limited government—or *public policies*—that are most congruent with biblical principles.

Categories of public policy

Public policy generally means government action, although it is better to distinguish policies by the categories of (1) reactive policy, (2) the inefficient provision of genuine market goods and services, and (3) proactive policy. Proactive policies may be categorized by three varieties: (i)

---

[17] So he purposed: "'I will do this: I will pull down my barns and build greater, and there I will store all my crops and my goods.' And I will say to my soul, 'Soul, you have many goods laid up for many years; take your ease; eat, drink, and be merry'" (Luke 12:18-19; cf. 1 Corinthians 15:32; Ecclesiastes 8:15).

[18] Two other related passages include: "The steps of a good man are ordered by the Lord, and He delights in his way" (Psalm 37:23), and "Trust in the Lord with all your heart, and lean not on your own understanding; in all your ways acknowledge Him, And He shall direct your paths" (Proverbs 3:5-6).

ones aimed at changing behavior, (ii) ones aimed at changing the way people think, and (iii) ones dedicated mostly or wholly to income and wealth redistribution. Before fleshing out these categories, something must be known about the rights theories that support the bulk of them.

Positive and negative rights

Many policies have to do with the implementation of some *positive right*: a right granted to people by the state, a right that people do not have naturally, and a right that other people must pay to sustain. Sometimes positive rights are couched in terms of "social justice" or sublime "public interest" planning objectives. In his book *Turn Neither to the Right nor to the Left* (2003),[19] Dr. Eric Schansberg outlines the major sub-categories of public policies based on positive rights theory using the terms "legislating morality" (LM) and "legislating justice" (LJ). He eloquently explains why Christians should avoid promoting policies of the former and only with great caution (and guided by strong principles) encourage ones of the latter.

Examples of positive rights include rights to minimum standards of health care, food or nutrition, income, and a "decent" education. These rights may be found in statements like the United Nations *Declaration of Rights* (1945), as well as in Marxian writings and elsewhere. These rights can also include things like a "livable" wage (a minimum wage or greater), a crime-free and unpolluted environment, and even "reasonable air conditioning" in a rental unit.[20] Thus, positive rights obligate one class of people to provide benefits for another. Hence, they are *artificial* in nature.

---

[19] The book is available in paperback and in e-book (PDF) format from Alertness Books at http://policyofliberty.net/checkout/products.php.

[20] For instance, the Virginia Residential Landlord and Tenant Act, amended in 1987, provides for "reasonable air conditioning" if air conditioning is provided in the unit. Va. Code 55-248.13(a)(6).

Conversely, *negative rights* are fundamentally construed to be "natural" or "fundamental" rights that people have to life, liberty, and property. Such rights-bearing has been extolled by political philosophers such as John Locke and Thomas Jefferson, and one may make a strong argument for negative rights by substantiating them in the Scriptures.

For instance, we find prohibitions against murder and support for capital punishment, in the Old Testament (e.g., Genesis 9:6)—even prior to the Law of Moses. The Ten Commandments, of course, prohibited murder, theft, and fraud, with penalties spelled out for them (and related crimes) in other parts of the Pentateuch. Moreover, we find throughout the Bible references to self-defense and warfare, especially under the theocracy, but also for self-preservation against predators and intruders. Therefore, the idea of negative rights is enshrined and buoyed in the Scriptures and the corollary importance of self-defense in order to prevent violation of negative rights is implied.

Self-defense: a paramount doctrine

Perhaps more than any other single doctrine, one's theology of public policy rests upon his understanding about the doctrine of self-defense. After all, in its most basic form, civil government exists as the collective means of self-defense. Indeed *if self-defense cannot be justified then neither can civil government itself be justified.* Christians might as well promote political anarchy (meaning preferring the implementation of no formal political apparatus to oversee society). After all, just what would a state do if it did not defend its citizens? Would it merely redistribute wealth, run public enterprises, certify products, and issue edicts for politically correct conduct? How could Christians prefer having such a state of affairs over having tax-free and regulation-free political anarchy? If the civil authority

20

can not or will not defend its citizens (us Christians in particular) then it is not worth having around.

Consequently, building a case for self-defense from the Scriptures—especially the New Testament—is both fundamental and of paramount importance to any Christian theology of public policy. As well, making a case for the rightness of self-defense by individuals or collectively through civil government is certainly doable, as delineated in chapter 7.

Significantly, in Luke 22:36, Jesus told His Apostles: "But now, he who has a money bag, let him take it, and likewise a knapsack; and he who has no sword, let him sell his garment and buy one". This statement indicates that self-defense would become a necessity after His time on earth was over. Swords were not used to hunt or fish, or to punish children. They were weaponry used to attack and kill other men.

Other key components of the doctrine of self-defense in the New Testament are readily identified. Jesus praised the great faith of a Roman centurion in Capernaum (Matthew 8:5-13; Luke 7:2-10) and did not rebuke him for being in the profession of warfare. Neither did John the Baptist rebuke the soldier for being a soldier in Luke 3:14. In Luke 14:31, Jesus says "Or what king, going to make war against another king, does not sit down first and consider whether he is able with ten thousand to meet him who comes against him with twenty thousand?" Moreover, one could probably make a case that Jesus Himself was not wholly opposed to warfare—even if he did tell *individuals* to turn the other cheek when wronged (Matthew 5:29; Luke 6:29), and even though he warned that "all who take the sword will perish by the sword" (Matthew 26:52b). Therefore, one would be hard pressed to make a case that the Bible opposes negative rights—or self-defense—and only with considerable difficulty make a case for biblical pacifism. Indeed, the biblical case for pacifism is shallow.

Reactive policy

Negative rights theory mandates that people restrain themselves from acting against the natural rights of others in society. Yet unlike positive rights they are costless; no person has to pay to maintain the negative rights of other people. That is why they are often said to exist *naturally*.

Reactive policy is action by government designed to provide collective self-defense against predators: a social service that the market cannot provide well. There are really only three "pure" reactive policy categories: national defense, the establishment and enforcement of legal rules to facilitate social certainty and commerce (which are based on the common law of property, contract, and tort), and criminal justice. Domestic defense against any predator—even infectious microorganisms—would qualify as well. These policies are reactive in the sense that they react to, or become effectual when there is, a violation of someone's negative rights by a clearly nonconsensual act (e.g., murder, rape, or robbery). Conformably, Frederic Bastiat in his famous book *The Law* terms these kinds of actions *defensive* policies, because they are designed to defend people from others who would harm life, liberty, or property.[21]

Such policies are devoid of behavior modification objectives or schemes, but instead provide safeguards that are perceived to be collective boons or "public goods". Of course, there is a "proactive" by-product in these policies, namely that predators are *deterred* from bad behavior. But only through such an abstraction (i.e., where the policy inadvertently ends up changing bad behavior) may they be

---

[21] Frederic Bastiat (1990 [1850]), *The Law*, The Foundation for Economic Education: Irvington-on-Hudson, New York, p. 28.

considered proactive. Nevertheless, since the operation of such policies only becomes effective after a rights violation occurs, they may reasonably be maintained as having an essentially reactive character.

The government is called upon to provide these collective goods either because the market "fails" to provide them well or, perhaps, because such collective action is itself the result of market provision. Accordingly, minimal state libertarians or "minarchists" and political conservatives (or constitutionalists) typically argue that reactive policies are the *only* necessary and just forms of government action. Many of them would restrict policy to defense from predators, together with lethal or noxious microorganisms perhaps, and criminal justice. Markets could provide civil procedure services and courtrooms, as well as local rules or laws to facilitate commerce.

Policies of inefficient public provision

It is often possible for government to provide a genuine good or service that is normally provided by the market. However, following economic theory, such provision will likely be inefficient since (1) bureaucrats face different incentives than managers or entrepreneurs in competing firms and (2) bureaucrats are protected from the discipline of the market. Thus, public enterprises tend to focus less on quality improvement and cost cutting, and often are over-staffed with over-paid employees (especially at higher levels of government). This predicament ends up driving up prices that consumers must pay for those goods and services, which in turn lowers social welfare. Such policies are usually neither proactive nor reactive, but they might be either proactive or reactive in some instances.

Most tariffs, quotas, and "dumping" laws probably fall under this policy category, since the protectionism they foster promotes inefficient provision in a country's private sector.[22] However, such "hidden taxes" on consumption are complicated, and must be judged on a case-by-case basis as to what category they belong. Examples of professions that devolve from these policies include the county recorder, postal service workers, mechanics who repair city vehicles, building safety inspectors, workers in dams and public utilities, road construction crews, public defenders, and the staff of a country's central bank. (Note that when taken generally, the actions of a central bank, along with legal tender laws, deposit insurance, and currency monopolization may comprise proactive policy during its course of facilitating indirect taxation by inflation.)

Proactive policies aimed at changing behavior or thinking

The first two divisions of proactive policy are action by government designed to alter people's behavior or way of thinking. These policies are not usually implemented because the targeted behavior is harmful to other people as much as it is antithetical to some lofty philosophical meta-goal. Proactive policy seeks to alter behavior that would otherwise be commonplace, normal, typical, and not harmful to others. The targeted behavior is simply designated as something naughty by a legislature or by some state bureau, usually upon the expert advice of academics, policy pundits, or pressure groups (lobbyists). Conversely, curtailing most recidivistic or criminal behavior (e.g., murder, assault, etc.) would more likely be a function of reactive policy rather than this species of proactive policy.

Sometimes such proactive policies are derided as "big brother" actions. They are so-called because people are compelled to behave in a manner not of their own choosing (as if an older and wiser person were providing

---

[22] See James Bovard (1991), *The Fair Trade Fraud: How Congress Pillages the Consumer and Decimates America's Competitiveness*, St. Martin's Press: New York. He demonstrates how consumers are harmed by tariffs, quotas, and dumping laws. The beneficiaries of such policies are political actors and industry special interests.

direction for a child). In this sense, someone in government and/or academia has determined that certain behavior is detrimental to the individual, society, or both.

Accordingly, proactive policies can be actions that aim at changing social institutions based on the suggestion of some academic theory (e.g., Marxism) or the wrangling of some activists (e.g., protesters from the Sierra Club, the Audubon Society, Greenpeace, the National Organization for Women, etc., or corporate and government "watchdogs" like Ralph Nader and Noam Chomsky). Examples of proactive policies include hate crimes and sodomite union legislation, marriage licensing, seat belt laws, smuggling and gambling restrictions, "sin" taxes on cigarettes and alcohol, regulation requiring "fairly" priced and decent housing, environmental "protection" (e.g., for certain species or the ozone layer), prohibition of alcohol or drug use, compulsory attendance in government schools (which Dr. Bruce Shortt rightly calls "pagan seminaries"),[23] and constabulary or offensive (aggressive) military operations.[24]

Also included in this proactive category are policy projects and institutions designed to serve higher social goals or "the public interest". Items that are deemed to be "public goods" or that result from the occurrence of "negative externalities" are used to rationalize public interest policies.[25] A negative externality occurs when a person

---

[23] Bruce N. Shortt (2004), *The Harsh Truth About Public Schools*, Vallecito, California: Chalcedon Foundation.

[24] Note that a proactive policy may also include minor reactive elements. For instance, protecting others from "second-hand smoke", shielding society from ozone depletion, and defending potentially innocent victims from intoxicated drivers all have (arguably) reactive qualities. Nevertheless, the central tenets of such policies remain proactive, aiming at coercing change in behavior or thinking.

[25] "A 'public good' is a good or service which is characterized as non-excludable and non-rival in consumption. That is, if a public good is provided to one person, it may be provided to all at no additional cost, such that people who do not pay for it cannot be prevented from consuming it (i.e., a positive externality). Examples of public goods often include national defense, law and order, pollution abatement, flood control, and perhaps building safety and quality. It is common for government to either provide (or at least regulate) such goods, based on the rationale that markets do not make adequate provision of them, and that it is not fair or efficient that some people should be free

25

who is not involved with the beneficial market exchange of others ends up bearing some of the costs of that bargain without receiving any of the benefits. The classic example is a woman who bears the cost of having her laundry soiled by the smokestack of a nearby factory but gets no benefit from the factory's production.

Another example, although it is not usually recognized as such, would be a person who pays taxes for the education of children when he has no school-age children. He pays for the costs of "production" without *directly* receiving any of its benefits. He probably does receive *indirect* benefits from the production, such as living among a literate population, but that does not disqualify the policy from being a negative externality in theory.

The woman with the laundry might also have indirect benefits from the smokestack because it creates jobs for others. Yet the smokestack is still considered in theory to be a negative externality. If the smokestack would cease production, there would be more jobless (and poorer) men, which might increase robberies. Instead, men working at the factory improve her community as their spending bolsters the quality of local commerce. Accordingly, some public policies can be considered, at least abstractly, to be negative externalities too. Hence, the specious idea of market failure stemming from pervasive negative externalities in turn provides a specious rationale for proactive policy.

Proactive policy aimed at redistribution

The third major division of proactive policy is redistributive policy. It entails proactive action by government designed to coercively transfer the wealth of one or more individuals (or segments of society) to others in con-

---

riders (leading to underproduction of the public good). Thus, some scholars contend that such market 'failure' obliges government intervention." John M. Cobin (1997), *Building Regulation, Market Alternatives, and Allodial Policy*, Avebury Press: London, pp. 81-82.

junction with a higher or meta-social goal. In other words, government uses its power to extort money from (typically) "the haves" against their will and to give it to "the have-nots" in a sort of modern Robin Hood role. Moreover, a socially detrimental payoff is also often available to quasi-government agencies, politicians, bureaucrats, regressive entrepreneurs, or private suppliers who participate in the transfer process—what economists call "rent seeking".[26]

Such legal extortion policies (for which Bastiat coined the term "legal plunder") are typically based on a positive rights theory, if not an outright socialist ideology. These proactive policies are popularly described as "welfare state" policies. They have an overarching societal or moral meta-goal, rather than just a goal of improving lifestyle risks, ensuring "fair" prices and information, providing public goods, or alleviating negative externalities. Like all proactive policies, this species is accomplished by direct taxation, indirect or hidden taxation (e.g., inflation), or by regulation (e.g., restricting the use of private property and thus lowering its value—also known as "takings", or by taking away private property in order to remove urban blight, spur new development, and increase local tax revenue as in the infamous 2005 U.S. Supreme Court decision *Kelo v. City of New London*).

Examples of redistributive policy programs include food stamps, Aid to Families with Dependent Children (welfare), Social Security, subsidies to farmers or other

---

[26] Rent seeking diverts useful resources into activities that redistribute surplus from exchange. Gordon Tullock defines rent seeking as "the manipulation of democratic [or other types of] governments to obtain special privileges under circumstances where the people injured by the privileges are hurt more than the beneficiary gains". Gordon Tullock (1993), *Rent Seeking*, The Shaftesbury Papers, 2, Brookfield, Vermont: Edward Elgar Publishing Co., p. 24, cf. p. 51. Thomas DiLorenzo specifies that, "in every industry the less efficient competitors can be expected to snipe at their superior rivals, and in many instances sniping turns into an organized political crusade to get the government to enact laws or regulations that harm the superior competitor. Economists call this process 'rent seeking'." Thomas J. DiLorenzo (2004), *How Capitalism Saved America*, New York: Crown Forum, p. 126.

groups, most unemployment "insurance", subsidized housing, public (state) education, university-level grants, and many student loan programs. Some proactive policies of redistribution are frequently mistaken as simply being policies of inefficient provision, in particular Social Security (or old-age) benefits, unemployment insurance, and university student loans. Yet they are clearly proactive because they involve the direct plunder of one group in society in order to benefit another group.[27]

Table 1: Policy types and their philosophical bases

Type of public policy	Rights basis
1. Reactive (defensive)	Negative
2. Inefficient public provision	Negative, positive, or neither
3. Proactive	
(i) to change behavior	Positive (typically)
(ii) to alter ways of thinking	Positive (typically)
(iii) to foster redistribution	Positive

Social Security and unemployment tax contributions are used to create a savings or insurance fund that an individual can draw upon when in need. Thus, they feel justified when accepting Social Security and unemployment benefits[28] since they think that they have "paid-in" to the program for many years. In reality, they have not paid-in anything. They were forced to participate in a state-run

---

[27] For instance, in passing legislation for the collection of Social Security (and unemployment) "contributions" or taxes, government may mandate that the employee and the employer *each* pay one-half. However, the reality is that the employee pays the tax in its entirety. When employers hire their employees they evaluate the labor services they expect to receive against the *total* cost they expect to have to pay for those services. By implication, an employee's wages would likely be higher if the firm did not pay his Social Security and unemployment "contributions". See Eric Schansberg (1996), *Poor Policy: How Government Harms the Poor*, Boulder, Colorado: Westview Press, p. 74.

[28] There may be some unemployment policies that actually are savings or true insurance plans—just as in Chile the national social security plan is privatized (albeit regulated). But these are exceptions rather than the rule.

28

Ponzi scheme[29] that facilitates income redistribution. Recipients are not *getting back* any of their own money; they are getting money from other people who are currently working.

University student grants work the same way, but their character as welfare is more evident. But educational loans for university study are frequently misunderstood by Christians to be justifiable because money is paid back to the state with interest. However, upon closer analysis, it is clear that many (but not all) student loans are forms of welfare for two principal reasons. First, "the government"— viz. taxpayers—is forced to pay the interest on the loan while the student is at the university. Second, they offer a lower rate of interest than a typical student would be able to acquire in the marketplace. Notwithstanding this fact, if an educational loan were taken out by a parent for his child, based on the parent's credit rating, and the interest was paid back by the parent from the outset; such a loan (if offered or backed by the state) would be inefficient provision rather than proactive policy.

The reader should now be prepared to distinguish reactive, inefficient provision, and proactive policies based on their leading characteristics. Some policies will be easier to discern than others because many policies have mixed objectives. Yet useful classification is still possible.

For instance, public health policy might have a reactive component, such as staving off infectious disease, while the rest of public health policy is proactive. Thus, when classifying the policy, one can split it into two parts:

---

[29] Charles Ponzi (1882-1949), a short (5 ft., 2 in.) Italian immigrant to the United States, was one of the greatest swindlers in American history. He was an incurable liar and possessed boundless self-confidence. Although there was a huge discrepancy between Ponzi's grand opinion of himself and his actual talents, he was an extraordinary con artist. He had a big smile and a fast line of talk. Ponzi's sales pitch for his pyramid postal coupon scam (offering huge returns on investment) was smooth and low-key, suckering many Americans and later became known as the original "Ponzi scheme".

(1) public health for infectious disease control—reactive and (2) public health for behavior modification—proactive.

Man's nature is the same regardless of his profession

Does the nature of man change on account of the ballot box or a political appointment? For years scholars in disciplines like political science and history have taught so. The basic idea is simply that a man who succeeds in being elected to office would reasonably be the "cream of the crop"—able to govern his fellow man with virtue—and subordinating his own self-interest motives for publicly-spirited ideals. Paradoxically, the mass of self-interested and often selfish voters would evidently elect such a virtuous man from their own dissolute ranks. Democratic processes and majority voting may thus bring about optimal social results, especially when "the voice of the people" has been heard through large voter turnouts.

However, this questionable notion has come under extensive attack by economists during the last several decades. Inspired by the libertarian-leaning writings of Nobel laureate Friedrich Hayek, and especially Austrian economist Ludwig von Mises, "public choice" economists such Gordon Tullock, James Buchanan, and Robert Tollison—as well as many "hybrid" economists espousing aspects of both the Austrian and public choice schools—began to promote a simple, but radical new idea. They extended the work of Adam Smith in *The Wealth of Nations* (1776) and other economists to conclude that being elected or appointed to office does not affect man's nature. Men still pursue their own self-interest in the political arena just as men in the private sector would. And why would any Christian think otherwise? The Bible never indicates that the nature of political actors is different than other men. Surely the fact that rulers like Nero and Herod are "ordained by God" (Romans 13:1) does not mean that they had human natures with less corruption! Indeed, Edmund Opitz reminds us of the inevitable legacy of corruption and privilege peddling by political leaders.

> As long as the state, the agency of coercion, stands over society offering to dispense economic privilege to those who pay it homage, conferring an advantage on some men at the expense of other men, the misuse of political power should be the first line of attack for the moralist. It is inevitable that political privilege will be used in this way if it is available and begging to be used. No people has ever resisted it who have been led into this temptation.[30]

Consequently, relying on both public choice economic theory and the Bible, we can safely conclude that there are never truly any so-called "statesmen". Rarely, if ever, is a man so publicly-spirited that he is able to subordinate his self-interest in favor of the "public interest". Most men desire public office primarily on account of self-interested motivations (e.g., money, power, or prestige). Few men today come close to exhibiting the public servant ideals of the Founders in their vision of establishing limited government. As Dr. Steven Yates notes:

> [W]hile politicians have never been our noblest or most honest, I do not believe most people today even expect much in the way of honesty or personal integrity from those seeking or holding high public office. They see politicians as pragmatists and judge them accordingly...Both dominant parties became repositories of pragmatism and expediency instead of principle and

---

[30] Rev. Edmund Opitz (1999), *The Libertarian Theology of Freedom*, Tampa, Florida: Hallberg Publishing Co., p. 84.

31

honorability long ago. Both see massive government [state] actions as the solution to problems, disagreeing only on the details—and again never looking beneath the surface of events or questioning premises.[31]

Moreover, economists in the Austrian school tradition have long pointed out the impossibility of men to accomplish public interest projects (whether socialism or other proactive policies). No man—or even a committee of brilliant men with a thousand computers and aides—can possibly harness the requisite knowledge to plan or regulate the economy in order to promote the public interest. On the one hand, there is no *public* interest. There are only individual interests. One man may like five aircraft carriers but another man only one. One man may like student loan programs and another may not. There is no way to aggregate individual preferences. Thus the term "public interest" is merely a euphemism for the preferences of a political party, a special interest group (or coalition), or any particular ruler making a decree.

On the other hand, no man (or junta) has enough knowledge by himself to produce anything. Even something as inexpensive and common as a pencil requires the cooperation of thousands of individuals with specialized knowledge to produce: graphite and brass mining and refining, forestry and woodworking, fine painting and lacquering, transportation, marketing, and much more. There is simply no way that any man (or any committee) would know what is needed to produce even the most basic goods. Thus, planners and regulators face an impossible task on account of this "knowledge problem". The most that can ever be expected of a man as a governor, representative, judge, juror, or sheriff—none of which qualify as states-

---

[31] Steven Yates (2005), *Worldviews: Christian Theism versus Modern Materialism*, Greenville, South Carolina: The Worldviews Project, pp. 51-52.

men—is to provide for the reactive functions of defending constituents from predators and providing a system of criminal justice.

Accordingly, economists have developed a two-pronged general critique of economic regulation and planning. First, if rulers and planners were angelic or nearly altruists with hearts of gold—being publicly-spirited and full of good intentions—they will still fail to plan correctly or efficiently on account of the knowledge problem. Second, if rulers and planners were not like angels, but instead serve their own self interests (rather than mainly the public interest) like the rest of humanity, they will fail to plan correctly or efficiently on account of public choice problems. Hence, good theory would lead us to conclude that proactive policies will fail to serve their stated purpose and instead only serve to benefit the state and political actors.

Perverse incentives lead to failed state policies

Sometimes a little economic theory can go a long way toward improving our understanding of the world we live in. The following application is adapted from a topic in *A Primer on Modern Themes in Free Market Economics and Policy* (1999), an upper-level economics text.[32]

Government planners—like all human beings—have a self-interest motive, and are typically not altruistic servants of the public interest. Therefore, public choice economic theory suggests that self-interested political actors will be subject to perverse incentives. For instance, planners have a perverse incentive to be ineffective. Governments never lose profits from being poor regulators, but the opposite is likely to be true. If regulation were com-

---

[32] The book is available in paperback through Amazon.com and in e-book (PDF) format (2003 rev. ed.) from Alertness Books: http://policyofliberty.net/checkout/products.php.

pletely effective at eliminating social problems then there would no longer be a need for it. A regulator or planner who wants to maintain his employment (and we can assume that they do) has an incentive to maintain some minimum levels of social problem in order to preserve his job.

In addition, planners have a perverse incentive to encourage adverse public information that suggests that current regulation is failing. The typical response to this information will be increased calls for government to augment regulation, likely leading to larger budgets and salaries for planners. Thus, planners might perversely view some regulatory failures as successes, while consumers and taxpayers will not concur.

Example of air pollution

The perverse incentives problem can be illustrated by a hypothetical example of air pollution levels (and regulatory constraints) for a major city. Let us suppose that (1) clean air is a "normal" good that people choose to buy more of as their incomes rise, (2) peoples' earnings continue to rise over time, (3) all production produces some smog, either directly or indirectly, and (4) that the urban area is growing (along with its production) over time.

As the city develops, people will enjoy rising incomes and will be willing to accept higher amounts of air pollution to sustain that income—up to a certain point of contentment C. However, as the level of smog rises above point C, people start becoming concerned, and a few will even become preoccupied, about the smog problem.

But most are still willing to tolerate the dirtier air because of the other benefits they have from urban life, at least up to point P. At smog level P they become critically preoccupied, although intense complaining might not begin right away. Accordingly, as the smog level surpasses point P, people might not complain or change their smog producing behavior in the short run if they believe that the rise above point P is only temporary. However, once people realize that the level of smog is permanent they will take steps to alleviate the problem. Two options are feasible.

Figure 1: Clean air levels constrained by public policy

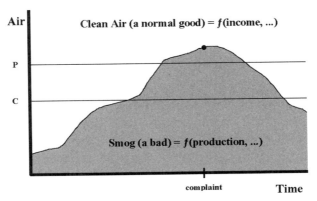

The first option is to simply let entrepreneurs and market institutions develop spontaneously to solve the pollution problem. Since clean air is a "normal" good, people will prefer to buy more of it as their incomes rise. Above point P, people will tend to trade some of their relatively high incomes for cleaner air. Consequently, pollution control experts and entrepreneurs will emerge to meet the demands of consumers, and competition will cause improvements in technology that make pollution abatement increasingly cheaper. Over time, the lower price will mean that more clean air can be acquired by trading the same percentage of income, and the result will be a smog level that continually declines, probably at a decreasing rate. The level of smog might be reduced to zero someday, but it is unlikely because the opportunity cost of doing so will be rising at an increasing rate. Thus, the costs of purity are often sufficiently high to deter people from achieving it. However, it is likely that the level of smog will remain

35

somewhere below point C, where there would be little public uneasiness from smog.

The second option is for voters to demand that proactive public policies be initiated to deal with the smog problem. The "public interest" would be invoked citing both positive rights to clean air and negative rights to protection from the pollution and its negative external costs. Vote-seeking politicians will respond to the demands of voters and special interest groups by (1) creating a bureaucracy to "solve" the problem and (2) taxing away incomes to support it. Personal freedom (or utility) will also be diminished by the regulation it generates. The new bureaucrats (and those who consult with them) will probably be experts in pollution abatement, and people will be forced to comply with their public interest objectives. As a result, the level of smog will decline, just as it would under the first option. Once people perceive that the long run level of smog has fallen below point P, they will stop complaining. Hence, bureaucrats will have an incentive, either directly or through the pressure of vote-seeking politicians, to reach that point as soon as possible. When they succeed, voters will be happy with the regulatory effectiveness and will in turn laud the politicians who initiated it.

However, with the level of smog below point P, the bureaucrats are faced with a perverse incentive. If the smog level should drop below point C, social uneasiness would diminish sufficiently far that people would begin to complain more about the taxes and regulation pertaining to the bureaucracy than the smog. People would prefer to have more disposable income and freedom from the smog-induced regulation. Hence, the bureaucrats, who want to keep their jobs and maximize their departmental budgets, will realize the importance of maintaining the smog level above point C, and will choose policies and favor technologies that achieve that goal. Therefore, smog problems will likely be alleviated by public policy (and evidence of urban regulation today often confirms this fact). But public choice theory suggests that smog will never be eliminated or brought to a level below point C in the long run. Political intervention to eliminate smog problems will simply tend to make an uncomfortable yet tolerable amount of smog a *permanent* part of social life.

Consequently, perverse incentives will naturally guide self-interested political actors to lead society in ways that run counter to the true public interest in favor of benefiting personal and private interests. No matter what agency the politician or bureaucrat endeavors to promote, his self-interest motives will trump public interest ones. Government planners will make smog a permanent fixture. Police departments will have an incentive to *control* crime and consensual vices like prostitution and drug abuse but never *eliminate* them (lest they also eliminate their jobs). Bureaucrats who are handed departmental budget cuts will find ways to maintain their budgets by creating public outcry against politicians, in order to secure their power base and personal career advancement opportunities. Judges will rule with their own self-interest and future promotion in mind rather than allowing the true public interest to dominate.

Applying theory to practice and ancillary exegesis

If economic theory and what the Bible teach about human nature are correct, then no Christian should be in favor of maintaining public enterprises or permitting public policies designed to change people's way of thinking and behavior or to redistribute wealth. The best that people can hope for in government is to limit its sphere and scope to protecting them from the dishonest, treacherous, and inordinate actions of others. And Christians should have no other political conviction than to see this end achieved.

Accordingly, vigorous biblical analysis of public policy will be easier with this chapter's basic tools from economics and public policy theory in hand. A Christian can thus utilize this knowledge to help him determine what policies are just and what policies are unjust or immoral. This knowledge will help him formulate a well-reasoned and appropriate response to most policies he encounters. As well, the applying these theories will help him decide whether or not a Christian should bother promoting some policy or not based on his prediction about its likelihood of success and the kind of outcome that it will tend to spawn.

Power tends to corrupt. Absolute power corrupts absolutely.
—Lord Acton (1834-1902)

Sometimes it is said that man cannot be trusted with the government of himself. Can he, then, be trusted with the government of others? Or have we found angels in the forms of kings to govern him? Let history answer this question.
—President Thomas Jefferson (1743-1826)

Because the regime is captive to its own lies, it must falsify everything. It falsifies the past. It falsifies the present, and it falsifies the future. It falsifies statistics. It pretends not to possess an omnipotent and unprincipled police apparatus. It pretends to respect human rights. It pretends to prosecute no one.
—Czech President Vaclav Havel (1978)

... the chief business of the greatest part of governments on the whole earth has been to abbreviate life, to poison and imbitter [sic] its sweetest pleasures, and add new pungency to its anguish.
—Vicesimus Knox (c. 1795)

2 Public Policy Theology in Historical Context

Understanding the first century audience and context

How would the statements by the Apostles Paul and Peter (in Romans 13:1-7, Titus 3:1, and 1 Peter 2:13-17) have differed if they had been modern day Americans rather than living under the Roman state? The study of history, economics, political science, world religions, literary forms, and philosophy are important for proper biblical interpretation. Without a good grasp of the facts revealed by these fields of endeavor, the interpreter is prone to make errors in judgment, including errors in applying the doctrinal rules regarding submission to authority under a modern "democracy" (or republic) rather than an autocracy.

For instance, the synoptic Gospel accounts say that the death of Christ occurred at the "sixth hour" (Matthew 27:45; Mark 15:33; Luke 23:44), while John 19:14 says that He was still with Pilate at that time. How can one reconcile the difference in time? Is the discrepancy proof that the Bible contains errors? By applying knowledge from fields such and history along with deductive reasoning, one will find that John's Gospel was written much later than the other three accounts—after the fall of Jerusalem in AD70. That cataclysmic event crushed, among other things, the

Jewish manner of keeping time. For a Jew, a day began at 6AM instead of midnight (the latter being both the Roman convention and ours today). Thus, in Jewish time the sixth hour corresponded to noon in Roman time. John would have used Roman time in his gospel and so there is no contradiction in the Bible.[33] Accordingly, biblical interpretation can be facilitated and enhanced by careful utilization of the tools from other disciplines.

That is not to say that all doctrines of the Bible require tools from disciplines like the sciences or the humanities to be well understood. In particular, the doctrine of salvation and the nature and attributes of God may be clearly manifest to even the most uninformed reader. But some theology and specific doctrine requires hard work to flesh out appropriately—including the use of analytical tools and knowledge gleaned from other disciplines. Thus, a good grasp of economics, public policy theory, and history are a boon in developing a biblical theology of public policy.

"Honor the king" (1 Peter 2:17) is Peter's terse apostolic admonition to first-century Christians, "pilgrims of the dispersion" (1 Peter 1:1), whom Nero had exiled to Asia Minor from Rome. The admonition includes the specific objects and extent of their acquiescence: "submit yourselves to every ordinance of man...to the king as supreme, or to governors..." (1 Peter 2:13-14a). In the same vein, the Apostle Paul wrote in more general terms to the Christians at Rome and Gortys (the capital of the province of Crete), using the language "rulers and authorities" (Titus 3:1, cf. Romans 13:1-3). As noted in the introduction, Paul surely had in mind the imperial Caesar Nero, as well as various lesser authorities who ruled Rome's provinces, such as Herod, Felix, and Agrippa.

---

[33] Note: even if John's gospel were written earlier, he could have opted for using what scholars call *Judean* time (where a day starts at midnight) if his audience were mostly non-Jews living in the Empire, instead of *Galilean* time where the day starts at 6am.

On the one hand, one must be cautious about employing history and culture in his biblical exegesis. God's Word is valid for all peoples of all times, and it is an error to arbitrarily ignore or modify portions of His Word based on one's understanding of history and culture. On the other hand, it is impossible to fully understand or appreciate the Scriptures apart from the historical and cultural context in which they were written. Indeed, a lack of cultural and historical understanding can lead to faulty exegesis.

Historians refer to the phase of the ancient Roman state in apostolic times as the *Principate*. The Emperor was

Emperor Nero
AD54-68

Caesar and, as such, held autocratic dominion. Although high-handed rule dominated, a number of decentralized forms and conventions still existed—leftovers from the oligarchic self-government of the Roman Republic (which effectively ended in 27BC). Thus, wealthy Plutarchs were called upon by the Emperor to handle various administrative functions in each province of the Empire (totaling 50 million inhabitants). It is important to realize that the Apostles were writing to Christians who lived under an autocratic, brutal state, rather than the famous Roman Republic that had ended some 80 years earlier. Sure, the memory of the old Republic likely filled the imagination of many citizens, but it was no longer a reality.[34]

Nero's character; politics, history and economics

Nero reigned in Rome from AD54 to AD68, and the Apostles Paul and Peter wrote Romans 13:1-7 and 1 Peter

---

[34] In the same way that some Romans might have mused about their glorious Republic of old, so some modern American patriots fondly muse about the liberty-loving American republic before 1861.

2:13-17 (to Roman believers) during that period. Nero was an insane, pompous criminal, who instigated chaos in society by his public policies. He burned the city, murdered his mother and other relatives, and cruelly assailed Christians.

Nero's activities were so base that the Roman Senate proclaimed him to be the prime enemy of the people. Not surprisingly, rioting and other grievous social upheavals were commonplace in Rome under Nero. The fact that Paul wrote to the Roman Christians during a time when their city was undergoing a famine and riots should have an important bearing on our interpretation of Romans 13:1-7 (which is applied in the concise commentary in chapter 6). Perhaps the social circumstances led Paul to exhort the Roman Christians to not participate in the "envying", "rioting", and "strife" around them (Romans 13:13).

Nero's character and public policies

In AD63, Nero made his famous appearance in a public stage performance, and allegedly fiddled while he burned at least two-thirds of Rome. Nero falsely blamed the Christians for the conflagration, and Peter thus alludes to the "fiery trial" (1 Peter 4:12) that would come upon believers on account of the ensuing persecutions. The Roman historian Tacitus relates something of Nero's public policy toward Christians: "Covered with the skins of beasts, they were torn by dogs and perished, or were nailed to crosses, or were doomed to the flames. These served to illuminate the night when daylight failed." Both Paul and Peter were likely martyred during Nero's reign. Nero committed suicide, after the Senate declared him a public enemy (AD68).

Since culture and history must have some bearing on the interpretation of Romans 13:1-7 and 1 Peter 2:13-17, a brief inquiry into the character and public policies of Nero will help us understand the context in which the Apostles wrote to the Roman Christians. Clearly, Nero did *not* uphold the Law of God or punish people on God's behalf who broke His rules. On the contrary, Nero violated God's law in both his personal life and in his public policies. Nero was not just an imperfect ruler who tried his best to do the right thing. He was an impenitent evildoer who viciously and overtly opposed God's ways. The Roman historian Josephus gives the following account of Nero:

> Now as to the many things in which Nero acted like a madman, out of the extravagant degree of the felicity and riches which he enjoyed, and by that means used his good fortune to the injury of others; and after what manner he slew his brother, and wife, and mother, from whom his barbarity spread itself to others that were most nearly related to him; and how, at last, he was so distracted that he became an actor in the scenes, and upon the theater, —I omit to say any more about them, because there are writers enough upon those subjects every where.[35]

Other accounts of Nero's life are similar, such as the descriptions in *Quo Vadis: A Narrative of the Time of Nero*. Nero was noted to be a rotten monster.[36] He was considered to be unmerciful.[37] He was considered to be a malicious madman.[38] He was pompous, fantasizing about

---

[35] Flavius Josephus (1999), *The Wars of the Jews*, William Whiston, trans., book II, 13:1, Grand Rapids, Michigan: Kregal Publications.

[36] "'I have revered the gods so far,' said he; 'but at this moment I think that not they are over the world, but one mad, malicious monster named Nero.' 'Aulus,' said Pomponia. 'Nero is only a handful of rotten dust before God.'" Henryk Sienkiewicz (2002), *Quo Vadis: A Narrative of the Time of Nero*, Jeremiah Curtin trans., chapter IV, McClean, Virginia: Indypublish.com.

[37] Ibid. "...life is one twinkle of the eye, and resurrection is only from the grave; beyond that not Nero, but Mercy bears rule, and there instead of pain is delight, there instead of tears is rejoicing."

[38] Ibid., chapter XXVI. "He was a patrician, a military tribune, a powerful man; but above every power of that world to which he belonged was a madman whose will and malignity it was impossible to foresee. Only such people as the Christians might cease

his own glory after rebuilding the great city of Rome after he burned it.[39] His rule and his policy were cruel to his subjects.[40] He persecuted Christians and made it difficult for them to worship.[41] Tacitus elaborates on Nero's vicious, cruel, and sadistic persecution of Christians as follows:

> Therefore, to put an end to the rumor [that Nero was responsible for the burning of three-fourths of Rome] Nero created a diversion and subjected to the most extraordinary tortures those hated

---

to reckon with Nero or fear him, —people for whom this whole world, with its separations and sufferings, was as nothing; people for whom death itself was as nothing. All others had to tremble before him. The terrors of the time in which they lived showed themselves to Vinicius in all their monstrous extent…in such times only Christians could be happy."

[39] Ibid., chapter XXXVIII. "'How could the earth find place at once for the Apostle Peter, Paul of Tarsus, and Caesar? Tell me this. I ask because I passed the evening after Paul's teaching with Nero, and dost thou know what I heard there? Well, to begin with, he read his poem on the destruction of Troy, and complained that never had he seen a burning city. He envied Priam, and called him happy just for this, that he saw the conflagration and ruin of his birthplace. Whereupon Tigellinus said, 'Speak a word, O divinity, I will take a torch, and before the night passes thou shalt see blazing Antium.' But Caesar called him a fool. 'Where,' asked he, 'should I go to breathe the sea air, and preserve the voice with which the gods have gifted me, and which men say I should preserve for the benefit of mankind? Is it not Rome that injures me; is it not the exhalations of the Subura and the Esquiline which add to my hoarseness? Would not the palaces of Rome present a spectacle a hundredfold more tragic and magnificent than Antium?' Here all began to talk, and to say what an unheard tragedy the picture of a city like that would be, a city which had conquered the world turned now into a heap of gray ashes. Caesar declared that then his poem would surpass the songs of Homer, and he began to describe how he would rebuild the city, and how coming ages would admire his achievements, in presence of which all other human works would be petty. 'Do that! Do that!' exclaimed the drunken company. 'I must have more faithful and more devoted friends,' answered he."

[40] Ibid., chapter XLIII. "Meanwhile the rage and despair of the crowd turned against the praetorians, who for another reason could not make their way out of the crowd: the road was blocked by piles of goods, borne from the fire previously, boxes, barrels of provisions, furniture the most costly, vessels, infants' cradles, beds, carts, hand-packs. Here and there they fought band to hand; but the praetorians conquered the weaponless multitude easily."

[41] Ibid., chapter XLV. "'This, lord, that synagogues exist openly in the Trans-Tiber; but that Christians, in their wish to avoid persecution, are forced to pray in secret and assemble in ruined sheds outside the city or in sand-pits. Those who dwell in the Trans-Tiber have chosen just that place which was excavated for the building of the Circus and various houses along the Tiber. Now, when the city is perishing, the adherents of Christ are praying. Beyond doubt we shall find a countless number of them in the excavation; so my advice is to go in there along the road.'"

for their abominations by the common people called Christians. The originator of this name (was) Christ, who, during the reign of Tiberius had been executed by sentence of the procurator Pontinus [*sic*] Pilate. Repressed for the time being, the deadly superstition broke out again not only in Judea, the original source of the evil, but also in the city (Rome), where all things horrible or shameful in the world collect and become popular. So an arrest was made of all who confessed; then on the basis of their information, an immense multitude was convicted, not so much of the crime of arson as for hatred of the human race...Mockery of every sort was added to their deaths. Covered with the skins of beasts, they were torn by dogs and perished, or were nailed to crosses, or were doomed to the flames. These served to illuminate the night when daylight failed. Nero had thrown open the gardens for the spectacle, and was exhibiting a show in the circus, while he mingled with the people in the dress of a charioteer or drove about in a chariot. Hence, even for criminals who deserved extreme and exemplary punishment there arose a feeling of compassion; for it was not, as it seemed, for the public good, but glut one man's cruelty, that they were being punished.[42]

Alonzo Jones further notes that "This cruel subterfuge accomplished the purpose intended by the emperor, to deliver him from the angry suspicion of the populace."[43]

Surely, if we hold that the apostles were referring to the existing Roman state, then something more than a plain, cursory understanding of the texts in Romans 13:1-7, 1

---

[42] Cornelius Historiae Tacitus (2003), *The Annals and the History*, 15.44.2-8, Alfred John Church and William Jackson Brodribb trans., New York: Modern Library Press.

[43] Alonzo T. Jones (1891), *The Two Republics or Rome and the United States of America*, Battle Creek, Michigan: Review and Herald Publishing Company, p. 114.

Peter 2:13-17 and Titus 3:1 must be considered when taking into account Nero's nefarious reign and persecution of Christians. Otherwise, what would we make of the Apostolic doctrine that says: "rulers are not a terror to good works, but to evil...Do what is good, and you will have praise from the same. For he is God's minister to you for good" (Romans 13:3-4a), indeed "for the praise of those who do good" (1 Peter 2:14b)? Nero's actions, which must have been manifestly clear to the Apostles, make a mockery of any doctrine based on a plain, exact, absolute or literalistic understanding of these texts, for he was one of the most evil villains in history.

On the one hand, Nero *was* a terror to those who did well in God's sight. Peter alludes to Nero's punishment of those who did well in 1 Peter 2:20, where some Christians were, apparently, doing good and suffering for it. On the other hand, Nero did *not* punish those who did evil in the sight of the Lord. He himself was a murderer, an adulterer, a proud and covetous man, a man who dishonored his parents, and a man who was public enemy number one.

Indeed, wicked Nero was God's enemy who "served" God in the same way that the devil serves Him—until the final day when he will be dispatched forever in the lake of fire. Perhaps seventeenth century English playwright Matthew Gwinn has summed it up best: "Nero is wholly composed of crime. But he will pay the price for his crimes, as is fair, and as will happen soon."[44]

Political context of the first century

Interestingly, Paul had written 1 Corinthians and 2 Corinthians around the same time (AD55 to AD57) as the epistle to the Romans, but the Apostle gives no practical

---

[44] Matthew Gwinn (1997 [1603]), *Nero*, Act V, Scene 4 [Act II, Scene 1], Volusius Proculus, Epicharis: Dana F. Sutton (translator).

47

treatise on Christians and the civil authority in those epistles. However, he does address both churches about the issue of the weaker brother and eating meat sacrificed to idols. The Corinthians had a litany of sinful problems, but evidently reminding them to be submissive to their local rulers was not a pressing issue for the Apostle. Paul does mention obedience to authorities to Titus, who was left in Crete for a while, but does not mention it to Timothy who was left in Ephesus (on the western coast of modern Turkey); both epistles were written about the same time.

While Crete was not of great economic importance in the Roman world, its south central city of Gortys (about 30 miles from modern Rethymno) did serve as capital for the province of Crete and Cyrenaica (the coast of modern Libya), which was formed in 74BC. Given Gortys' political importance, its proximity to Roman trade routes, and the Cretans' famous propensity to indulge in revelry as: "liars, evil beasts, lazy gluttons" (Titus 1:12), Paul exhorted Titus to tell Cretan believers to be careful to "be subject to rulers and authorities, to obey, to be ready for every good work" (Titus 3:1).

A key supposition: it seems that Paul wanted to shut down any possible excuse for the Roman state to persecute believers. If there was to be persecution, it must come as a result of hatred for Jesus Christ and His church (Revelation 12:17), and not because of the sinful behavior of Christians. When social instability and lack of food produced rogues and riots in Rome, Christians were to have no part of it. As Matthew Henry comments:

> Our Lord Jesus was so reproached, though he told them his kingdom was not of this world: no marvel, then, if his followers have been loaded in all ages with the like calumnies, called *factious, seditious,* and *turbulent,* and looked upon as the troublers of the land, their enemies having

found such representations needful for the justi-
fying of their barbarous rage against them. The
apostle therefore, for the obviating of this reproach and the clearing of Christianity from it,
shows that obedience to civil magistrates is one
of the laws of Christ, whose religion helps to
make people good subjects; and it was very unjust to charge upon Christianity that faction and
rebellion to which its principles and rules are so
directly contrary.[45]

David Brown concurs:

But since Christians were constantly charged
with turning the world upside down, and since
there certainly were elements enough in Christianity of moral and social revolution to give
plausibility to the charge, and tempt noble spirits, crushed under misgovernment, to take redress into their own hands, it was of special importance that the pacific, submissive, loyal spirit
of those Christians who resided at the great seat
of political power, should furnish a visible refu-
tation of this charge.[46]

The Bible's political context is important because it
profoundly influences our theology of public policy. Yet
the clear contextual differences between the political organization and public policies of first century Rome and the
present day seems to be missed by many pastors and Christian leaders today. Some of them apparently presume that
the Apostles lived under a state similar to ours. However,
it is manifestly clear that they did not, and proper biblical
interpretation must be tempered accordingly.

---

[45] Matthew Henry (1721), *Commentary on the Whole Bible*, vol. VI, Grand Rapids,
Michigan: Christian Classics Ethereal Library (e-book reprint).
[46] David Brown in Robert Jamieson, A. R. Fausset and David Brown (1871), *Commentary Critical and Explanatory on the Whole Bible*, Grand Rapids, Michigan: Christian
Classics Ethereal Library (e-book reprint).

Consider the differences in the form of government then and now. We do not have a "king". While the principle of submitting to those in authority, even in a Constitutional Republic, can rightly be inferred from the passages pertaining to obedience to the state and honoring the king, it is quite possible that structural changes in governmental forma and structure can lead to corresponding changes in our response to the state and its policies. Some Bible doctrines are either dependent on or subject to contextual considerations, meaning that with some commands only principles survive without the exact form of obedience.

Historical and cultural context of the first century

While cultural considerations are not paramount in proper biblical interpretation, they do play an important role. For example, modern Christians do not literally buy a "sword" for use as a weapon to fulfill Christ's command in Luke 22:36; because of technological improvements they can buy a gun. Likewise, Paul commanded Roman, Achaean, and Macedonian Christians to greet each other with a "holy kiss" (Romans 16:16, 1 Corinthians 16:20, 2 Corinthians 13:12, 1 Thessalonians 5:26). The command was given four times—one more time than the Apostles commanded Christians to be submissive to state authorities. Yet modern Christians do not have the exact practice of greeting-by-kissing because the culture has changed. Only the principle of affectionate salutation has been retained.

In many cases, cultural context is significant for proper interpretation. Consider the following passages from the Bible to see the importance of understanding context:
1. the mandate to give holy kisses (Romans 16:16, 1 Corinthians 16:20, 2 Corinthians 13:12, 1 Thessalonians 5:26, 1 Peter 5:14) and mandatory greetings (Philippians 4:21, Titus 3:15, Hebrews 13:24);

2. Old Testament practices brought into the New Testament (Acts 15:28-29, Romans 14:5, Colossians 2:16);
3. issues of Christian indebtedness (Romans 13:8); self-defense (Romans 12:19, cf. Luke 22:36);
4. the requirement to eat any meat sold in the meat market (1 Corinthians 10:25);
5. practices of women in church (1 Corinthians 14:34, cf. 1 Timothy 2:11) and with women's hair and head coverings (1 Corinthians 11:5-6, cf. 1 Timothy 2:9);
6. mandates regarding prophecy and tongues-speaking (1 Corinthians 14:39, 1 Thessalonians 4:20-21);
7. principles of order in worship (1 Corinthians 14:40);
8. mandates about when to bring offerings (1 Corinthians 16:2);
9. requirements of temporal contentment (1 Timothy 6:8);
10. Paul's personal commands to Timothy (2 Timothy 4:9, 13, 21a);
11. mandates to entertain strangers or angels (Hebrews 13:2);
12. obligations to pray for prisoners (Hebrews 13:3);
13. admonitions to the wealthy class acting wrongly (James 5:1);
14. admonitions to confess our sins to other believers (James 5:16);
15. prohibitions about letting heretics into one's home (2 John 1:10-11);
16. requirements to give away one's clothing (Matthew 5:40) or to acquire tools and provisions (Luke 22:36);
17. mandates to not attempt to change one's social class or status (1 Corinthians 7:24); and

18. directives to not despise leaders (Titus 2:15b, 1 Timothy 4:12).

Plus there are those curious directives to be ignorant (1 Corinthians 14:38), unjust, unholy, filthy, righteous, and holy (Revelation 22:11), as well as the exhortation to figure out what the numerology of 666 might mean (Revelation 13:18). Surely cultural (and historical) context matters in interpreting such passages, as well as the rest of the New Testament.

Many theological issues and ecclesiastical problems were specific to a particular church, culture, or geographic region. Indeed, many of the early churches were afflicted by particular troubles, usually mimicking the culture that surrounded them. For instance, Corinth was a resort town renowned for lasciviousness and lewdness, and it is such behavior that infiltrated the Corinthian church: sexual immorality, marital issues, lawsuits among believers, abuses of the Lord's Supper, dissention and contentions, and dealing with weaker brothers. Churches in Galatia and Palestine were combating legalisms introduced by Jewish infiltrators.

Christ specifically rebuked the Smyrnan church for not acting appropriately with wealth, and James similarly reprimanded his readers. Jude warned against the intrusion of heretics into the ranks of the faithful, as Christ points out to the churches at Pergamos and Thyatira. John corrected churches that had been permeated by incipient Gnosticism. Christ rebukes the churches in Sardis and Ephesus for their formalism and deadness. Similarly, the church at Rome, being the seat of government power and a huge center of trade, was influenced by the activities of the culture surrounding it, and Paul and Peter counsel the Roman believers in this regard in Romans 13:1-7 and 1 Peter 2:13-17. Understanding some of the facets of the cultural context of Rome is essential in understanding the issues particular to the Roman Christians, as well as to properly interpreting the apostolic doctrine regarding submission to civil government.

Economic context of the first century

The political context of the Apostles differed greatly from the situation of the modern West. Not only do most Western countries not have an autocratic state, the rules of interventionism have changed. Rome had no welfare state. This fact is important for Christians because welfarism is based on the notion of "positive rights". This political philosophy justifies plundering one group of citizens in order to benefit another, and is therefore an abomination to the Christian faith.

Would the Apostles have encouraged modern Christians in the West to participate in welfare state programs or employment schemes? If we take the Scriptural admonitions against theft seriously, the answer must be "No". The Bible clearly prohibits theft: "You shall not steal, nor deal falsely, nor lie to one another" (Leviticus 19:11), "You shall not steal" (Exodus 20:15; Matthew 19:18, Romans 13:9), "Let him who stole steal no longer" (Ephesians 4:28a); and it forbids idleness: "If anyone will not work, neither shall he eat" (1 Thessalonians 3:10).

The fact that the state legalizes plunder through extortive taxation policy does not justify the theft, nor does the state's rewarding of idleness excuse complacent joblessness. Recipients may not receive welfare and be innocent any more than a woman or her abortion "doctor" can be guiltless of murder when performing a "legal" abortion. How can a Christian rightly contend that the Apostles would have contradicted their teaching against theft by allowing looting through the political process? The bottom line is that a Christian cannot be righteous while *voluntarily* requesting welfare state benefits like Social Security,

Aid to Families with Dependent Children, food stamps, educational grants, or subsidized housing.

Furthermore, the existence of democratic processes under a constitutional republic does *not* alter the malevolent nature of proactive public policies or the bad behavior of government agents. Representative government does *not* preclude Christians from championing causes against bad legislation, evil decrees, or nefarious rulers. Neither does it prevent them from disobeying foul edicts that would cause them to sin or violate the Constitution. There is nothing in Scripture that would lead one to believe that state-sponsored extortion or state-sanctioned murder (e.g., abortion and euthanasia) are cleansed (or are no longer wrong) because they have been approved through a representative process. And it is inconsistent for Christian leaders to arbitrarily decry abortion policy but not extortion policies.

Another key supposition: the Apostles simply did not envision (and could not have imagined) Christian submission to the state entailing us Christians advocating or *voluntarily* supporting and benefiting from state-sanctioned thefts, murders, unjustified aggression, fraud, or malice. Had the Apostles been able to foresee what would transpire under modern "democracies" in the name of "the general welfare" or the "public interest", they would have both condemned the policies as evil and certainly discouraged Christian participation in them. This supposition is derived from the extension of apostolic teachings regarding theft, sloth, slavery, doing "good", and peacemaking. Further, the Apostles would have doubtless called believers to be those who stand up against such evil policies, whenever prudent, as a matter of maintaining integrity in their Christian lifestyles and their commitment to the Truth (Proverbs 23:23). Nowadays pastors and church leaders, rather than Apostles, are left with the charge of calling Christians to maintain integrity. The big question is: "Are they willing to do so?"

Applying the submission doctrine to modern believers

So how should American Christians "honor the king"? They have no monarch. Does that fact invalidate apostolic doctrine about submission to state rulers? No, the *principle* of submission still stands. Culture does not wipe out biblical theology, even if the application of doctrine must be adapted to technological and cultural changes— like swords and holy kisses becoming guns and hand-shakes.

Other important questions remain however, including the reason *why* Christians should submit and *what* Christians should submit to. In *Bible and Government*, Christians are said to submit for reasons expedient or "pragmatic" (in the sense of being *practical*). The Bible in several places calls believers to exercise practical wisdom—perhaps even insincere and superficial performances—before rulers (Proverbs 23:1-3; Ecclesiastes 8:2-5; Matthew 17:27). Interpreting Scripture with Scripture, one may conclude that the kind of performance mandated for Nero and his cronies should correspond to those mandated in these other passages.

In America, a case can and should be made that the proper object of Christian submission are the Constitution and the Declaration of Independence since they comprise our formal government. Presidents, Supreme Court justices, and congressmen are not kings. Our political structure is not autocratic but rather a republic based on a contract between "We the People". The *political* allegiance of an American Christian is not to the President or to Congress, but to the republican contract established by the people. On this point, theonomist Greg Durand is on the right track:

> The Apostle Paul wrote the Roman epistle to a people who were under the subjection of a dicta-torship. The Roman emperor was the "higher

55

power" spoken of and, as far as he ruled justly and did not command that which was contrary to God's Law, Christians were bound to submit to him. We in America, however, are not under a dictatorship, but a Constitutional Republic which was explicitly founded upon biblical principles and modeled, in many ways, after the Israelite theocracy of the Old Testament. Therefore, Romans 13:1-7 cannot be made to apply in exactly the same way as it did to Paul's initial audience without grossly twisting its intent. In American law, the people which form the several states are the "higher powers," not the Federal government.[47]

Therefore, an American Christian can submit to the principles of the Constitution, for instance, and still dishonor, condemn, or even—as a last resort—overthrow the state rulers or government actors who oppose it (as detailed in chapter 12). This idea would have been unfathomable in the context of the first century, even for those acquainted with the Roman Republic era. Yet it is part and parcel of the American civil society that Providence has decreed.

---

[47] Greg Loren Durand (1996), "The Liberty of Conscience: Civil Disobedience in Light of Romans 13:1-7", Dahlonega, Georgia: Crown Rights Book Company, 28p., FBS Library Online: http://train.missouri.org/~newlife/romans13.htm.

The greatest danger to liberty today comes from the men who are most needed and most powerful in modern government, namely, the efficient expert administrators exclusively concerned with what they regard as the public good.
    —*Friedrich von Hayek (1960)*

We have placed too much hope in politics and social reforms, only to find out that we were being deprived of our most precious possession: our spiritual life.
    —*Alexander Solzhenitsyn (1918-)*

If a nation expects to be ignorant and free, in a state of civilization, it expects what never was and never will be.
    — *President Thomas Jefferson (1743-1826)*

To meliorate the condition of human nature can be the only rational end of government.
    —*Vicesimus Knox (c. 1795)*

3 The Four Christian Views of the State and Public Policy

A Christian's judgment about how Tories or Benedict Arnolds should be treated, or about how one should respond to revolutionary movements in general, will depend on his presuppositions regarding the nature of the state and what is entailed in appropriate Christian response to public policy. Christians can be orthodox and Evangelical with respect to the fundamentals of the faith and the doctrine of salvation and still disagree widely in their public policy theology. This doctrinal divergence was manifest between the Christian patriots and the Christian Tories, and it is still seen in modern American Christianity.

There are two historical schools of Evangelical thought regarding the nature of the state and public policy: (A) the Integrated Authority School and (B) the Competing Kingdom School. The former school views the state as (at least) a potential ally of the family and church in establishing or advancing God's kingdom in the world. The state's role may be as small as simply restraining what God thinks is evil or as large as actively clearing the way for the establishment of true religion in a country. Some integrated authority adherents believe that a strong nexus between church and state is necessary for a godly society, where the church preaches to the state regarding what it should enforce and the state upholds the biblical standard it receives via the power of the sword.

The latter school views the state, encompassed in the biblical terminology as "the kingdoms of this world", running a course that is antithetical to God's. Whether driven by its own cultural norms or Satan himself, the state *competes* against God. Nevertheless, God holds the ultimate reigns on the state and uses it to accomplish certain ends in this world, such as bringing terrestrial judgment upon sinners or sanctifying His church through state persecutions. Perhaps illogically, some competing kingdom adherents also view the state as restraining civil evil at times.

Both of these schools have two branches (or subclassifications) which make up a total of four Christian perspectives of public policy. The two branches of the integrated authority school are (1) the theonomy view or Christian Reconstructionism and (2) the revitalized or reshaped divine right of kings view. These views may be condensed to simply the terms *theonomy* and *divine right*. The two branches of the competing kingdom school are (1) the Anabaptist (strict separationist) or pacifist view and (2) the liberty of conscience view.

Professor Mark Noll's work *Christians and the American Revolution* is especially helpful in forming a historical perspective on these positions.[48] The instigators of the American "Revolution" were largely theonomic Presbyterians and Congregationalists, along with liberty of conscience Baptists. These groups took an active role in transforming their world, albeit for very distinct reasons.

Integrated authority or competing kingdom

There is one key question that will determine which school a Christian will align himself with: "Is the state a

---

[48] Also see *Bible and Government: Public Policy from a Christian Perspective*, supra.

special sphere of authority along with the family and the church?" The responses will be diverse enough to make some rather strange bedfellows. Christians who have sharp disagreements over the millennium or predestination may find themselves in agreement with respect to public policy theology.

Table 2: Bases for the four Evangelical public policy paradigms

Historical School	Integrated Authority		Competing Kingdom	
Paradigm/Perspective	*Theonomy*	*Divine Right*	*Anabaptist*	*Liberty of Conscience*
Views the state as a special sphere of authority like the family and the church?	Yes	Yes	No	No
Views the state as a transformable institution under the "dominion mandate" (Gen. 1:26-27)?	Yes	Yes	No	No

Unlike soteriological and other theological concerns which divide easily along Reformed or Dispensational lines, such as the propensity of Presbyterians to be Calvinists, the propensity of Baptists to be dispensationalists, or the propensity of charismatics to be premillennial, one will find far more diversity in the theology of public policy. For instance, being Calvinistic and amillennial does not provide a tendency to any one particular public policy view. Such a Christian may hold to any one of the four views of public policy and civil government.

There is, however, at least a logical tendency for paedobaptists (Presbyterian, Reformed, Methodist, and Anglican) to be within the integrated authority school and for those who hold a baptistic and/or congregational view to be in the competing kingdom school. But there appear to be too many exceptions to this rule to make it of much value generally. Indeed, it appears that the vast majority of

60

modern pastors and theologians from all denominations embrace the integrated authority school. However, that lopsidedness has not always been the case, as evinced by publicly-stated views during the American War for Independence.

Table 3: Evangelical public policy paradigms (historical categories and their main branches)

Category by Disposition / Action	Integrated Authority	Competing Kingdom
Transformational / Involved	Theonomy	Liberty of Conscience
Non-Confrontational / Passive	Divine Right	Anabaptist

It is important to emphasize that each of the four views are Evangelical. They are held by people who would vehemently defend the authority of the Bible and the fundamental doctrines of the Christian faith. At least in terms of basic orthodoxy, having one view or another of public policy has not affected one's Evangelical commitment.

The integrated authority school

The integrated authority school views the state as a special sphere of authority along with the family and the church. The state has a useful purpose in directly advancing the kingdom of God in the world. In his famous *Institutes of the Christian Religion* (book 4, chapter 20), John Calvin stated that the Christian finds himself under two governments: one secular and the other ecclesiastical. The secular or civil government has the obligation to be godly and promote the Christian religion. The ecclesiastical government provides spiritual discipline and administers the sacraments. Since the civil government (state) punishes those who are condemned as evildoers by God's Word, they must know God's rules. Thus, in order for the state to know what it should promote and condemn, the church has a responsibility to preach the Word of God to civil rulers. The state is thus a transformable institution under the dominion mandate of Genesis 1:26-27. As English Preacher Vicesimus Knox (1752-1821) succinctly claims:

> There can be no good reason assigned why government should not be, like every thing else, continually advancing to all the perfection of which it is capable. Indeed, as the happiness of mankind depends more upon well-regulated and well administered government, than on any thing subordinate in life or in arts, there is every reason for bestowing all the time which every passing generation can bestow, in bringing government to its utmost point of attainable perfection.[49]

Theonomy (or Christian Reconstructionism) forms the first, and most sophisticated, branch within the integrated authority school. Although its doctrine is far more refined than Calvin's, theonomy (which is almost exclusively Reformed) has consistently carried Calvin's ideas. Theonomy embellishes Calvin by including all of the Old Testament laws that are not explicitly repudiated in the New Testament (although there is some disagreement between theonomists about what has been repudiated, e.g., dietary rules). Revolution is a proper and useful function, so long as an alternative authority structure is preserved, in order to maintain a godly quality in civil government. Furthermore, after godly rulers have been installed, the state has a role in punishing infidels, as Oliver Cromwell and John Owen vivified in their practice of (or support of) wars of righteous conquest:

---

[49] Vicesimus Knox (1824 [1795]), *The Works of Vicesimus Knox*, vol. VI, Section XXXVIII, "That All Opposition to the Spirit of Despotism Should Be Conducted With the Most Scrupulous Regard to the Existing Laws, And to the Preservation of Public Peace and Good Order", London: J. Mawman, p. 133.

Before the troops had left England, John Owen had justified their violent involvement in Irish politics on exactly that basis. The 1641 rebellion, he claimed, had demonstrated Old English populations were the enemies of God, and therefore the duty of the Puritan soldiers was to execute God's justice upon them: 'Ireland was the first of the nations that laid in wait for the blood of God's people,' he claimed, so 'their latter end shall be to perish forever.' they were the sworn vassals of the man of sin, the followers of the beast. Owen held that in opposing and then executing the king as well as in the invasion of Ireland and then Scotland the army had been doing the will of God...Indeed, the battles fought and the victories won, were clearly prophesied in Revelation 17-19 as part of God's programme for the last days. Cromwell himself understood that his Irish campaign fulfilled a prophecy made in the 100th Psalm.[50]

Some of the major Evangelical proponents of theonomy include Greg Bahnsen, Gary North, R. J. Rushdoony, Baptist Pastor John Weaver (an outspoken modern American "patriot"), John Calvin, John Knox, John Owen, Oliver Cromwell, Cotton Mather, William Bradford, James Willson, Greg Loren Durand and, it seems, Charles Hodge. Theonomy holds a transformational, active or involved theology of public policy, and is characteristically postmillennial. Greg Bahnsen describes the fundamental philosophy of theonomy:

[T]heonomy teaches that civil rulers are morally obligated to enforce those laws of Christ, found

---

[50] Crawford Gribben (2003), *The Irish Puritans: James Ussher and the Reformation of the Church*, Auburn, Massachusetts: Evangelical Press, p. 95. He is citing John Owen in Goold, W.H., ed. (1850-3), *The Works of John Owen*, vol. viii, London: Johnson and Hunter, pp. 231-235.

63

throughout the [Old and New Testament] Scriptures, which are addressed to magistrates (as well as to *refrain* from coercion in areas where God has not prescribed their intervention). As Paul wrote in Romans 13:1-10, magistrates—even the secular rulers of Rome—are obligated to conduct their offices as "ministers of God," avenging *God's wrath* (compare 13:4 with 12:19) against criminal evil-doers. They will give an account on the Final Day of their service before the King of kings, their Creator and Judge. Christian involvement in politics calls for recognition of God's transcendent, absolute, revealed law as a standard by which to judge all social codes and political policies.[51]

In chapter 19 of *Theonomy in Christian Ethics*, Bahnsen holds that passages like Romans 13:1-7 apply to an idealized state. For instance, Paul was stepping out of a very practical section of his treatise to the Romans to describe what a good government *should* be like either now or in some future golden age. Paul was not describing the actual, current experience of the Christians in Rome, nor was he reveling in some fancy that Nero was serving the Lord by upholding His law. Instead, he was explaining what a proper civil government *should* look like in the world (and what it will be like during the postmillennial golden age). Thus, theonomists avoid the problem of reconciling the plain meaning of the text with the fact that Nero was in power by viewing Romans 13:1-7 as an abstraction.

The second branch within the integrated authority school is what could be termed the **revitalized (or reshaped) divine right of kings** view—denoted simply as *divine right* for short. Evangelical proponents of this view

---

[51] Greg L. Bahnsen (1994), "What is Theonomy?", *New Horizons* (April), Covenant Media Foundation, sec. 5.

include: Samuel E. Waldron (a leading Reformed Baptist), John Eidsmoe (a constitutional lawyer, theologian, and famed keynote speaker with the Institute on the Constitution), Pastor John Macarthur, Irish Pastor Ivor Oakley, English Baptist John Gill, and, most likely, both Vicesimus Knox and Charles H. Spurgeon (although they loathed aggressive war like a competing kingdom school adherent would). Martin Luther probably held this view too, who would otherwise be a theonomist. An internet search of electronic texts on the subject of civil disobedience and Romans 13 indicates the divine right position of many other preachers and commentators: Bob Deffinbaugh (Bible.org), David Guzik, Matthew Henry, B.W. Johnson, Harold S. Martin (Church of the Brethren), noted dispensationalist William R. Newell, John Piper, Charles Stanley (Southern Baptist), and Ray Stedman. Recall too the Tory preacher (mentioned earlier) who proclaimed that "Rebellion against authority is rebellion against God." He holds a divine right perspective.

According to this view, the state is a special sphere of authority along with the family and the church. However, like the family and church, the state is imperfect because it is comprised of sinful men. And, like the family and the church, the state's imperfections (even crass criminal activities) are basically passed over in the same way that imperfections in the church are passed over. After all, a divine institution run by sinners cannot be expected to be perfect. Christian duty is simply to make the best of whatever rulers and public policies Providence has given to us.

Not all institutions are ordained by God and require obedience and respect. The Mormon church, for instance, must be treated differently because it is not a divine institution. Christians are called upon to dispel Mormon doctrine and disobey Mormon precepts in a way that they never should do in the case of the state—even though Mormons and their organization may be more righteous and have doctrine and practice closer to the truth than do rulers and the state.

Thus, the divine right view rests on the premise or assumption that God has ordained the state to look after civil society for Him. Therefore, Christian action must be generally obedient, supportive of state institutions, passive in most forms of resistance, participatory, and respectful. As John Eidsmoe explains in his book *God and Caesar*, rulers are to receive special respect from Christians.

> [W]e should not pray only for those whom we like. It is easy to pray for the leader whom we respect or with whom we agree. It is much harder to pray for the leader whose personality is offensive, whose ethics are questionable, who takes the "wrong" position on every issue, or who is in the "wrong" party. Yet these leaders are also ministers of God. They don't necessarily deserve our vote, but they do deserve our respect and prayers.[52]

Similarly, Vicesimus Knox proclaimed Toryism after the American Revolution and decried the French Revolution based on divine right premises.

> I most earnestly admonish all who are instigated by these motives to seditious language, writing, or action, to consider that they are insulting the King of kings; who delights in order and tranquility, and whose gracious Gospel particularly

---

[52] John Eidsmoe (1984), *God and Caesar*, Westchester, Illinois: Crossway Books, p. 28. Of similar interest, Dr. Ivor J. W. Oakley (1929-2003), former pastor of Strandtown Baptist Church, Belfast, Northern Ireland, stated the divine right view with respect to modern welfarism (sermon notes of May 14, 1978): "Not only does the state preserve order and prevent anarchy, but it also confers on us other benefits. Wide range of services, which individually we could not enjoy. Supposing we had to supply our own water, light, sewerage, education for children, social security, public transport and roads. These are only obtainable when men agree to live together in one state and under one government, which organizes life. In the light of all of this, we have a duty to the state." Online source: http://www.ivoroakley.com/Romans/romans_131-10.htm.

require as peaceful submission to the laws of a country, and to the powers legally established. Confusion and every evil work are the consequence of the unruly passions of envy and strife, when they direct their force against the civil government and its proper administrators. "Fear God, and honour the king" are commands joined together in the Scriptures so closely, as to induce one to conclude, that to honour the king, is to perform a duty, at least approaching to the nature of a religious office. But if this should not be allowed, yet it is certainly true, that to disturb good government, is contrary to the duty of a good man, and particularly inconsistent with the character of a good Christian; who should study to be quiet, and to mind his own business, and not follow those who, from envy and strife, are given to change, or unnecessary innovation.[53]

The state has a useful purpose in directly advancing the kingdom of God in the world, but the parameters under which the state must operate or decree public policy have not been very well delineated theologically. Unlike theonomy, where the state and church are more closely linked, the state serves God directly without necessary intervention from the church, restraining chaos and sin in society. Believers owe allegiance to the state and nation in a way that is tantamount to their allegiance to their local church. The American flag is proudly displayed in church sanctuaries, and pastors fondly commemorate national holidays.

The state becomes a sort of oracle of God, although not in a fully inspired sense. Christians must obey virtually any command of public policy as if the decree had come from God Himself. For a divine righter, breaking either the "letter of the law" or the 'spirit of the law" is sin. For ex-

---

[53] Vicesimus Knox (1824 [1795]), *The Works of Vicesimus Knox*, vol. V, Sermon XVII, "On the Wickedness and Misery of Envy and Contention", London: J. Mawman, pp. 248-249.

ample, speeding, hiring an illegal alien, or not coming to a full and complete stop before the limit line before the stop sign would be morally wrong (in countries where such activities are illegal).

In the divine right view, the state is benign or even innocuous. Like a television set, the state can be good when good things (men) participate in it. But when evil things (men) dominate then the state will be evil. A few favored biblical rules are declared to be within the proper range of civil government function. However, the biblical principles that underlie state rules often end up being an arbitrary selection of favorite behavioral ideals (e.g., (1) enforcing the Ten Commandments, or (2) just the 5th through the 9th Commandments, or perhaps (3) enforcing all New Testament rules as well as a few Old Testament ones regarding sodomy, bestiality, homosexuality, etc.). Unlike theonomists, which are more consistent in selecting what biblical principles apply to the state, the divine righter becomes the arbiter of what is right and wrong in a social sense and, therefore, what particular moral issues should be enforced by the state and which ones should be left to church discipline.

Revolution and civil disobedience are frowned upon, including the American Revolution and the so-called Civil War. The instigation of either war is widely considered to have been sinful. Hence, divine right holds a passive or non-confrontational view in terms of public policy theology. To the divine righter, the decrees and actions of rulers are part of "general revelation", even though the Bible makes no clear indication of their inclusion in it. With respect to apostolic doctrine, divine right seems to have the most difficulty of the four views in avoiding the problem of reconciling the plain meaning of Romans 13:1-7 and 1 Peter 2:13-17 with the fact that Nero was in power.

As incredible as it might seem, some argue that Nero *was* (albeit imperfectly) punishing those who did evil in the sight of the Lord and rewarding those who did well in God's sight. Others seem to have never really thought about the implications of what the words *good* and *evil* might mean in the cultural context of Nero's Rome. For instance, divine right adherents John McGarvey and Philip Pendleton make excuses for the state, especially when it has pursued its normal course of persecuting Christians. They argue that states have never intentionally quelled good and exalted evil but rather have only done so through ignorance, just as Saul persecuted the church:

> A good man may suffer [at the state's hand] through misunderstanding, the machination of evil men, or even maladministration, but he can never suffer *as* a good man. Even Nero punished Christians *as* evil-doers (2 Tim. 2:9). History presents no instance where any government set itself to put down righteousness and exalt evil *as such;* though there are myriads of cases where human ignorance, prejudice and bigotry mistook the wrong for the right, and made havoc of the good, supposing it to be evil. Paul himself, as an executive of the Jewish Government, had been party to such an error (Acts 8:3; 9:1, 2; 1 Tim. 1:13). Intentional punishment of the good and countenancing of the evil would be governmental insanity and suicide.[54]

However, this sentiment is surely naïve and mistaken. Such divine right thinking is both uninformed and spiritually precarious. Nero was not a well-meaning but ignorant dolt that ended up punishing Christians by blunder. He willfully blamed Christians for social maladies and intended to harm them. He sought what he thought was best

---

[54] John W. McGarvey and Philip Y. Pendleton (1916), *Thessalonians, Corinthians, Galatians and Romans*, vol. 3, chapter IV, "The faith-life discharging civil duties, and recognizing the divine ordination of governments", Cincinnati: The Standard Publishing Company, p. 508.

for Nero rather than what was in the best interests of good people in Rome. He was, in short, exactly what historians described—and what economists would have expected—him to be. The same thing may be said of other rulers in history, from the most benign to most despotic.

Consequently, although popular, the divine right view is an embarrassment for American Christianity. Although it is convenient, amicable, and mollifying, the divine right view is also naïve and lacks a cogent and consistent understanding about the nature of the state and the Christian's response to public policy.

The competing kingdom school

The competing kingdom school views the state as an entity entirely distinct from the church and family insofar as promotion of the Kingdom of God is concerned. Some proponents of this school would see the state as benign, although it often rears up its ugly side to assail the church of God. Others would view it as significantly aligned with Satan's kingdom and his efforts in the world. Either way, the state is *not* a special sphere of authority along with the family and the local church.

The first branch of this school is the **Anabaptist** (strict separationist) or pacifist view. Leading Evangelical theologians of this perspective include Menno Simmons, Mark Roth, Harold Bender, Heinrich Bullinger, and evidently the founder of dispensationalism John Nelson Darby. Submission is passive for the Anabaptist, and even though rebellion is unavoidable in most lifetimes (as Christians inevitably come into contact with trying public policies), armed revolt is never the role of a Christian. Hence, the Anabaptist view holds a passive or non-confrontational public policy theology. However, like the divine righters, the Anabaptists do not make a very compelling or consistent case for reconciling the plain meaning of Romans 13:1-7 and 1 Peter 2:13-17 with the fact that Nero was in power.

The Anabaptist view is the least sophisticated branch of the competing kingdom school and at some points (like divine right) is attenuated by some apparent logical contradictions in its structure. For instance, the Anabaptist preacher tells believers that it is sinful to be involved with the state's "social security" plan, running for office, jury participation, military service, or voting because the state is effectively evil. The state is also exposed as the frequent afflicter of the church, persecuting God's people. Yet many of this persuasion hold, paradoxically, that the malevolent state is in some way doing God's bidding by restraining evil in the world and punishing criminals—even though it is not doing so! While Anabaptists view the state as a separate, competing kingdom (some even see it as having a satanic nexus), they also see the state (even in Nero's Rome presumably) as an instrument of God to punish criminals or those who do evil in God's sight. This fact is rather odd given that Anabaptists, who are presumably the good guys in general, have suffered more persecution at the hands of state than perhaps any other Christian group.

The second branch of the competing kingdom school may be aptly termed **liberty of conscience**. Although this term has not been commonly used historically to describe theological views of public policy, many theologians and pastors have held it. Proponents include Baptists at the time of the American War for Independence such as Isaac Backus, John Leland, and John Wallers; as well as Roger Williams and probably John Bunyan (who at least held the seeds of the liberty of conscience view). Vicesimus Knox curiously held to the seeds of the liberty of conscience view of the nature of state rulers and, along with Spurgeon, that view's excoriation of unjust war. Yet

Knox, like Spurgeon, still held a divine right view of the purpose of the state and its transformability.

Any Christian who holds to a dispensational or a "new covenant" Calvinistic perspective of biblical interpretation will tend to embrace this view, along with most Baptists (at least historically). Such Christians prize volunteerism and freedom of thought among believers and in society, shunning the notion of using Old Testament law or public policy to coerce people into behaving in a proper manner. For instance, few of them would want to force people to abstain from working on Sunday and to attend church services instead. Few of them would want to enlist the tools of the state to better Evangelism by compelling people to hear the Gospel. Only God has a right to "compel" sinners to come to Him (Luke 14:23; Psalm 65:4). Conversely, all integrated authority school adherents want at least *some proactive* interference by the state in people's lives.

The liberty of conscience view is developed and applied in a practical way in *Bible and Government* and in greater depth in this book. In the same way that theonomy is the logical outcome of a Presbyterian and postmillennial theology, liberty of conscience is the logical outcome of a Baptist theology (whether premillennial or amillennial). More resolutely than its Anabaptist counterpart, liberty of conscience views the state as evil, having a strong link with Satan and his kingdom. Yet Christians are left to their liberty with regard to where and when to resist the state, work within the state, or participate in revolution. Like theonomy, liberty of conscience holds a transformational, active or involved view of public policy theology. It is morally wrong at times to rebel against the state, but not always. Yet the state is never viewed as something to be transformed or that can ever become anything other than evil. The state is not the benign entity of the divine righters.

Moreover, those who hold a liberty of conscience view have a well worked out and cogent view of the words good and evil used in Romans 13:3-4 and 1 Peter 2:13-14. Unlike the divine righters, they do not try to make Nero into an overall bad ruler that nonetheless did imperfectly bring law and order to society. And unlike the Anabaptists, they do not try to impose a godly role on the state as an occasional punisher of criminals. They do not share the theonomic quest to idealize the passages and push them off as a theological abstraction with little practical significance for the Christians at Rome. Instead, they interpret the words good and evil to mean good and evil as defined by the state (or Nero) rather than as defined by God. So a state may consider Christians to be "evil" and punish them with the sword (as Nero did), while rewarding adulterers, idolaters, and murderers that it deems to be "good".

Christian submission to the state and public policies is *expedient* (or pragmatic/practical). In other words, Christian obedience is triggered when the believer faced with any particular policy (legislation, ruling, executive order) that threatens him. The bottom line is that Christians obey in order to avoid incurring the state's wrath. They do not want to incite Leviathan to break out against them on account of their public disobedience to a policy. Their objective is to minimize earthy entanglements (2 Timothy 2:4) or any action that detracts from the glory of God.

The liberty of conscience perspective explained

Despite the state's crass waywardness, the Apostles do command Christians to submit to the state and the apostolic command has moral ramifications. Even if the rule has to be applied differently depending on the historical and cultural context, in principle it still stands for all believers at all times. Disobeying apostolic teaching must, therefore, have a moral implication (i.e., it involves sinning). However, it is doubtful that the Apostles were telling Christians that a believer sins when he does not follow the "letter of the law" of the state's policies. On the contrary, there are clear cases when Christians *must* violate public policy, such as prohibitions of Gospel preaching, mandates to kill children, and so forth.

Submission to the state is not an absolute command. Therefore, one cannot say that a Christian has sinned *necessarily* because he has violated some public policy—especially things like speeding, not coming to a complete stop behind the limit line at a stop sign, or hiring an illegal alien. What makes violation of these public policies sinful?

The liberty of conscience view permits Christians to disobey public policy at times. *Even though the general rule is for them to submit to rulers and public policies,* Christian submission to civil government must be *passive* rather than *active.* The Greek verb ὑποτασσέσθω, translated "be subject" in Romans 13:1, is in the present tense, passive voice in the original language. Likewise, Paul uses the passive voice in Titus 3:1 (ὑποτασσέσθαι), as Peter in 1 Peter 2:13 (ὑποτάγητε). **Christians react to the state by submitting—mainly after they have been acted upon.**

In other words, Christians are to obey whenever directly called upon to do so, so long as God is not defrauded or any sin committed, but it is not their duty to *actively* pursue a course wherein they scour the "law of the land." They do not need to make sure that they are in compliance with every point of public policy if the state does not directly pressure them to do so. Accordingly, Christians do not sin by violating government rules *per se.* They sin if their actions sidetrack them from their primary mission, cause harm to a neighbor, or detract from the glory of God. Being unduly harassed by the state for things of miniscule importance (from an eternal perspective) must not be the primary focus of a kingdom-minded saint. But disobedient acts—even revolution—are both permissible and righteous.

Many early English and American Baptists held an infant form of the liberty of conscience perspective. *The First London Confession*, published in 1644 (revised in 1646) by seven Particular (Calvinistic) Baptist churches in London, sets forth a more primitive version of the liberty of conscience view, citing about 90 percent from New Testament passages as its authority. Articles XLIX and LI demonstrate the crux of this Baptist position on civil government (although there were other coeval Baptist groups in Holland and elsewhere who held a more theonomic or a divine right view).

> The supreme Magistracie of this Kingdome we beleeve to be the King and Parliament freely chosen by the Kingdome, and that in all those civill Lawes which have been acted by them, or for the present is or shall be ordained, we are bound to yeeld subjection and obedience unto in the Lord, as conceiving our selves bound to defend both the persons of those thus chosen, and all civill lawes made by them with our persons, liberties, and estates, with all that is called ours, although we should suffer never so much from them in not actively submitting to some Ecclesiasticall Lawes, which might be conceived by them to be their duties to establish which we for the present could not see, nor our consciences could submit unto; yet are we bound to yeeld our persons to their pleasures.
>
> But if God with-hold the Magistrates allowance and furtherance herein; yet we must notwithstanding proceed together in Christian communion, not daring to give place to suspend our practice, but to walk in obedience to Christ in the profession and holding forth this faith before mentioned, even in the midst of all trialls and afflictions, not accounting our goods, lands, wives, children, fathers, mothers, brethren, sis-

ters, yea our own lives dear unto us so we may finish our course with joy; remembering alwayes we ought to obey God rather then men, and grounding upon the commandement, commission and promise of our Lord and master Jesus Christ, who as he hath all power in heaven and earth, so also hath promised, if we heed to his commandments which he hath given us, to be with us to the end of the world; and when we have finished our course, and kept the faith, to give us the crowne of rightiousnesse, which is laid up for all that love his appearing and to whom we must give an account of all our actions, no man being able to discharge us of the same.

This Confession evinces a very practical disposition for Christians confronted by the state. They generally must obey state decrees but not always—especially when a decree defies a matter of liberty of conscience with respect to religious practice. Submission to the state is thus held with a loose hand, making this Baptist declaration a prototype of the liberty of conscience position.

Aside from tolerating a larger role for the Holy Spirit (than the integrated authority school views would) in convicting the believer of sinning, or leading him to obey or disobey, the liberty of conscience perspective has a clear means of determining when civil disobedience is sinful. No public policy, unless it mimics the law of Christ, is morally binding on believers. Submission is commanded by the apostles for ancillary and practical reasons, and its extent depends on the culture and times in which a Christian lives. Christians obey because it is most expedient to do so.

Civil disobedience done from a rebellious attitude is always wrong. Otherwise, civil disobedience is only sinful if it meets certain criteria (gleaned from biblical principles). First, one's action of civil disobedience must be public and flagrant in nature (a precursor to sin). Second, one's action must involve a cavalier disregard for apostolic reasoning for obedience, in particular when it causes harm to a neighbor. Third, one's action must blatantly detract from the glory to God. Only when all three of these elements are present does an act of civil disobedience necessarily miss the mark.

In sum, the Apostles are concerned that disobedient believers should not sin by: (1) dishonoring God in the sight of others; (2) harming the testimony of Jesus Christ in society; (3) bringing wrath unnecessarily upon believers and their families; (4) acting foolishly—or least without the appropriate amount of wisdom and prudence; (5) being poor stewards of God's provisions; (6) giving the state an excuse or reason to single out Christians for persecution; (7) worrying about what the state might do to them and thus violating the teaching of Christ in Matthew 6:25; and (8) beginning to engage in ostensibly benign activities that (a) might eventually lead to temptation to do sinful things or (b) might at least have the appearance of evil deeds to onlookers. The expediency camp does not look to the letter of the public policy to determine what is sinful or not. Instead it considers the fallout from behavior on the more important areas of life and personal character. Civil disobedience that causes Christians to not bring glory to God, to harm their neighbors or family, and to act foolishly is sinful because of its consequences.

When may Christians disregard the state's rules?

Absolute submission to the state and its public policies (per Romans 13:1-7, 1 Peter 2:13-17, Titus 3:1) is not an Evangelical posture. Indeed, violating morally innocuous public policy would not be sinful if done discreetly, privately, clandestinely, wisely, prudently, and carefully (or perhaps when done through ignorance of the policy). Whether or not a Christian's disobedience to the state or public policy is sinful will depend in large part on the cultural context in which he lives. Disobeying curfew rules while living under Nero or Stalin is one thing, but running a stop sign at 2AM in rural North Dakota is another.

As noted in chapter 10, trying to pull off a revolution under a powerful Caesar or Czar might be suicide, and thus not glorify God. But revolting against King George actually brought American Christians greater freedom and has given more glory to God in the long run, especially in light of America's boon to worldwide missionary endeavors, the printing of Christian books, and the promotion of theological study. In brief, the choice to revolt, or even to what extent a Christian may prudently disobey, depends on the political, technological, and economic context in which he finds himself.

However, a Christian who unintentionally or inadvertently offends men—state officials in particular—or gives occasion for reproach of Christ on account of his disobedience to such policies (even if the policy is considered asinine, like prohibiting spitting on the sidewalk or requiring using a seatbelt before driving down the block at midnight), must be willing to apologize quickly and humbly make amends when confronted.

Unless one is willing to claim that the Apostles were out of their minds, or that their teaching was and is largely irrelevant for practical living today, the liberty of conscience view holds that the cursory (and common) interpretation of Romans 13:1-7, 1 Peter 2:13-17, and Titus 3:1 is wayward and must be rejected. Sometimes nationalism and an Americanized theology can cloud proper interpretation of biblical texts. Christians are not compelled by the Apostles to be exemplary keepers of *any* and *all* public policy, going out of their way to abide by every rule, and spending time and resources exacting out every aspect of compliance as a "good citizen". Only in exceptional places like America would such notions arise. The vast majority of Christians have faced an entirely different political experience. Since the Bible was written for all cultures and times, one must be careful to not confound proper interpretation with his cultural context. What was truth in Paul's day in Rome was true in Iceland during its anarchic period, in twentieth century Cambodia under Pol Pot or Chile under Salvador Allende, and is true in modern-day Iraq and South Africa.

The character and role of the state: a jarring, distinct view

The last key motif of the liberty of conscience perspective is perhaps the most shocking for contemporary Evangelicals. As developed in the ensuing chapter, the state is held to be evil by nature. This view is confirmed by: (1) the biblical record of public policies that indicate that some 90 percent of public policies (outside of the Old Testament theocracy) were wicked, opposed to God's Kingdom, and to the detriment of God's people; (2) the historical record of public policies that shows overwhelmingly that the vast majority of civil governments (states) too have been evil, tyrannical, and oppressive for the last several thousand years; (3) the doctrine of Revelation 13:1-9, where kings are represented as a grotesque "beast" (drawing from the beast from the sea, lion, bear, leopard, ten horns of Daniel 7:1-28), proving a connection between Satan and civil government and public policy, and (4) the fact that civil rulers, who martyred Jesus Christ and nearly all of the Apostles, are without exception the stated enemies of Christ when he returns in glory (see Revelation 6:15; 16:14; 18:9; 19:16-21): "The kings of the earth set themselves, And the rulers take counsel together, Against the Lord and against His Anointed [Christ]" (Psalm 2:2; Acts 4:26) and "the beast, the kings of the earth, and their armies, [will be] gathered together to make war against Him [Christ] who sat on the horse and against His army" (Revelation 19:9).

The state is not a special sphere of authority to promote or enhance the kingdom of God. As part of the competing kingdom, it is an agent of the kingdom of Satan that God ordains and uses primarily as His servant to bring terrestrial judgment on sinners. Accordingly, disobedience to the evil state is *never* sin in cases when public policy would compel us to violate a clear commandment of God or to disregard our Scriptural convictions. In all other cases, disobedience to the state might be sinful—but not because of disregard of a public policy *per se* (as if disobeying the state is tantamount to disobeying God Himself *per se*). Again, civil disobedience would be sinful if it were public and flagrant—especially during dire times such as the ones Christians faced under Nero—and if it involved careless or cavalier disregard for God's glory and the apostolic concerns.

At this point in time, at least so far as thinking Christians are concerned, there are only two serious contenders for a proper public policy theology: theonomy and liberty of conscience. The other views (divine right and pacifism), as they stand today at least, lack both Scriptural thoroughness and logical coherency. Moreover, the liberty of conscience view arguably provides the most believable interpretation of the apostolic doctrine set forth in Romans 13:1-7, Titus 3:1, and 1 Peter 2:13-17, especially with regard to the words "good" and "evil". It also has the strongest biblical and historical support for defining the nature and purpose of the state.

PART II

LIBERTY OF CONSCIENCE PERSPECTIVE PARTICULARS

What is history but the story of how politicians have squandered the blood and treasure of the human race?
—Thomas Sowell (1930-)

I believe that all government is evil, and that trying to improve it is largely a waste of time.
—H.L. Mencken (1880-1956)

A young man should say what he means and mean what he says. Avoid the demeaning examples of politicians, government bureaucrats, and lawyers.
—Gen. Robert E. Lee (1807-1870)

For the bureaucrat, the world is a mere object to be manipulated by him.
—Karl Marx (1818-1883)

I would rather be exposed to the inconveniences attending too much liberty than to those attending too small a degree of it.
—President Thomas Jefferson (1743-1826)

How deplorable, when government becomes so perverted as to increase the evil it was designed to cure. Yet this has been, and is now the case on a great part of the globe.
—Vicesimus Knox (c. 1795)

4 The Nature of the State

The distinction between government and the state

Albert Jay Nock (1870-1947), although relatively obscure today, was one of the foremost journalists and political philosophers of his day. He founded what would become *The Freeman* in the early 1920s[55]—one of the strongest and most consistent pieces of advocacy journalism for liberty and free markets available. He was also ordained as a minister in the Episcopal Church in 1897.

A.J. Nock

Jeffrey A. Tucker praises Nock's sophistication and genius in his tribute: "Albert Jay Nock, Forgotten Man of the Right" (2002).[56] "The phrase Man of Letters is thrown around casually these days, but A.J. Nock was the real thing. Born in Scranton, Pennsylvania, he was home-schooled from the earliest age in Greek and Latin, unbelievably well read in every field, a natural aristocrat in the best sense of that term. He combined an old-world cultural sense (he despised popular culture) and a political anarchism which saw the state as the enemy of everything civilized, beautiful, and true. And he applied this principle con-

---

[55] See http://www.fee.org for details.
[56] See http://www.lewrockwell.com/tucker/tucker23.html.

83

sistently in opposition to welfare, government-managed economies, consolidation, and, above all else, war."

In his *Memoirs of a Superfluous Man* (1943), Nock writes about the anomalous nature of government: "We were supposed to respect our government and its laws, yet by all accounts those who were charged with the conduct of government and the making of its laws were most dreadful swine; indeed, the very conditions of their tenure precluded their being anything else." Nock was altogether discomfited by the reality of the state. He saw it as a great evil in the world; tragically unavoidable and, in a nearly fatalistic sense, the manifest, gloomy downfall of all great civilizations. He envisaged that the rise of state power would gradually reduce the great roads of New England to the desolate, overgrown Roman roads of Old England.

In his classic essay *Our Enemy, The State* (1935), Nock develops his main thesis: there is a great difference between *government*, which is established by men to protect "social power" and peaceful, mutually-beneficial cooperation, and the *state*. The state is the ever-growing mutation of government that results in the favor-brokering, benefit-peddling, business-protecting nuisance that now plagues modern society. On the one hand, men have natural rights, antecedent to the creation of government, that are to be protected by the collective power of government. As Thomas Jefferson put it, "We hold these truths to be self-evident, that all men are created equal, that they are endowed by their Creator with certain unalienable Rights, that among these are Life, Liberty and the pursuit of Happiness. That to secure these rights, Governments are instituted among Men, deriving their just powers from the consent of the governed." On the other hand, states are cancerous outgrowths that thrive by plundering inalienable rights. States are parasites and predators that dole out privileges and siphon off prosperity through taxes and regulation.

Nock says: "At the outset of his pamphlet called *Common Sense*, [Thomas] Paine draws a distinction between society and government. While society in any state is a blessing, he says, 'government, even in its best state, is but a necessary evil; in its worst state, an intolerable one.' In another place, he speaks of government as 'a mode rendered necessary by the inability of moral virtue to govern the world.'" Government might originate by the common understanding and agreement of society aimed at securing "freedom and security". But government power should be limited to these two elements and should never degenerate into any "positive intervention upon the individual, but only a negative intervention." For Nock, "the whole business of government" should be to protect our inalienable rights and nothing more.

Nock is right. The vision of the American Founders could not have been clearer. Yet the defiant state has materialized—despite the Founders' good intentions—originating "in conquest and confiscation." The resulting anti-social order of the state and its administrators would have to be judged by ethics and common law as "indistinguishable from a professional-criminal class." Nock continues: "So far from encouraging a wholesome development of social power, it has invariably, as [James] Madison said, turned every contingency into a resource for depleting social power and enhancing State power. As Dr. Sigmund Freud has observed, it can not even be said that the State has ever shown any disposition to suppress crime, but only to safeguard its own monopoly of crime...with unconscionable ruthlessness. Taking the State wherever found, striking into its history at any point, one sees no way to differentiate the activities of its founders, administrators and beneficiaries from those of a professional-criminal class."

If liberty-lovers adopt a Nockian view of the state, they are left with no alternative than to recognize that the ideal of government envisioned by the Founders has been obliterated. Far more than when Nock wrote 70 years ago, the mutant American state has been transformed into nothing more than a band of thugs. If the right of self-defense is justified and the principles of Jefferson are still valid, then the destruction of the present American state is both justified and a worthy objective of those who love liberty. The state should be replaced with a limited constitutional government congruent with the vision of the Founders and built on the biblical premise of self-defense. After all, if the state is truly something evil, then no Christian should back it.

The satanic nature of the state

Is the state run by Satan? What do we know about the nature of the state? According to the Bible, the state's power comes from Satan through the "spirits of demons". In Revelation 13:1-4,[57] "a beast rising up out of the sea" with "a blasphemous name" on his heads emerges to rule civil society. This ruler is empowered by "the dragon", also "called the Devil and Satan" (Revelation 12:9, cf. 20:2), who gives him "his power, his throne, and great authority". As Royce Gruenler correctly notes, "Revelation 13 characterizes Rome as the demonic beast from the abyss."[58] At the time of the writing of the book of Revelation, Domitian was likely Caesar, noted for the band of gold he wore on his head containing the blasphemous inscription "Dominus et Deus" (i.e., "Lord and God").[59] Satan empowered this

---

[57] Good Protestant hermeneutics mandates that doctrine should primarily be derived from didactical parts of Scripture such as the law, Christ's parables, and the apostolic epistles. Other revelation should be either supportive or secondary in forming doctrine, having its best purpose to clarify, enhance, or bolster principles. The book of Revelation is an inspired portion of the Scriptures, and therefore "profitable for doctrine" (2 Timothy 3:16), with this kind of supportive role. It contains many passages that relate to the state, and thus is helpful in forming a biblical understanding of public policy.

[58] Royce Gordon Gruenler (1989), *Evangelical Commentary on the New Testament*, Walter A. Elwell (ed.), Grand Rapids, Michigan: Baker Book House.

[59] See Herman Hoeksema (1969), *Behold He Cometh: An Exposition of the Book of Revelation*, Grand Rapids, Michigan: Reformed Free Publishing Assoc., pp. 451ff.

ruler "beast", as he does all the "kings of the earth". James Willson concurs:

> And the prophet Daniel, and afterwards the apostle John, expressly and frequently denominate the Roman Empire a "beast." The former, a "beast, dreadful and terrible, and strong exceedingly; and it had great iron teeth: it devoured and brake in pieces, and stamped the residue with the feet of it." (Dan. 7:11.) The latter, a "beast having seven heads and ten horns, and on its horns ten crowns, and on its heads the name of blasphemy," (Rev. 17:1.) Surely such a description was never given of a government that could lay any solid claim to be "ordained of God;" at least, in any other sense than the pestilence is God's ordinance, existing in his providence, but to be shunned and banished as soon as possible.[60]

But the beast does not only refer to a particular Roman Caesar or even to the entirety of the Roman state. Revelation 16:14 (cf. 19:19) says that the "spirits of demons" emerging from this beast and Satan "go out to the kings of the earth and of the whole world, to gather them to the battle of that great day of God Almighty." And the devil presently uses the state to do his bidding, including casting Christians into prison (Revelation 2:10)—as was the case when Peter and John were condemned for preaching the Gospel (Acts 5:17-29). Plainly, the nature of the state—along with all of the "kings of the earth"—is satanic.

Accordingly, when tempting Christ, the devil was probably not lying, and his claims were not exaggerated, when Satan said that he controls the state. "Then the devil, taking Him up on a high mountain, showed Him all the kingdoms of the world in a moment of time. And the devil

---

[60] James M. Willson (1853), *Civil Government: An Exposition of Romans xiii. 1-7*, section 2 (re verses 1 and 2), Philadelphia: William S. Young.

said to Him, 'All this authority I will give You, and their glory; for this has been delivered to me, and I give it to whomever I wish. Therefore, if You will worship before me, all will be Yours.' And Jesus answered and said to him, 'Get behind Me, Satan! For it is written, "You shall worship the Lord your God, and Him only you shall serve""" (Luke 4:5-7).[61] In Revelation 17:11-14 the connection between great states and the figurative beast is evident, where the beast is identified as the eighth successive king. These beasts stand against the kingdom of God and will be cast into hell (Revelation 19:20-21). Therefore, the state can be generally viewed as an agent of the kingdom of Satan and empowered by the devil—even if it is ultimately ordained by God (in the sense of Romans 13:1).

How then can the Bible say that states are "ordained" or "appointed" by God to be his "ministers" (Romans 13:1-2, 4, 6)? Briefly, divine appointment to God's service does not imply that the person or institution appointed is holy or godly. After all, Satan himself is ordained by God, and his actions are bounded by Providence (e.g., as the Bible describes in Job's trials and the protecting of Peter from being sifted "as wheat" by the devil in Luke 22:31).[62] The state is ordained by God but the Bible indicates that its most intimate relationship is with the devil (Revelation 18:9), and the state has generally served Sa-

---

[61] The parallel passage in Matthew 4:8-11 states: "Again, the devil took Him up on an exceedingly high mountain, and showed Him all the kingdoms of the world and their glory. And he said to Him, 'All these things I will give You if You will fall down and worship me.' Then Jesus said to him, 'Away with you, Satan! For it is written, "You shall worship the Lord your God, and Him only you shall serve."' Then the devil left Him, and behold, angels came and ministered to Him."

[62] The Bible is replete with examples of this fact. Ungodly Old Testament era kings were God's controlled servants, including Pharaoh (Exodus 4:21), the Assyrian king (Ezra 6:22), Nebuchadnezzar king of Babylon (Jeremiah 43:10), and Cyrus king of Persia (Isaiah 44:28; 45:1; 2 Chronicles 36:22; Ezra 1:1). The demons had to ask Christ's permission to be cast into the swine (Matthew 8:31) instead of the "dry places" (Matthew 12:43; Luke 11:24). Satan is said to be "bound for a thousand years" by God's angel (Revelation 20:2). God used Michael the archangel to withstand the devil in his wiles (Daniel 10:13; Jude 1:9).

tan's evil designs throughout history, even if God ultimately directs the state and disposes of it as He wills.

The satanic nexus with the state is also described or implied in Daniel 10:13, Ezekiel 28:12-19, and Revelation 17:1-7. In these passages, Satan is called "the prince of kingdom of Persia" and the "King of Tyre". Plus, the "kings of the earth" are described as having an intimate and illicit relationship with Satan by way of his "scarlet beast" and the "woman" who is carried by it. So once again we find a direct link between Satan and the earthly rulers that God ordains. The devil certainly controlled these kings, assuming they were historical figures. Perhaps he even possessed them. Hence, we have more evidence to suggest that the state may credibly be considered part of the kingdom of Satan, and only ordained by God in the sense that the devil himself is ordained by God—to fulfill His purposes and to glorify Him. As James Willson confirms:

> All physical power—all executive energy, in every department of creation, is from God [including the state which is divine ordained]. "In Him we live, and move, and have our being." (Acts 17:28.) In this sense the power of evil beasts and even of the devil, is from God. "By Him all things consist," (Col. 1:17.) Again, if we understand by "power," the possession of the reins of government, it is, certainly, through Him that kings are permitted to occupy their thrones and that, whatever the steps by which they may have succeeded to the seat of authority. Pharaoh was "raised up" in the course of that providence which controls all the affairs of men. God "gave the kingdom" to Jeroboam. The same hand "raised up" Cyrus, and our Lord expressly declares to Pilate, the unholy Roman governor, "Thou couldest have no power at all against me, except it were given to thee from above," (John

19:11.) Even the devil has "power," in this sense, from God.[63]

The Scriptures indicate that the state is often a "minister" of judgment ordained by God (cf. Isaiah 3:4-5, 12-15). To varying degrees, in each judgment situation, the state becomes "the rod" of God's "anger" and "the staff" of His "indignation" (Isaiah 10:5). It receives a "charge" from God to punish the people who are objects of His terrestrial "wrath" (Isaiah 10:6). The Bible says that Lord himself brings "calamity" on people (Isaiah 45:7). The state is often a judgment against the people over which it rules (particularly outside of the theocracy of Judah), although God has also used the state to judge foreigners during the Old Testament theocratic kingdom.[64] Yet the states that serve God in this way are often at least as wicked as the ones they judge, showing that not all of God's ordained servants (cf. Romans 13:4) are upright in character. Casting aside popular myths to the contrary, the state's evil nature and bad character are realities to be expected.

Angry and wicked rulers in the Bible

Not only are the great majority of rulers recorded in the Scriptures wicked, they also share certain common immoral character traits. And such bad behavior even arose in otherwise good theocratic rulers. While it is said that "anger rests in the bosom of fools" (Ecclesiastes 7:9), it also seems to rest in the bosom of kings and other civil authorities. Pharaoh got "angry" (Genesis 40:2; 41:10) and King Saul became both "angry" and "displeased" (1 Samuel 18:8), as did King David (2 Samuel 13:21) and the

---

[63] James M. Willson (1853), *Civil Government: An Exposition of Romans xiii. 1-7*, section 2 (re verses 1 and 2), Philadelphia: William S. Young.

[64] Sometimes a state is more evil than the people it afflicts (Isaiah 10:10, Habakkuk 1:4-11) but God uses it for judgment nonetheless.

90

princes of the Philistines (1 Samuel 29:4). Good King Asa was likewise affected, being enraged with a seer and oppressing some of God's people (2 Chronicles 16:10), and King Uzziah was angry with the priests over the divine technicalities of a ritual (2 Chronicles 26:19). Nebuchadnezzar responded "in rage and fury" to the faithful Jews (Daniel 3:13). King Ahasuerus's "anger burned in him" after Queen Vashti refused to obey him (Esther 1:12). Sanballat was angered by the Jews' rebuilding Jerusalem's walls "and took great indignation" (Nehemiah 4:1, 7). The "princes" were angry with the Prophet Jeremiah, beat him, and cast him into prison (Jeremiah 37:15). Herod was "exceedingly angry" with the Magi (Matthew 2:16). Herod had also been "very angry with the people of Tyre and Sidon" (Acts 12:20a). Herod hated Jesus too and desired "to kill" Him (Luke 13:31). Perhaps political power tends to promote the sin of anger? Or is this tyrannical anger induced from within a ruler by the hateful adversary of good, viz. the devil?

Instead of being for "praise" to those who do "good" in God's sight (cf. Romans 13:3)—as many Christians today mistakenly suppose the civil authority should be—rulers have proven to be a violent and terrifying foe of good people. From the time of His birth, even Jesus Christ was assailed by bad public policy: "...for Herod will seek the young Child to destroy Him" (Matthew 2:13). Eventually, the civil authority did abuse Jesus: "Then Herod, with his men of war, treated Him with contempt and mocked Him, arrayed Him in a gorgeous robe, and sent Him back to Pilate" (Luke 23:11). Moreover, since a servant is not above His master (Matthew 10:24), the church also suffered persecution by the hand of the state. "Now about that time Herod the king stretched out his hand to harass some from the church" (Acts 12:1). A civil junta of "the priests, the captain of the temple, and the Sadducees" (Acts 4:1) hated the Apostles and had determined to "severely threaten them" (Acts 4:17, 29). Enraged, Satan pledged to "make war" with the church by means of his "beast" of civil authority (Revelation 12:17-13:1).

Alternatively, Jesus Christ was never angry. While civil rulers became enraged as a result of self-indulgence in their own lusts and pride, Jesus only assailed other men (e.g., harassing the money changers in the Temple or mocking the Scribes and Pharisees) when "zeal" to please His Father inspired him (John 2:14-17). Angry civil rulers throw tantrums when they do not have their way, but Jesus—and all Christians who desire to imitate Him—only participate in social upheaval out of a zeal for the glory of God. So it was for the Christian Founders in America. The King had violated the commonly believed obligations he had to his subjects, giving them a reason to resist him. They fought tyrannical taxation and regulation for the glory of God. As a result of their efforts, we enjoy the fruits of prosperity for our lives and the Gospel that has been unparalleled in the history of the world. While God is glorified in all events, the American experience has been unique.

Harry Stout postulates: "When understood in its own times, the American Revolution was first and foremost a religious event."[65] At the time of the War for American Independence, perhaps eighty percent of the 2.3 million free Americans attended Protestant churches regularly (with the overwhelming majority being Calvinists). Baptists and Methodists were growing rapidly, and would eventually eclipse all other denominations. They dominated Virginia and overwhelmed areas of the South and elsewhere (notably Pennsylvania and Rhode Island) with Evangelicalism. And preachers *en masse* backed the revolt against King George III. Were the faithful sinning? Was the Christian church dreadfully backslidden? Tory preach-

---

[65] Harry S. Stout (1996), "How Preachers Incited Revolution", *Christianity Today*, Issue 50 (May), vol. 15, no. 2, p. 10. http://www.christianitytoday.com/holidays/fourthofjuly/features/50h010.html.

ers affirm this sentiment and pronounce that God was merely working through—and in spite of—the sinful actions of the rebellious colonists in order to bring about His purposes. That's euphemistic parlance meaning "Yes, the American colonists sinned but we still like the results anyway." But perhaps their actions were not sinful.

Jesus taught his disciples to not only be concerned about the evil doctrine emanating from false religion but also to beware the evil public policies of the civil authority. "Then He charged them, saying, 'Take heed, beware of the leaven of the Pharisees and the leaven of Herod'" (Mark 8:15). Herod's *leaven* of social evil was taught and promulgated through wayward public policy (rather than in the synagogues where the Pharisees promulgated their bad ideas). Christians have many enemies in the world, both religious and secular (or civil). If Christians cannot flee (Luke 21:21), then perhaps some of them will have opportunity to defend their families from criminals and tyrants. If they can neither flee nor fight, then they will surely become martyrs to the Glory of God (Revelation 2:13).

Ultimately, Christians win. The Bible says that "kings of the earth" and the "rulers" take a stand "against the Lord and against His Christ" (Psalm 2:2; Acts 4:26), but their actions (as any other action of Satan) are under the control of God's foreordained and predetermined purpose (Acts 4:27-28). The Bible teaches that satanic forces hold sway over civil rulers and turn them against God's Kingdom: "For they are spirits of demons, performing signs, which go out to the kings of the earth and of the whole world, to gather them to the battle of that great day of God Almighty" (Revelation 16:14, cf. 13:1). Nevertheless, civil authorities will not prevail against God or His people. "It shall come to pass in that day that the Lord will punish on high the host of exalted ones, and on the earth the kings of the earth" (Isaiah 24:21).

The state has been a vile nuisance for civilized men, and the Bible gives us no reason to believe its evil nature can be changed. The psalmist recognized that states legislate evil policies when he wrote: "Shall the throne of iniquity, which devises evil by law, have fellowship with You?" (Psalm 94:20). Historically, the state usually reigns by iniquity, stimulating and fomenting evil schemes. And, in the end, God will destroy the evil and "twisted" state, the beast from the sea (akin to the one mentioned in Revelation 13:1). As He says in Isaiah 27:1: "In that day the Lord with His severe sword, great and strong, will punish Leviathan the fleeing serpent, Leviathan that twisted serpent; and He will slay the reptile that is in the sea." Indeed, the Bible teaches that hell (Tophet) was "prepared" for the king (Isaiah 30:33), and designates the lake of fire as the ultimate end of defiant earthly kings (Revelation 19:20).

With conviction, the Bible indicates that the state is always created according to God's permissive will: "The king's heart is in the hand of the Lord, like the rivers of water; He turns it wherever He wishes" (Proverbs 21:1). By God's wisdom, "kings reign, and rulers decree justice" (Proverbs 8:15). Indeed, "All the inhabitants of the earth are reputed as nothing; He does according to His will in the army of heaven and among the inhabitants of the earth" (Daniel 4:34-37). Thus, even the most vicious and evil rulers are subject to God's decree, even though their lust for greed and power fosters conscription, taxation, power brokering, and oppression—just as Samuel prophesied (1 Samuel 8:11-18).[66]

---

[66] 1 Samuel 8:4-22: Then all the elders of Israel gathered together and came to Samuel at Ramah, and said to him, "Look, you are old, and your sons do not walk in your ways. Now make us a king to judge us like all the nations." But the thing displeased Samuel when they said, "Give us a king to judge us." So Samuel prayed to the Lord. And the Lord said to Samuel, "Heed the voice of the people in all that they say to you; for they have not rejected you, but they have rejected Me, that I should not reign over them.

Biblical accounts of public policy clearly indicate that state acts in the Bible were mostly evil, concurring with other historical manifestations over the last few thousand years. As shown in *Bible and Government*, over 90 percent of the recorded acts of states (outside of the theocracy) were clearly evil. That is to say, public policies recorded in Scripture are usually perverse or opposed to God's law and righteousness, or are directed against God's people. "Summarizing the biblical data, we can conclude that non-theocratic state policy actions were evil 90.2 percent of the time. Theocratic ones were evil 60.3 percent of the time. Overall, state acts were evil 78.4 percent of the time."[67]

The Bible does not support the popular notion that the state is generally a benign—if not benevolent—upholder of social order. The state has not generally been the guardian of God's law or even an arbitrary selection of it. Moreover, the Bible hardly supports the notion that men

---

According to all the works which they have done since the day that I brought them up out of Egypt, even to this day—with which they have forsaken Me and served other gods—so they are doing to you also. Now therefore, heed their voice. However, you shall solemnly forewarn them, and show them the behavior of the king who will reign over them." So Samuel told all the words of the Lord to the people who asked him for a king. And he said, "This will be the behavior of the king who will reign over you: he will take your sons and appoint them for his own chariots and to be his horsemen, and some will run before his chariots. He will appoint captains over his thousands and captains over his fifties, will set some to plow his ground and reap his harvest, and some to make his weapons of war and equipment for his chariots. He will take your daughters to be perfumers, cooks, and bakers. And he will take the best of your fields, your vineyards, and your olive groves, and give them to his servants. He will take a tenth of your grain and your vintage, and give it to his officers and servants. And he will take your male servants, your female servants, your finest young men, and your donkeys, and put them to his work. He will take a tenth of your sheep. And you will be his servants. And you will cry out in that day because of your king whom you have chosen for yourselves, and the Lord will not hear you in that day." Nevertheless the people refused to obey the voice of Samuel; and they said, "No, but we will have a king over us, that we also may be like all the nations, and that our king may judge us and go out before us and fight our battles." And Samuel heard all the words of the people, and he repeated them in the hearing of the Lord. So the Lord said to Samuel, "Heed their voice, and make them a king." And Samuel said to the men of Israel, "Every man go to his city."

[67] John M. Cobin (2003), *Bible and Government: Public Policy from a Christian Perspective*, Greenville, South Carolina: Alertness Books, p. 98.

have learned to govern themselves better over time—such that the evils of the past are less likely to be repeated in the future. On the contrary, the Bible teaches that the heart of man is the same in all ages, resulting in social decay.

Does history confirm the Bible's doctrine regarding the nature of the state? Indeed, it does so emphatically! Throughout history, rulers have typically been malevolent and often cruel. Some have been hedonistic; others have been sadistic. Some have been ideologues or masterful demagogues; others have been rapacious conquerors. Such are the standout traits of power and authority in history. Vicesimus Knox notes that there have been hundreds of evil rulers, some of whom have masqueraded as Christians.

> Pope Julius the Second appears to have been one of the very worst princes that ever reigned. He delighted in war, while he professed to be the representative of the Prince of Peace. He was guilty of oppression and injustice; and while he pretended to be feeding the sheep of Christ, gave himself no other concern but how he might secure the fleece. Yet all his conduct was palliated, by the politicians around him, from the plea of state necessity. Morality and religion gave way to the system of political ethics; and he, who ought to have blessed mankind, and to have preached peace, became their oppressor, despot, and unrelenting murderer. I mention Julius only as a striking instance, and hundreds may be adduced, of the depraved system which rules cabinets, and which, for the gratification of the few, renders the many miserable. No Machiavels can ever justify, in the eyes of God, or of men uninfluenced by corruption, any politics, however subtle and able, which, for the sake of aggrandizing a nation, (an abstract idea,) much less of gratifying a court, render all the individuals of

the nation so to be aggrandized, poor, wretched, insecure, and slavish.[68]

Renowned economist Ludwig von Mises notes that interventionist public policy by states "has caused wars and civil wars, ruthless oppression of the masses by clusters of self-appointed dictators, economic depressions, mass unemployment, capital consumption, [and] famines."[69] For Mises, "collectivism is a doctrine of war, intolerance, and persecution" where the people "become mere soulless pawns in the hands of a monster."[70]

The Bible substantiates this observation. "If you see the oppression of the poor, and the violent perversion of justice and righteousness in a province, do not marvel at the matter; for high official watches over high official, and higher officials are over them" (Ecclesiastes 5:8). Jesus Christ confirmed the vicious behavior of rulers too: "You know that those who are considered rulers over the Gentiles lord it over them, and their great ones exercise authority over them" (Mark 10:42; cf. Matthew 20:25).

The record of state abuses indicates that social learning has hardly improved the state or the demeanor of its rulers—from the Roman Empire to the Dark Ages down to the present. The state remains the foremost enemy of humanity and, along with false religion, the foremost ally of Satan. Thus, the permanent satanic nature of the state presented in the Bible implies the futility of trying to

---

[68] Vicesimus Knox (1824 [1795]), *The Works of Vicesimus Knox*, vol. VI, Section XXXII, "On Political Ethics; Their Chief Object Is to Throw Power into the Hands of the Worst Part of Mankind, and to Render Government an Institution Calculated to Enrich and Aggrandize a Few, at the Expense of the Liberty, Property, and Lives of the Many", London: J. Mawman, p.121.

[69] See Ludwig von Mises (1996 [1966/1949]), *Human Action: A Treatise on Economics*, fourth revised edition, Irvington-on-Hudson, New York: The Foundation for Economic Education, p. 855. Modern socialists have finally admitted that these things were true: "It turns out, of course, that Mises was right." Robert Heilbroner (1990), "After Communism", *The New Yorker*, September 10, p. 92.

[70] Ludwig von Mises, (1985/1957), *Theory and History: An Interpretation of Social and Economic Evolution*, Auburn, Alabama: The Ludwig von Mises Institute, p. 61.

"transform" it into a godly institution (under the dominion mandate of Genesis 1:26-27). Christians should not expect that a leopard will change its spots or that a poisoned spring will produce fresh water.

The evil nature of the state is clearly manifested by the carnage of totalitarian and communist regimes during the twentieth century. Dr. Rudolph Rummel has demonstrated in his book *Death by Government* (and later articles) that, in the twentieth century alone, states around the world were responsible for the killings of at least 262 million—up to an estimated 350 million—of their own civilian, non-combatant populations.[71] This figure does not count the more than one billion slain by state-sanctioned abortion worldwide, or the over 40 million military personnel slain through state-sponsored aggression, during the same period. The state has been the most lethal institution in human history.[72] And history illustrates the fact that twentieth century states have been the most evil of all time in terms of (1) loss of life and property and (2) persecution of the church.

Clearly, the state has been more lethal than any infectious disease, plague, or religious inquisition in the history of mankind. In a July 1997 interview with *The Freeman: Ideas on Liberty*, Rummel stated: "Concentrated political power is the most dangerous thing on earth. During the twentieth century, 14 regimes murdered over a million people" each. "So much for the notion of state benevo-

---

[71] Rudolph Rummel (1994), *Death by Government: Genocide and Mass Murder Since 1900*, New Brunswick, New Jersey: Transaction Publishers. The low figure was adjusted up from 169 (or 174) million by new data received by Dr. Rummel in 2005.

[72] Steven Yates points out that bad philosophy led to such tragedy: "Political systems designed along specifically materialist lines have always turned out to be systems in which totalitarian coercion and sometimes genocide was unleashed in its bloodiest fury...Left in the hands of power-hungry intellectuals (Marxist or otherwise), materialism removes all moral restraints on responsibility (which emerged out of Christian theism) and hence on power. In the last [20th] century this led to worse consequences than anything Hobbes could have imagined!" Steven Yates (2005), *Worldviews: Christian Theism versus Modern Materialism*, Greenville, South Carolina: The Worldviews Project, p. 58.

lence. Powerful states can be like gangs, stealing, raping, torturing, and killing on a whim."

Many Christians have been murdered by states, including Jesus Christ and nearly all of the Apostles. Yet the relatively peaceful, anomalous American experience has stymied American Christians from appreciating this fact. The truth of the matter is just the opposite: states have proven to be destructive to property and a great nuisance to the church and gospel preaching throughout the ages down to the present time. Christian leaders would do well to be better apprised of history (especially as it relates to states and public policy) and basic economics. When it comes to facing unmitigated state power, ignorance is not bliss.

State evil is likewise evident from the poisoned and baneful redistributive policies of modern welfare states, the confiscatory taxation used to accomplish proactive policy, and much moral blight—such as the condoning of manic abortion or the excesses of the Clinton administration in America. Moreover, the imperialistic, unjust, and unconstitutional wars in Iraq and Afghanistan conducted by Bush family presidencies prove that there has been no end to the apparent bloodthirsty quest for power and economic benefit by American rulers beginning with Abraham Lincoln.

Even in America, civil liberties and constitutional rights are frequently eroded by all branches of the state, through court cases undermining private property and the right to life, legislation curtailing the Bill of Rights—under the guise of "fighting terrorism" or warring against vices like drug trafficking, and executive orders that encourage police state brutality and barbarism. Thus, the United States of America is fast devolving to the equilibrium point of interventionism and "security" that humans have coddled for centuries. In doing so, citizen-subjects fail to realize the deadly outcome of centralized and unrestricted state power.

Those Christians who errantly view the modern state as God's colleague, upholding part of His law, must face a double dilemma.[73] First, the Bible indicates that the state is generally evil, having a satanic origin, and often serves God by bringing terrestrial judgment upon people. Second, it is very rare (if not impossible) to find historical examples of states that have ever come close to upholding God's law in the world. Given that the earthly institutions of God designed to expand His kingdom must at least resemble His ways and serve His cause, the state—which is eminently wayward—cannot fall into this category.

Accordingly, adherents of the liberty of conscience perspective are wary of confiding in the state to do anything good, including legislating morality (LM) or promoting any other proactive policy in the "public interest". Moreover, while they favor the Ten Commandments as God's Word, they do not advocate posting them on state buildings or courtroom monuments. Jesus states: "For a good tree does not bear bad fruit, nor does a bad tree bear good fruit. For every tree is known by its own fruit. For men do not gather figs from thorns, nor do they gather grapes from a bramble bush" (Luke 6:43-44).

If the state is inherently evil, therefore, how can it be possible to expect any lasting good to come from it? If it has the power to legislate Christian morality today, then what kind of morality will the wayward state legislate tomorrow? It is better that the state legislate no moral principles at all—other than to enforce ones which protect citizens from predators (e.g., murder, theft, rape, kidnapping)—than to open Pandora's Box by giving it proactive authority that will likely be turned against Christians at

---

[73] Specifically referred to are adherents of the revitalized or reshaped divine right of kings perspective discussed later in this book. Theonomists would never attribute such confidence to the modern state; even if they hope that one day it will become such an attendant of righteousness. Likewise, those pacifists who hold that the state is a competing kingdom against God's kingdom would also cast a vote of no confidence in the modern state—for good reason. Regrettably, there are relatively few Christian leaders today who reject the divine right perspective. A discussion of these different perspectives is contained in chapter 3 and Appendix 1.

some point. Dr. Eric Schansberg aptly sums up the liberty of conscience position:

> I used to be more tolerant of the belief that Christians should legislate morality. I remain tolerant in the sense that many evangelicals have been deluded into worshipping the State as an agent of social change—by surface logic and the prodding of politically active religious conservatives. And as a teacher, I can empathize with how easy it is to avoid saying tough things from the "pulpit" and instead, to appeal to the audiences "itching ears". But to believe in this idol after the last two chapters [on what the Bible says about LM, what Jesus would do, and the high practical costs of any LM program] requires that one downplay important practical considerations and make some curious assumptions about the Bible, Christ's life, and their application to our lives. It is the pursuit of a forced morality for others, using a method that is difficult, if not impossible, to defend biblically.[74]

Consequently, Christian leaders are leading people astray who promote the modern state, in America or elsewhere, as a companion of the church or an apt legislator of morality. On the contrary, they should warn Christians about the evil nature of the state, about the statist schemes of Satan, and tell them to be on their guard against the state—one of the church's most lethal enemies in history. Lamentably, only a few Christian leaders have been dutiful to proclaim this sort of warning.

Christian leaders must also be about the business of proclaiming God's way of caring for the poor and needy, for promoting peace, and for defending ourselves against

---

[74] D. Eric Schansberg (2003), *Turn Neither to the Right nor to the Left*, Greenville, South Carolina: Alertness Books, pp. 100-101.

the intrusions of the state. Regrettably, rather than being active agents in transforming their culture, ignorant Christian leaders have been willing to abandon it to the mischief and folly of statists.

The day is coming, dear Christian, and dear lover of liberty, that you too might join the ranks of the Founding Fathers in resisting tyranny. Are you really prepared to take a stand against the "kings of the earth"? If not, now's the time for a paradigm shift in your public policy theology.

To sit back hoping that someday, someway, someone will make things right is to go on feeding the crocodile, hoping he will eat you last—but eat you he will.
—President Ronald Reagan (1911-2004)

No man's life, liberty, or property is safe while the legislature is in session.
—Mark Twain (1866)

To be free, a government must rest on the consent of everyone who participates in it. Any government can call itself free, and it is to those who voluntarily support it. But when a government resorts to force and coercion—no matter how just or noble the cause—it becomes a tyranny to those compelled to support it against their will.
—Lysander Spooner (1867)

The ballot...is a mere substitute for a bullet.
—Lysander Spooner (1870)

5 The Divine Ordination of State Criminals and Legalized Crime

Implications of divine ordination of state rulers

Just what does divine appointment imply about public policy, particularly proactive varieties? Are rulers (or states) generally good men (or institutions) simply because they are *ordained* by God? How can a God-ordained institution persist in legalizing crime and legitimizing the criminal behavior of rulers?

Thomas Jefferson candidly observed, "Sometimes it is said that man cannot be trusted with the government of himself. Can he, then, be trusted with the government of others? Or have we found angels in the forms of kings to govern him? Let history answer this question." In *Common Sense*, Thomas Paine agreed: "...could we take off the dark covering of antiquity [pertaining to the origin of kings and of the State] and trace them to their first rise, we should find the first of them nothing better than the principal ruffian of some restless gang; whose savage manners or pre-eminence and subtlety obtained him the title of chief among plunderers; and who by increasing in power and extending his depredations, overawed the quiet and defense-

Thomas Jefferson

less to purchase their safety by frequent contributions." Likewise, as noted in chapter 4, Sigmund Freud (cited by Albert J. Nock in *Our Enemy, the State*) observed: "Taking the State wherever found, striking into its history at any point, one sees no way to differentiate the activities of its founders, administrators and beneficiaries from those of a professional-criminal class." History teaches us that rulers and states everywhere have typically advocated evil policies and have behaved in ways that would be categorized as criminal if done in the private sector.

Although states *can* (and often do) legalize crime, God does not sanction such policy. For example, abortion, euthanasia, assisted suicide, sodomite unions, marriage licensing, divorce (for reasons other than adultery or abandonment), family control rules (e.g., prohibitions against spanking, truancy "laws"), public (pagan) education, affirmative action, taxation (legalized theft) of non-privileged earnings, farm and other subsidies (financed by extortion), welfare and other relief that requires the looting of one person in order to benefit another (e.g., Social Security, food stamps, Pell grants, etc.), and aggressive warfare (murder)[75] are immoral policies but are still legal—and even endorsed by the state. Yet God condemns them in His word.

From before the time of Christ, nearly every state has promulgated such evil policies. And the variety of evil policies is growing. Given this unshakable fact, how should we understand the Bible's teaching that states are "or-

---

[75] For further discussion on the immorality and evil of aggressive warfare, see Laurence M. Vance (2005), *Christianity and War and Other Essays Against the Warfare State*, Pensacola, Florida: Vance Publications. "[M]ilitary chaplains asking God to bless troops on their missions of death and destruction are taking God's name in vain" (p. 18). "To say, as some Christians do, that because "the Lord is a man of war" (Exodus 15:3), and God allows wars between [political] nations, that it is honorable for Christians to enthusiastically participate in U.S. wars of aggression is about the most profound demonstration of biblical ignorance that one could manifest" (p. 29). "Cursed is he that taketh reward to slay an innocent person" (Deuteronomy 27:25 KJV).

dained" or "appointed" by God (Romans 13:1)? Divine ordination simply indicates that Providence directs all things. As historic Baptist and Presbyterian confessions of faith declare: "God hath decreed in himself, from all eternity, by the most wise and holy counsel of His own will, freely and unchangeably, all things, whatsoever comes to pass."[76] Surely, the Apostle Paul did *not* purport that all particular states then (and ever since) have been characteristically good or good for society. History evinces the opposite.

Consider state rulers of the last century alone—mega-murderers—such as Mao Tse-tung and Chiang Kai-shek (China), Josef Stalin (U.S.S.R.), Adolf Hitler (Germany), Pol Pot (Cambodia), U Ne Win (Burma), Marshal Josip Broz Tito (Yugoslavia), Yahya Khan (Pakistan), Tojo Hideki (Japan), Mustafa Kemal Atatürk (Turkey), and Idi Amin (Uganda). Of course, evildoers are not confined to the state. One may also note prolific (private sector) serial killers such as David Berkowitz (the "Son of Sam"), Ted Bundy, John Wayne Gacy, and Pee Wee Gaskins of the United States; Moses Sithole and Norman Afzal Simons of South Africa; Bruno Ludke of Germany; Javed Iqbal of Pakistan; Luis Alfredo Gavarito and Pedro Alonso Lopez of Colombia; Andrei Chikatilo of Russia; Anatoly Onoprienko of the Ukraine; Bela Kiss of Hungary; Arnfinn

Chiang Kai-shek

---

[76] Article III of the 1689 (Second) *Baptist Confession of Faith* says: "God hath decreed in himself, from all eternity, by the most wise and holy counsel of his own will, freely and unchangeably, all things, whatsoever comes to pass; yet so as thereby is God neither the author of sin nor hath fellowship with any therein; nor is violence offered to the will of the creature, nor yet is the liberty or contingency of second causes taken away, but rather established; in which appears his wisdom in disposing all things, and power and faithfulness in accomplishing his decree." Article III of the 1644 (First) *Baptist Confession of Faith* says: "That God has decreed in Himself from everlasting touching all things, effectually to work and dispose them according to the counsel of His own will, to the glory of His name; in which decree appears His wisdom, constancy, truth, and faithfulness." Article III of the 1649 *Westminster Confession of Faith* says: "God from all eternity did, by the most wise and holy counsel of His own will, freely, and unchangeably ordain whatsoever comes to pass: yet so, as thereby neither is God the author of sin, nor is violence offered to the will of the creatures, nor is the liberty or contingency of second causes taken away, but rather established."

106

Pee Wee Gaskins

Nesset of Norway. We live in an "evil age" (Galatians 1:4). So much bloodshed brings to mind the solemn words of Scripture: "For man also does not know his time: like fish taken in a cruel net, like birds caught in a snare, so the sons of men are snared in an evil time, when it falls suddenly upon them" (Ecclesiastes 9:12). Nevertheless, at least in terms of raw numbers, states and their rulers have been the foremost manifestations of "cruel nets" and "snares" that men have had to face, far and away exceeding the evil of all serial killers combined. While serial killers murder a small number of people, state rulers murder them by the thousands and even millions.

In the case of states, God has ordained evil men to rule to accomplish His purposes in the world. Divine appointment or ordination includes that which is evil and nefarious. Many will no doubt be shocked by the Bible's plain, clear doctrine: the fact that God ordains all things does not necessarily mean that all the things that God ordains are *good*. For instance, Satan, the demons, various false religions, genocidal rulers, and prolific serial killers were all ordained by God yet clearly none of them were good. Clearly, divine ordination does not necessarily imply even a tendency toward institutional goodness in the state. Indeed, God ordains the state in the same sense that He ordains the devil himself.

Yahya Khan

Divine ordination and the rightness of state decrees

May a state legalize crime or actions that God says are wicked? Does God give the state permission to break His laws by virtue of the fact that it is the appointed civil authority—elected or otherwise?[77]

---

[77] As mentioned earlier, and documented in *Bible and Government*, the insidious nature of the state with its public policies is manifest in over 90 percent of the occurrences of

Since the closing of the canon, the menacing nature of public policy and states has continued to be manifest. As the Bible instructs us: "If you see the oppression of the poor, and the violent perversion of justice and righteousness in a province, do not marvel at the matter; for high official watches over high official, and higher officials are over them" (Ecclesiastes 5:8).

We should concur with the premises of Dr. Francis Schaeffer in *A Christian Manifesto* and those of the Christian Founding Fathers: Christians may oppose the state when it decrees evil public policies, either passively or actively, even to the point of armed resistance under the right circumstances. Both Tory doctrine and the neo-orthodox pietism of Dietrich Bonhoeffer are wrong. These passive positions are mistaken by suggesting that Christians must not be involved in any overthrow of the divinely ordained civil authority, under any conditions, or that Christians should withdraw from engaging the carnal world of public policy, instead preferring to mind heavenly things. The appropriate Christian posture is activism in all areas of life (see chapter 15). Accordingly, the biblical premise of Operation Rescue may rightly be applied to us today: "If you faint in the day of adversity, your strength is small. Deliver those who are drawn toward death, and hold back those stumbling to the slaughter. If you say, 'Surely we did not know this,' does not He who weighs the hearts consider it? He who keeps your soul, does He not know it? And will He not render to each man according to his deeds? (Proverbs 24:10-12). And God commends those

Francis Shaeffer

Dietrich Bonhoeffer

---

implemented public policies in the Bible (outside of the Old Testament theocracy). The Apostles lived under Nero, who was certainly one of the most evil rulers in history, along with local draconian rulers like Herod. They had no delusions about the nature of the state which often persecuted them.

who uphold His righteous ways in the world regardless of whether their actions defy the mandates of the state.

God alone (apart from the state) defines right and wrong

Who defines criminal behavior? The state may have its definition, but God's definition differs (see chapters 4 through 6). Nowhere in the Bible is the state held out to be the great decider or legislator of what God thinks is right or wrong. God takes care of that task through His revealed will in the Scriptures. The principles of right and wrong, good and evil, transcend culture and technology. We know that pornography and abortion are wrong because the principles of God's Word can be applied to them.

Nero tormented the Christians (whom he considered to be criminals), Hitler eradicated Jews, Stalin obliterated Kulaks, Turks annihilated Armenians, and Lincoln ravaged and castigated "rebel" southerners, for their "crimes". These rulers decided what was right and they legislated what they believed to be proper. Yet in the mind of God, all of these "ordained" rulers were criminals while their victims, by and large, were not. The state cannot make any action moral or immoral by its decrees. The best that limited government can do is repeat God's Word after Him by decreeing right and wrong based on what God says is right and wrong.

And what should we think of those American leaders who brought down liberty and replaced it with tyranny by means of oppression? Abraham Lincoln and Franklin Delano Roosevelt were among the greatest American criminals, yet they are revered and venerated today. Lincoln was responsible for slaughtering hundreds of thousands of Americans. Roosevelt legalized wholesale plunder and redistributive theft.

Tragically, on account of statism and false ideologies fomented in state schools (or pagan seminaries), people are confused about who the real villains are. Assassins of rulers are considered criminals in the eyes of the state. But are they, like Ehud, also criminals in the eyes of God (see chapter 12)? Would killing state criminals be any less just than killing a robber in your home? Why should rulers enjoy amnesty (as heads of state) unlike other criminals?

Rulers are often divinely-ordained swine and thugs

Yes, evil rulers are ordained by God. But that fact does not mean that they are *good* for society. They are exalted criminals with immunity, what Albert J. Nock called "most dreadful swine"; a cohort that Lysander Spooner referred to as "open robbers and murderers". No surprise that rulers love divine right doctrine[78] promoted by Evangelical Tories then and now. Only within the mechanism of the state can a man legally be a thug without reprisal or public shame. Yet God ordains such thugs: "to the intent that the living may know that the most High ruleth in the kingdom of men, and giveth it to whomsoever he will, and setteth up over it the basest of men" (Daniel 4:17). Vicesimus Knox wrote about the character of rulers:

Lysander Spooner

> Happy indeed would it be, if those who are exalted to honourable offices of state, were elevated, because they were eminent examples of all moral virtue. They are too often forced into offices, by their own restless ambition, and the furious zeal of deluded parties; or, when they are chosen, it too often happens, that ability, and not virtue, determines the choice.[79]

---

[78] See chapter 3 and Appendix 1 for discussion on the revitalized divine right of kings view.

[79] Vicesimus Knox (1824 [1795]), *The Works of Vicesimus Knox*, vol. V, Sermon XV, "The Pride of Human Learning and False Philosophy, a Great Obstacle to the Reception of Christianity", London: J. Mawman, p. 226.

An honest heart is a surer and better guide, even for those who preside in government, than those boasted principles, which are often called Machiavelian [*sic*], but ought to be termed diabolical, policy. It can never be proved to the satisfaction of good men, that the Virtues which communicate happiness in the civil, social, and commercial intercourse of men, are not the most productive of good in the political department. Indeed, the reason that men of corrupt morals and abandoned characters have frequently guided a nation, is, that such men are the most turbulent and ambitious; ready to destroy the community, by the power which their wealth affords, if they are not permitted to guide its councils, to engross its honours, and to divide its emoluments among themselves and the instruments of their aggrandizement.[80]

In a very real sense, ruling a state is a low, sneaking business. God often appoints "the basest of men", particularly unprivileged in character, to rule. Historically and biblically speaking, it is evident that divine ordination has only rarely led to godliness among rulers since the Babylonian Empire. Indeed, the opposite seems to be true: God ordains wicked men—knowing that they will do evil—to rule this world. As Psalm 12:8 states: "The wicked prowl on every side, when vileness is exalted among the sons of men." Yet God uses such rulers to accomplish His temporal purposes: "The king's heart is in the hand of the Lord, like the rivers of water; He turns it wherever He wishes" (Proverbs 21:1)—even mega-murderers.

God's temporal purposes seem to primarily accomplish two objectives: (1) the sanctification of His beloved

---

[80] Vicesimus Knox (1824 [1795]), *The Works of Vicesimus Knox*, vol. V, Sermon VIII, "Good Intentions the Least Fallible Security for Good Conduct", London: J. Mawman, p.118.

111

church and/or (2) the terrestrial judgment of the hated workers of iniquity that anger Him (Psalms 2:1-5; 5:5, 7; 7:11). In this sense the state serves a nonrandom purpose. God certainly knows the futile thoughts and plans of the wicked (Psalm 94:11) and can turn them to work for His appointed designs according to His "determinate counsel" (Acts 2:23). "He catches the wise in their own craftiness, and the counsel of the cunning comes quickly upon them" (Job 5:13). Nevertheless, a state *may not* legalize crime or actions that God says are wicked. Such legalization would be immoral and would reflect the evil nature of the state. God does not give the state *permission* to break His laws by virtue of its divine appointment as the civil authority—elected or otherwise—even though it routinely does so.

Many are appalled when they read statistics about how many members of Congress have been convicted of crimes like assault, fraud, shoplifting, or who have gone bankrupt (or have very bad credit), or otherwise have been of low character. But such is far more the norm for states and rulers than the exception. How can anyone who is knowledgeable about political history, public choice economics, or the biblical depictions of states and public policy be surprised by the criminal behavior of rulers?

Right is right, even if everyone is against it, and wrong is wrong, even if everyone is for it.
—*William Penn (1644-1718)*

Unthinking respect for authority is the greatest enemy of truth.
—*Albert Einstein (1879-1955)*

6 A Concise Commentary on Romans 12–14 and 1 Peter 2 Manifesting the Liberty of Conscience Framework

The following comments on the key New Testament passages regarding submission to civil government are not intended to form a comprehensive, exegetical commentary. Instead, they are intended to show how the liberty of conscience framework is established in the text so that the crucial points and issues brought up in this book are addressed in a consistent way—perhaps as an auxiliary to traditional commentaries for serious students of the Word.

It is striking to see how many commentators default to the divine right perspective. Many of them presume, perhaps without much reflection, that the state does a reasonably good job punishing criminals and benefiting those who behave well. They imagine, as Royce Gruenler says, that the Apostle Paul has distinguished "the state as a gift of God's common grace to guarantee civil order and to restrain uncontrolled evil."[81] The divine right camp apparently postulates that public policy is generally effective in promoting the "public interest". Adherents like Gruenler further assert that a "cooperative servanthood" exists between the state and the church, where the state provides social order that facilitates successful promotion of the Gospel.

---

[81] Royce Gordon Gruenler (1989), *Evangelical Commentary on the New Testament*, Walter A. Elwell (ed.), Grand Rapids, Michigan: Baker Book House.

> It is in this sense [that God is sovereign over the kingdoms of men] that Paul exhorts his readers to "submit to the governing authorities" (vv. 1, 5). Insofar as human authorities are the servants of God and provide a basis for order and the mission of the church, being indirectly at the disposal of God for the carrying on of his work, Christians are to respond in cooperative servanthood.[82]

However, each of these divine right suppositions is dubious at best—if not completely spurious—and subject to both historical verification and scientific (economics) challenge.

Accordingly, the comments in this chapter are intended to demonstrate how the theology of public policy is facilitated by proper interpretation of these passages (utilizing the principles discovered in both this book and *Bible and Government*). The proper application of cultural context, economics, public policy theory, and history are joined with the interpretive paradigm to provide a cohesive public policy theology through prudent exegesis.

Ancillary and topical exegesis of Romans 12:16–14:19

> *12:9* Abhor what is evil. Cling to what is good...*14* Bless those who persecute you; bless and do not curse.

These verses form an important prelude to the main focus of this chapter's commentary commencing with verse 16. In verse 9, Christians are exhorted to maintain good works as elaborated in God's Word, despite the fact that others around them are given over to misbehavior and wickedness (πονερός). Given the context at Rome, Paul is

---

[82] Ibid.

115

declaring that social mischief and roguery are evil and Christians must abstain from such behavior.

Recall from chapter 4, a major premise of the liberty of conscience perspective is that the state is evil. Thus, we are we to abhor the state, even though we must still submit to it in most policies in order that we are not distracted from the Christian life's main mission. There are many policies that must be submitted to in order to avoid being harassed or fined by the state. Some policies must not be submitted to since they would violate a clear command of God or a conviction that we hold from the Scriptures. And there are many other policies that can be disobeyed since they are not enforced or are archaic (and still not repealed).

At the time of writing (AD57), Rome was full of unrest and rioting. Paul makes clear in verse 14 that he did not want the Roman believers to partake in the mischief and chaos, as would have been so easy for them to do. Furthermore, Nero was harming Christians who were doing well. Thus, in order to stand out in society and glorify God as a city set on a hill that cannot be hidden (Matthew 5:14), Paul exhorts the believers to bless their enemies. Paul was applying the general teaching of Christ in the Sermon on the Mount to the specific circumstances in Rome at the time. Of course, as a general principle for all Christians, Paul's teaching is valuable as well—just as Christ's teaching is of general value even though it was directed specifically at the Jewish culture of the day.

> *12:16b* Do not set your mind on high things, but associate with the humble. Do not be wise in your own opinion. *17* Repay no one evil for evil. Have regard for good things in the sight of all men. *18* If it is possible, as much as depends on you, live peaceably with all men. *19* Beloved, do not avenge yourselves, but rather give place to wrath; for it is written, 'Vengeance is Mine, I

will repay,' says the Lord. *20* Therefore 'If your enemy is hungry, feed him; If he is thirsty, give him a drink; For in so doing you will heap coals of fire on his head.'

Christians might have been opportunists like their neighbors and taken advantage of the social upheaval, or they could have been tempted to resist with force those who were caught up in the insurrection that wanted to molest them. But Paul wanted the believers to behave differently in order to glorify God and have a good testimony. He also wanted to make sure that they did not lose their lives and damage their families in the face of Nero's wrath—that is a practical ("pragmatic") or expedient approach. Paul did not want believers to be a focal point in the eyes of the civil government, especially since Nero was already prone to blame Christians.

12:21 Do not be overcome by evil, but overcome evil with good.

Doing good works and not acting in the same manner as the rogues in Rome will bring glory to God. Moreover, orderly behavior by Christians will not provoke the civil authority to pour out his wrath on them. The Greek word here translated "evil" is κακόν, which may carry the milder meaning "misdeeds" (unlike the stronger word πονερός in verse 9 meaning wickedness), referring to the civil misdeeds of the rioters. Paul also uses κακόν in chapter 13:2-5 when referring to state punishment of evildoers.

Christian behavior should demonstrate how wickedness can be overcome by goodness. Paul is also giving a general principle that whenever we can subdue evil in the world and replace it with what is good we should do so, but only if we do not sin in the process.

13:1 Let every soul be subject to the governing authorities. For there is no authority except from God, and the authorities that exist are appointed by God.

Paul is essentially saying: "Do not mess with the state like others are doing. Realize that God has ordained it (and all authorities) for a purpose: judgment of sinners being one particular. So stay out of the way of God's minister of wrath on the rebels. The state is also ordained for the good of Christians; that is, their general sanctification" (as noted in Romans 8:28). Submission to the state is always qualified. We must obey in general, but many times we will disobey a policy on account of personal conviction, its obsolescence, or its non-enforcement. Furthermore, as Martin Luther notes, Christian submission to the state is superfluous in terms of engendering moral behavior:

> St. Paul teaches that one should honor and obey the secular authorities. He includes this, not because it makes people virtuous in the sight of God, but because it does insure that the virtuous have outward peace and protection and that the wicked cannot do evil without fear and in undisturbed peace. Therefore it is the duty of virtuous people to honor secular authority, even though they do not, strictly speaking, need it.[83]

The verb ὑποτασσέσθω ("be subject") is in the present tense, passive voice in the Greek in Romans 13:1, indicating that Christian submission to civil government occurs as a response to being acted upon (implied in the *passive* voice) rather than active seeking out ways to submit.

---

[83] Martin Luther (1972 [1545]), "Preface to the Letter of St. Paul to the Romans", Andrew Thornton (trans.), "Vorrede auff die Epistel S. Paul: an die Romer" in *D. Martin Luther: Die gantze Heilige Schrifft Deudsch 1545 aufs new zurericht*, Hans Volz and Heinz Blanke (eds.), Munich: Roger & Bernhard, vol. 2, pp. 2254-2268.

Christians must obey innocuous policies whenever they are directly called upon to do so, but they are not called upon to *actively* ensure compliance with every public policy. They need not be burdened to scour thousands of pages of legislation and executive orders to ensure that they have complied with every particular policy that applies to them.

All Christians agree that submission is qualified. Differences arise over the "why" (or what) and the "when." What policies can be disobeyed, why can they be disobeyed, and when should a believer employ *passive* or *active* resistance to any particular policy? The theonomists would allow resistance to any policy that does not comply with God's law set forth in the Old or New Testament.[84] The Anabaptist might passively resist any decree of the state, if it is considered contrary to the purposes of the kingdom of God.

The revitalized divine righter would permit rebellion only when a policy runs contrary to a "clear" teaching of Scripture, such as, prohibitions of Gospel preaching (Acts 4:19), eating forbidden foods (Daniel 1:8), bowing to false gods (Daniel 3:12), prohibitions of prayers to God (Daniel 6:7-10), selling one's possession when it is a special heritage from God (I Kings 21:3), and committing murder (Exodus 1:17). Other permissible rebellions may

---

[84] Some commentators, theonomists in particular, find support in the original language for their position that only *worthy* rulers must be submitted to. "The word (uperexousaij) here [in Romans 13:1 KJV] rendered 'higher,' properly signifies prominence, or eminence, and hence it comes to mean 'excellent,' or 'excelling,' and must be translated by these or equivalent expressions in a number of passages in the New Testament. 'Let each esteem other better (uperexontaj) than themselves,' (Phil. 2:3.) 'And the peace of God, which passeth (uperexousa) all understanding,' (Phil. 4:7.) 'For the excellency (dia to uperexon) of the knowledge of Christ Jesus my Lord,' (Phil. 3:8.) In fact, the passage now before, us, and Pet. 2:13, a parallel passage, are the only instances in which our translators have furnished a different rendering. Hence, some expositors have been disposed to lay no little stress upon this epithet, as distinctly defining the character of the powers here intended, and as limiting to such the subjection here enjoined, the 'excelling powers;' that is, powers possessing a due measure of the qualifications requisite to the rightful exercise of the power of civil rule." James M. Willson (1853), *Civil Government: An Exposition of Romans xiii. 1-7*, section 1 (re verse 1), Philadelphia: William S. Young.

119

be added to the list as well, including prescribing violations of a few of the Ten Commandments, mandating oath taking, or directing child-rearing and educational practices. Answers from divine righters will vary depending upon the one consulted (i.e., the accumulated list may show wide variance between them).

Nevertheless, from a liberty of conscience perspective, submission to the state always has the objective of being expedient and practical toward men and glorifying toward God. There is never a moral problem for disobeying a policy or revolting *per se*. Any sin problem for disobedience arises only when one's action is unwise, involves poor stewardship, requires neglecting one's family duties, or detracts from the believer's principal purpose in life (as noted under the Romans 12:9 comment earlier).

All four views would permit *passive* resistance to any morally repugnant policy, including fleeing on account of policies of persecution (Matthew 2:13; 10:23; 24:16; Mark 13:14; Luke 21:21; John 10:5)—although the divine righters would probably allow less passive resistance than other Christians. Surely, it is unimaginable that Roman believers would have obeyed policies requiring them to turn in their brethren to the authorities. The Roman Christians obviously disobeyed a policy designed to persecute them by not surrendering to authorities, preferring to flee to the Catacombs. The main disagreements in practical theology arise over when active resistance can be employed. At any rate, *none* of the four views of a believer's response to public policy takes Paul's teaching (or Peter's) to be *absolute*.

However, the liberty of conscience perspective developed in this book and in *Bible and Government* squares best with Paul's teaching in Romans 13:1-7 since it does not abide with inconsistencies like the other views. The theonomists have to relegate Paul's teaching to a golden age or an idealistic time when the state behaves as it should (even though they know that the state only very rarely if ever has behaved as it should). Most of the time, they will be able to justify revolt, making Paul's submission requirement rather lame or impotent for believers living under wicked rulers.

The Anabaptist view, although similar to the liberty of conscience view in some respects, does not seem to give much weight to Paul's mandate in practice. Almost any policy can be found wanting (and thus become nonbinding) in terms of their overarching desire for the advancement of the kingdom of God.

The divine righters are left with the uneasy position of demanding absolute disobedience to a few policies and absolute obedience to everything else. The problem for them arises in that there is no universally or even widely accepted list of policies that can be disobeyed (beyond a handful of "clear" ones). One will say that hiring a Christian who has entered the country illegally is sin while another will not. The same is true about policies for the military draft, giving preferential treatment for hiring homosexuals, prohibiting sexual practices in marriage, prohibiting working or shopping on Sunday, and many other policies. If representatives of each policy view were debating over hard policy questions, they would end up accusing each other of sinning at many points. (Some will conclude the crass position that almost anything *illegal* is sin.)

Furthermore, divine righters end up throwing Christians into bondage. For them, it is a *sin* to revolt or disobey *any* public policy that is not specifically on their "OK to disobey" list. It makes no difference that a believer is ignorant of the legislation and policies where he is situated. He sins whether he disobeys intentionally or not. In some places he sins if he spits on the street (as in Dunn, North Carolina), if he wears his grandfather's postal worker uniform to a costume party (USA), if he wears a military ribbon that he is not authorized to wear (USA), if he fails to wear his seatbelt for any reason in most states, if he throws a rock at a bird in Dublin, Georgia, or if he is under age 18 and plays pinball in South Carolina or Nashville, Tennessee.

There are a countless number of federal and state "laws" that he is obliged to obey. He must not have a cavalier attitude toward sin (cf. Romans 6:1) and thus must take seriously his obligation to be apprised of the local public policies wherever he goes. If he is tempted to sin and break a "law," God will provide a "way of escape" for him (1 Corinthians 10:13), and he must strive to find it. Hence, if the divine right doctrine is taken seriously, the bondage is severe.

The theonomists have an advantage of having a more or less exact list of good and bad polices from the Old Testament and from the Law of Christ. They do not think that it is sin to disobey a policy unless it is on the Bible's law code. Some of them might say that, under a covenantal view of society, a state that violates God's covenant forfeits its right to obedience by its subjects. Nevertheless, while there may be some bondage in the theonomic system, it is nothing like the bondage found under a divine right one.

The liberty of conscience view has the advantage of freeing the believer from bondage to men's rules. Any policy may be resisted if the need (or moral obligation from conviction) arises, so long as if there is no clear practical or expedient reason to obey public policy (unlike there was in Rome), and the believer does not commit any ancillary sin by disobeying.

Thus, it is not very difficult to reconcile Paul's rather absolute-sounding mandate with a liberty of conscience view. He exhorted the Roman Christians under Nero to be particularly careful to obey every policy they could, in order to minimize personal suffering and persecution. Some were banished by Nero, and perhaps many others fled the city, following the teaching of Christ (Matthew

10:23). Yet the fact remains that the coddled quasi-absolutist interpretation of the divine righters does not hold up well when one considers the whole counsel of God (Acts 20:27).

Even divine righters admit that there are times when rebellion against the state is required. Paul's tough language reflects the context in which the believers were living. Such a strong directive is not universal for all times and places. The principle stands of course, but its specific application will depend on the repugnancy of the policy in question, the strength of the state that enforces the policy, and the ability of the believer to wisely resist the policy (either actively or passively) within his cultural context. The liberty of conscience view also permits the greatest personal choice and responsibility in deciding which policies to resist, thus fomenting a tendency to promote policies of liberty as well.

> *13:2* Therefore whoever resists the authority resists the ordinance of God, and those who resist will bring judgment on themselves. *3* For rulers are not a terror to good works, but to evil. Do you want to be unafraid of the authority? Do what is good, and you will have praise from the same.

Here Paul is saying: "Do not cross state rulers and you will not have to face their wrath that is going to come down on the rioters. Instead, behave as they want you to and they will be pleased with you." The state has its own definition of what is good and evil, which is almost certainly antithetical to God's at most points. The state is an authority ordained by God, just as Satan is an authority, but this fact does not mean that its decrees will be generally or even occasionally godly in character.

Paul is pointing out to the believers at Rome that if one does something that the much-annoyed Roman state thinks is evil then he will suffer wrath for it. As pointed out in chapter 2, those who wish to divorce this teaching from its historical context, making Paul's teaching an absolute requirement in all cultures and eras, are greatly mistaken. They end up placing Christians under an inordinate bondage to public policy, just as do many adherents of the revitalized or reshaped divine right of kings doctrine.

> *13:4* For he is God's minister to you for good. But if you do evil, be afraid; for he does not bear the sword in vain; for he is God's minister, an avenger to execute wrath on him who practices evil.

Concurring with Dr. Greg Bahnsen's remarks in chapter 3, Greg Durand succinctly states the theonomic position: "this passage was intended to be prescriptive, not descriptive". In other words, the state is only truly God's minister when it obeys God's commands and behaves as God *prescribes*. Otherwise, "it is the duty of Christians to resist his unlawful rule as they would the rule of Satan himself".[85] However, the theonomists read too much into the text. There is no compelling reason to believe that Paul has in mind other rulers than those in first century Rome.

Indeed, Paul states the facts of life: "If you taunt the state it will bite you—hard." Paul knew how powerful Nero was and the damage he could inflict on the growing church

---

[85] Greg Loren Durand (1996), "The Liberty of Conscience: Civil Disobedience in Light of Romans 13:1-7," Dahlonega, Georgia: Crown Rights Book Company, FBS Library Online: http://train.missouri.org/~newlife/romans13.htm. The complete comment is: "When all is said and done, it is important to take into consideration that this passage was intended to be prescriptive, not descriptive. In other words, it speaks of what the 'higher powers' are supposed to be, not what they are intrinsically at all times. As 'God's minister,' the civil magistrate is obligated to obey God's Law and to properly apply it to the society which he governs. Conversely, any time the civil magistrate becomes 'a terror to good works,' and rewards evil rather than punishing it, he then has begun to 'bear the sword in vain.' To this extent, he is no longer 'God's minister to you for good' and it is the duty of Christians to resist his unlawful rule as they would the rule of Satan himself."

at Rome. (The same is true of lesser rulers like Herod, Felix, and Agrippa.) Nevertheless, Paul reminds the believers that the unrest around them, and the state's wrathful activities, would in the end produce more general sanctification in the sense of Romans 8:28: "And we know that all things work together for good to those who love God, to those who are the called according to His purpose."

> *13:5* Therefore you must be subject, not only because of wrath but also for conscience' sake.

The reason we *must* submit to government is to avoid wrath or worrying about being harmed by the state authority. God does not want us to be entangled with the affairs of this world to the point where such involvement detracts from our primary mission.

The word "conscience" is used to denote one's worry about doing something wrong. But in this case, as it was in Corinth where some weaker brethren worried about eating meat sacrificed to idols (1 Corinthians 10:23-31), the believers were worried about whether doing something that the Roman state considered to be wrong.

In terms of God's way, our conscience bothers us when we sin and reminds us of the Day of Judgment. In terms of the state, it bothers us when we are not in compliance with the policy and we worry that we might incur the wrath of the state. Remember, the state's definition of evil and God's definition of evil are often diametrically opposed.

While submission is generally *required*, it is not absolute. Nevertheless, Paul was writing to Roman believers in whose circumstances submission to rulers was especially important. Christians needed to show themselves to be different than their neighbors. Those few Christians would not have stood a chance in resisting the civil authority.

Might there be other times when believers might be able to participate in gaining the upper hand over an evil authority, such as the American Revolution? The liberty of conscience view holds that Scripture leaves room for such a possibility.

As noted in chapter 2, the peculiar submission to Rome in AD57 had special significance to the believers of that day, and as a principle to future situations, but not necessarily all situations. What a grief it is to modern believers when their church leaders bring them into bondage of having to be apprised of, and obey, every bit of legislation and executive or judicial decree that presents itself in their lives! What a grief it is to believers who are chided by some (based on a quasi-absolutist interpretation of this passage) for resisting or revolting against an evil state when they have a legitimate opportunity to overcome it!

Rather than such absolutism, one might argue that Paul generally permits Christians to "overcome" evil (authority) and be "free" from it—as developed in chapter 9. "Overcome evil with good" (Romans 12:21) and "Were you called while a slave? Do not be concerned about it; but if you can be made free, rather use it...You were bought at a price; do not become slaves of men" (1 Corinthians 7:20-23).

Thus, the primary reason God tells us to obey is to avoid facing overwhelming wrath and worry, but when Christians have the ability to resist an evil state and overcome it, as the Americans did in 1776, then they may by all means do so. Accordingly, Paul is not teaching that all resistance must be immoral. He is not saying that violating public policy is generally sinful, with a few exceptions (e.g., prohibitions of Gospel preaching and demands to commit murder). He is teaching that since any resistance by the Roman believers would be crushed by overwhelming power, and would give an excuse to begin a general persecution of Christians, they had to be careful to go above and beyond the call and submit to all policies that do not cause them to sin. As Peter would say to them later: "submit yourselves to every ordinance of man for the Lord's sake" (1 Peter 2:13).

> *13:6* For because of this you also pay taxes, for they are God's ministers attending continually to this very thing.

It is as if Paul were saying: "Consider submitting to the present policies in the same manner as you submit when paying taxes. You hate to pay taxes but you do so because you do not want to either experience the state's wrath or worry about it. Behave well, especially now given all the tumult (or perhaps the martial law) that is emerging."

Note that Paul teaches that suffering is part of the Christian life (Philippians 1:29, 2 Timothy 3:12; cf. Luke 6:22, John 16:33). But he does not teach that Christians should *seek* persecution. On the contrary, Christ taught us to flee persecution when possible (Matthew 10:23, 24:16; Mark 13:14; Luke 21:21), and in Romans 13:1-7 and 1 Peter 2:13-17 the Apostles admonish believers to comply with policy in order to minimize persecution and suffering. Paul demonstrated this objective when he utilized his rights as a Roman citizen to mitigate the persecution and suffering that he might face (Acts 25:11, 22:25-29, 23:27, 28:19).

Were the Christians who participated in the Boston Tea Party and other tax rebellions against England in violation of this mandate to pay taxes to an evil state? No! See chapters 7 through 12. Nero's rule was plainly evil too, but believers had no chance of overthrowing him. Were Isaac Backus (1724-1806)—a noted Baptist preacher, historian, and defender of liberty—and the other early American Baptists in violation of biblical principles by their active resistance to certain religious taxation? They were not, because the force of the teaching of Paul is neither absolute nor neatly transcendent across cultural contexts. And the Americans had a viable chance at achieving liberty—as Baptists like Backus, Wallers, and Leland must have realized (not to mention the plethora of preachers and theologians from other denominations).

> *13:7* Render therefore to all their due: taxes to whom taxes are due, customs to whom customs, fear to whom fear, honor to whom honor.

The word 'taxes' here is *tribute*, or a capitation tax charged in a township census. The government agents went house to house and counted the residents (or the residents registered at a local office, cf. Luke 2:1), and demanded immediate payment of the tribute. "Do not resist them," says Paul, "just pay it." "The same thing holds with any sort of indirect tax they charge you when you bring your goods to market to trade and they require a tariff at the gate of the city. Walk humbly past those state agents who have the power to harm you, and be outwardly fearful so as not to provoke them. Give honor to the authorities superficially so as not to peeve them and give them cause to assault you. Give them whatever money or respect they require of you during this tumultuous time."

Moreover, as a general principle for future circumstances, modern Christians should do the same. Yet it is not clear that Paul has in mind any sort of tax that would be levied but rather those levied visibly near their homes or in the marketplace. Nonpayment in public would classify them with the rebels and rogues of the day. Paul wanted them to avoid such public controversy so that they would not become objects of governmental wrath or detract from the glory of God.

But how does this apostolic teaching about taxes relate to our modern era when taxation is not always public as it was in Rome? Would Paul require that American Christians be scrupulous in reporting every dime for income and sales tax purposes (e.g., that they gain through private bartering or cash sales)?

The taxpaying requirement set forth in Romans 13:6-7 refers to circumstances in which paying a tax is demanded by the state on-the-spot, and where noncompliance would inevitably expose a Christian to facing the state's "wrath"—not to mention cause him much anxiety. Note that Jesus Christ was not *worried* about His tax liability (Matthew 17:27), even though (being God) He knew it existed. He might even have opposed paying taxes (Luke 23:2). He certainly manifested no qualms over avoiding taxes.

If the main principles in the passage that Paul teaches are (1) to avoid the state's wrath, (2) to be free from worry that the state will harass you, (3) to not make a public spectacle of resistance to public policy and thus give the state an excuse to persecute the church, and (4) above all, to glorify God by keeping His commandments, then it seems that many modern taxes may be avoided or even evaded without sinning or violating apostolic teaching. Tribute and tariffs are not representative of all kinds of taxes in all cultural contexts for all times. They were the public taxes of the Roman civilization.

This counsel from the Apostle Paul is very practical (or "pragmatic"), expedient, and advisable. As noted in this book and *Bible and Government*, Paul is not out of line with the similarly expedient directives regarding civil government elsewhere in the Scriptures (see chapter 2). Paul did not want believers to be entangled with the state. "No one engaged in warfare entangles himself with the affairs of this life, that he may please him who enlisted him as a soldier" (2 Timothy 2:4). Instead, a Christian should live a "quiet and peaceable life" (1 Timothy 2:2), being noticed only on account of his good works, love and faith. Impertinent speech was to be exchanged for "humility" (Titus 3:1) and gentleness.

Elsewhere in the Scriptures, there is important practical advice given regarding one's behavior regarding civil authority. Christians are to use wisdom and caution around rulers (Proverbs 23:1-3), to not "marvel" or fret over political corruption and oppression (Ecclesiastes 5:8), to not foolishly taunt rulers or openly challenge political authorities that might harm us (Ecclesiastes 8:2-5), and to comply with their petty decrees lest they be offended (Matthew 17:27). Indeed, it is not unusual to encounter practical instruction about Christian behavior around state rulers in the Bible. Therefore, it should not surprise us that the Apostles continue to embellish this practical teaching in places like the second half of Romans—especially given the instability of the times.

Accordingly, in order to avoid being needlessly harassed by the state (which could be suicidal), a Christian must conduct himself wisely, showing at least superficial respect to state leaders and public policies. Daniel appeared in the king's court and even accepted his (unsolicited) gifts, without overtly mocking any official who could have harmed him (cf. Ecclesiastes 10:20). Paul says that Christians who face Roman imperial threats should (passively) "be subject" as a matter of practical wisdom, resting in Providence.

Paul was *not* requiring unqualified submission to public policy. The early believers comprehended the practical nature of the instruction of Paul (and Peter). Surely, the Roman government upheld precious little of what was godly or pious. It set its own standards of good and evil, right and wrong, according to its pagan principles, and the Apostles were likely well acquainted with this fact.

13:8 Owe no one anything except to love one
another, for he who loves another has fulfilled
the law.

This precept not only applies to tribute and tariffs
that would be demanded, but also to any other person in
Rome at that unstable and difficult time. Paul is basically
saying, "Do not give anyone around you, whether politician, bureaucrat or rioter, a reason to assail you." This text
does not mean that under more tranquil times believers
were forbidden to borrow money. The best choice at that
time in Rome was to bless others with things that they had,
government agents and rioters included, and to thus demonstrate the love of Christ. As a principle, we might do the
same as the Roman believers were instructed (at least in
some cases).

13:9 For the commandments, 'You shall not
commit adultery,' 'You shall not murder,' 'You
shall not steal,' 'You shall not bear false witness,' 'You shall not covet,' and if there is any
other commandment, are all summed up in this
saying, namely, 'You shall love your neighbor
as yourself.' *10* Love does no harm to a
neighbor; therefore love is the fulfillment of the
law.

The law of Christ sums up in one phrase the entire
second table of the law: how we ought to treat our
neighbors. Paul says: "Apply that law of Christ now with
regard to your Roman neighbors caught up in the frenzy."

13:12 The night is far spent, the day is at hand.
Therefore let us cast off the works of darkness,
and let us put on the armor of light. *13* Let us
walk properly, as in the day, not in revelry and
drunkenness, not in lewdness and lust, not in
strife and envy.

131

Paul admonishes them: "Do not sin like most everyone else around you. Behave differently; as Christ would have you behave. Do not mimic their drunken parties, fighting, lusts, revelries, and riots, but instead act as a Christian should act and use the opportunity to show that you are different than the rabble of society."

> *13:14* But put on the Lord Jesus Christ, and make no provision for the flesh, to fulfill its lusts.

Paul effectively says: "Rather than take advantage of the situation for earthly gain, utilize the circumstances to glorify God, advance the cause of the Gospel, and promote your own sanctification."

> *14:1* Receive one who is weak in the faith, but not to disputes over doubtful things. *2* For one believes he may eat all things, but he who is weak eats only vegetables. *3* Let not him who eats despise him who does not eat, and let not him who does not eat judge him who eats; for God has received him.

Continuing his expedient teaching into Romans 14, Paul says: "With all of the turmoil going on around you, do not devour one another over minor issues." In terms of applying public policy theology to modern issues, one might also extend Paul's teaching to disputes over whether a Christian traveling three miles per hour over the posted speed limit is wrong, or whether or not a Christian physician can "break the law" by providing "free" medical care to indigent missionaries or middle class family members (which is against public policy).

> *14:4* Who are you to judge another's servant? To his own master he stands or falls. Indeed, he

will be made to stand, for God is able to make him stand.

Paul sums it up: "Respect Christian liberty on issues that are not absolutely clear in the Scriptures. God is his Judge, but God has also promised to preserve him as one of His elect."

14:8 For if we live, we live to the Lord; and if we die, we die to the Lord. Therefore, whether we live or die, we are the Lord's.

The Christian's life is in God's hands. He will make the believer persevere so that he will never be out of His favor.

14:12 So then each of us shall give account of himself to God. *13* Therefore let us not judge one another anymore, but rather resolve this, not to put a stumbling block or a cause to fall in our brother's way.

Paul admonishes the believers to be careful how they live and not to use their liberties in such a way that it causes a brother to have a conscience problem—even if the conscience violation he feels has no merit in reality—but is only on account of his weak understanding.

14:14 I know and am convinced by the Lord Jesus that there is nothing unclean of itself; but to him who considers anything to be unclean, to him it is unclean. *15* Yet if your brother is grieved because of your food, you are no longer walking in love. Do not destroy with your food the one for whom Christ died. *16* Therefore do not let your good be spoken of as evil; *17* for the kingdom of God is not eating and drinking, but righteousness and peace and joy in the Holy

Spirit. *18* For he who serves Christ in these things is acceptable to God and approved by men.

Paul is saying here: "Especially during unrest, your brethren are the most important supports in your lives. Do not nitpick and wrangle with them in a sort of spiritual revelry that rivals the vile and reprehensible revelry around you. Instead, show extra love and patience and do not grieve your brother."

19 Therefore let us pursue the things which make for peace and the things by which one may edify another.

The bottom line is: behave in a godly and peaceable manner in order to glorify God in this unstable world around us, and let us behave in a charitable and encouraging manner to the brethren. Pursue peace by limiting the state's desire to assail you. Under the right circumstances in modern times, if you can make a change in state policy, fight against those things which take away peace in the world (like socialism and interventionism through proactive policies). This action is part of what is implied in Paul's command: "pursue the things which make for peace". We make peace by upholding policy that promotes peace.

Ancillary and topical exegesis of 1 Peter 2:1-25

2:1 Therefore, laying aside all malice, all deceit, hypocrisy, envy, and all evil speaking, *2* as newborn babes, desire the pure milk of the word, that you may grow thereby, *3* if indeed you have tasted that the Lord is gracious.

Like Paul in Romans 13:12, Peter gives a similar list of follies and behaviors to shun. Instead of living for the flesh, Peter admonishes the Roman believers to use instability as an opportunity to improve Christian character.

2:7 Therefore, to you who believe, He is precious; but to those who are disobedient, 'The stone which the builders rejected has become the chief cornerstone,' *8* and 'A stone of stumbling and a rock of offense.' They stumble, being disobedient to the word, to which they also were appointed. *9* But you are a chosen generation, a royal priesthood, a holy nation, His own special people, that you may proclaim the praises of Him who called you out of darkness into His marvelous light; *10* who once were not a people but are now the people of God, who had not obtained mercy but now have obtained mercy.

The reprobates around the believers act out their part to defy God and reject Christ. Apparently, the Roman state's wrath was going to come upon them as a terrestrial judgment as well. By their bad behavior, they were asking for stripes. On the other hand, the elect in Rome were to realize who they were and act accordingly, ensuring that the glory of God remained their chief end.

2:11 Beloved, I beg you as sojourners and pilgrims, abstain from fleshly lusts which war against the soul, *12* having your conduct honorable among the Gentiles, that when they speak against you as evildoers, they may, by your good works which they observe, glorify God in the day of visitation.

Like Paul in Romans 13:1-7, Peter does not want the Roman believers to participate in the riotous living of those around them, or any protests against their exile. Instead, he wanted the believers to be seen by state rulers as compliant and not troublesome, to the end that the Gospel might be promoted even more.

> *2:13* Therefore submit yourselves to every ordinance of man for the Lord's sake, whether to the king as supreme, *14* or to governors, as to those who are sent by him for the punishment of evildoers and for the praise of those who do good.

Peter's teaching is similar to Paul's in Romans 13:1-7: "Do what the Roman government demands." Christians needed to realize that the rogues of Rome were in jeopardy of being judged by the powerful state, which disliked their misdeeds. States have seldom in history— and certainly not under Nero's Rome (AD54 to AD68)— punished people who broke God's law or harmed His ways, or who rewarded believers or those who promoted the kingdom of God.

The meaning here, as in Romans 13:1-7, is that the state punishes evil as it defines evil and rewards or praises good as it defines good. The message to believers is stay out of Leviathan's way so as to avoid having terrestrial wrath poured upon them. The verb ὑποτάγητε ("submit yourselves") is in the aorist tense, passive voice in the Greek again, indicating that Christian submission to civil government is to be *passive* rather than active—meaning that they do not go out of their way to find ways to submit but rather do so whenever confronted by rulers. As noted in the comments on Romans 13:1 above, Christians must obey innocuous policies whenever they are directly called upon to do so, but they are not called upon to *actively* ensure compliance with every public policy.

> *2:15* For this is the will of God, that by doing good you may put to silence the ignorance of foolish men—

Peter has in mind the same goal that Paul did. Behave differently in your culture during the uprisings and you will glorify God more and advance the Gospel by your good deeds.

2:16 as free, yet not using liberty as a cloak for vice, but as bondservants of God.

Peter alludes to his conversation with Christ about the temple tax in Matthew 17:24-27. "Free," ἐλεύθερος, is used in a similar way in both 1 Peter 2:16 and Matthew 17:26. Compare the passage in Matthew 17:

24 When they had come to Capernaum, those who received the temple tax came to Peter and said, 'Does your Teacher not pay the temple tax?' *25* He said, 'Yes.' And when he had come into the house, Jesus anticipated him, saying, 'What do you think, Simon? From whom do the kings of the earth take customs or taxes, from their sons or from strangers?' *26* Peter said to Him, 'From strangers.' Jesus said to him, 'Then the sons are free. *27* Nevertheless, lest we offend them, go to the sea, cast in a hook, and take the fish that comes up first. And when you have opened its mouth, you will find a piece of money; take that and give it to them for Me and you.'

Christians are "free" from having to obey legalisms or any authority but God in an absolute sense. Nevertheless, for both expedience reasons and for reasons of advancing the kingdom of God, Christians should also obey civil authority. This directive is compounded by Peter's actions which effectively bound Christ by oral contract into paying the tax that He obviously knew about (being omniscient) but saw no reason to pay.

Christians should not disobey many policies "lest we offend" rulers (Matthew 17:27). In this passage, Jesus was not worried about His unpaid tax liability. He was not merely testing Peter to see how he would perform and in turn pay the tax if Peter did the right and "honest" thing (by extension to the modern age, "Let's see if Peter will voluntarily declare all his income on a 1040 income tax form or not").

Offending state rulers only brings wrath, worries, and wastes our time and resources. And in Jesus' case not paying the Temple tax would have drawn undue attention to Him politically which would have detracted from His redemptive purpose. Offending the civil authorities unnecessarily throws our priorities in life out of whack. The same application may be made for joining rogues in their roguery. It is not fitting for saints who are in reality a royal priesthood (as Peter just described) to behave like rogues, who should be dedicated to glorifying God in everything.

> *2:17* Honor all people. Love the brotherhood. Fear God. Honor the king.

Similar to Paul's teaching in Romans 13:7-8, believers should go out of their way to love their brethren, especially during difficult times. And Peter calls on believers to show at least superficial honor to rulers or to their neighbors (even in the midst of debauched revelries and rogueries). The Apostle Paul was careful to maintain this outward respect toward the high priest (Acts 23:5). However, we see that this command is not absolute under any circumstance by looking at the lives of Christ, John the Baptist, and the Apostles. Jesus disparagingly referred to Herod as a "fox" (Luke 13:32), publicly dishonored the ruling scribes and Pharisees by calling them a "brood of vipers" (Matthew 23:33) and "sons of hell" (Matthew 23:15), and reproached the high priest (John 18:19-23).

Unlike Paul, Jesus did not make a conciliatory gesture when He was accused of reproaching the high priest and was struck on the cheek—partly because being struck on the face was a fulfillment of Isaiah 50:6. (We also see that the command to turn the other cheek in Matthew 5:39 is not an absolute requirement since Christ did not do so—nor did Paul when he was similarly struck in Acts 23:2.) Peter and John publicly derided the demands of the Jewish rulers, elders, scribes, and the high priest when they were asked to stop speaking about Jesus (Acts 4:18-19).

John the Baptist likewise called the ruling scribes and Pharisees a "brood of vipers" (Matthew 3:7; Luke 3:7), and was not afraid to rebuke and dishonor Herod publicly by saying that his brother Phillip was in sin for his involvement with Herodias in an illicit relationship (Matthew 14:4). His actions were congruent with the doctrine of the Apostle Paul: "Those who are sinning rebuke in the presence of all, that the rest also may fear" (1 Timothy 5:20), and John the Baptist was not out of line with many of the other Old Testament prophets who harshly confronted civil leaders.

> *2:18* Servants, be submissive to your masters with all fear, not only to the good and gentle, but also to the harsh. *19* For this is commendable, if because of conscience toward God one endures grief, suffering wrongfully.

More practical exhortation: "Believing slaves must not take advantage of the current unstable circumstances to procure benefits for the flesh." It makes no difference if one's master is a believer, benign, or cruel. The believers were to use the instability as an opportunity for testifying to others about God's grace, rather than to create a bad testimony by taking advantage of the situation. They should stay faithful and reverent; just like Paul and Silas who chose to not escape from the Philippian prison (Acts 16:25-34). Like them, if the Lord wills, they would have an opportunity to gain both their freedom and the souls of their masters.

> *2:20* For what credit is it if, when you are beaten for your faults, you take it patiently? But when you do good and suffer, if you take it patiently, this is commendable before God. *21* For to this you were called, because Christ also suffered for us, leaving us an example, that you should follow His steps: *22* 'Who committed no sin, Nor was deceit found in His mouth'; *23* who, when He was reviled, did not revile in return; when He suffered, He did not threaten, but committed Himself to Him who judges righteously; *24* who Himself bore our sins in His own body on the tree, that we, having died to sins, might live for righteousness—by whose stripes you were healed. *25* For you were like sheep going astray, but have now returned to the Shepherd and Overseer of your souls.

Clearly, Nero *was* a terror to those who did well in God's sight (viz. Christians). In verse 20, Peter alludes to the fact that Nero and his state at times punished those who did well. Christians were apparently doing good and suffering for it. Nero had exiled the Christians to whom Peter wrote to the southern shores of the Black Sea. Thus, public policy was opposed to God's way, at least in terms of directly promoting His kingdom in the world.

Of course, all rulers promote God's will in the world by bringing terrestrial judgment on sinners and by bringing trials to the righteous for their good (i.e. sanctification, cf. Romans 8:28). In sum, Christians are to expect, and rejoice in, suffering for Christ (Philippians 1:29; 2 Timothy 3:12; Luke 6:22; John 16:33). By imitating Him we glorify Him and advance His kingdom.

Closing remark regarding the liberty of conscience view

One final note of interest is that the liberty of conscience view of the state and public policy (presented in this book and in *Bible and Government*) is the proper heritage of Baptist Christians. That is not to say that the liberty of conscience view is incompatible with other the doctrinal positions of other denominations. It is compatible. But Baptists have had the great misfortune of aligning themselves with incompatible doctrines about public policy from other groups that has led to the acceptance of errors like the revitalized or reshaped divine right of kings doctrine.

Hence, it is fitting to conclude by noting what that famous English Baptist preacher, Charles H. Spurgeon proclaimed—a man who hated war and statecraft—about Baptist suffering at the hand of the state, as well as at the hands of Roman Catholics and other Protestants: "[O]ther than some occurrences among radical Anabaptist groups, Baptists have never made any alliance with the state—a kingdom that competes with the reign of their Lord.[86]

---

[86] "We believe that the Baptists are the original Christians. We did not commence our existence at the reformation, we were reformers before Luther or Calvin were born; we never come from the Church of Rome, for we were never in it, but we have an unbroken line up to the apostles themselves. We have always existed from the very days of Christ, and our principles, sometimes veiled and forgotten, like a river which may travel underground for a little season, have always had honest and holy adherents. Persecuted alike by Romanists and Protestants of almost every sect, yet there has never existed a Government holding Baptist principles which persecuted others; nor, I believe, any body of Baptists ever held it to be right to put the consciences of others under the control of man. We have ever been ready to suffer, as our martyrologies will prove, but we are not ready to accept any help from the State, to prostitute the purity of the Bride of Christ to any alliance with Government, and we will never make the Church, although the Queen, the despot over the consciences of men" (*The New Park Street Pulpit*, volume VII, p. 225).

141

PART III

KEY ISSUES

There is no distinctly native American criminal
class...save Congress.
—Mark Twain (1835-1910)

Of government, at least in democratic states, it may
be said briefly that it is an agency engaged whole-
sale, and as a matter of solemn duty, in the perform-
ance of acts which all self-respecting individuals re-
frain from as a matter of common decency.
—H.L. Mencken (1880-1956)

Government is best that governs least.
—Henry David Thoreau (1817-1862)

All government which makes not the advancement of
human happiness, and the comfort of the individuals
who are subject to its controul [sic], *the prime pur-*
pose of its operations, partakes of despotism.
—Vicesimus Knox (c. 1795)

7 The Christian and Self-Defense against Criminals—Including the State

Christians and self-defense

Do Christians have a right of self-defense? If so, under what circumstances may they defend themselves? May they only defend themselves against criminals or against civil authorities too? Are there any instances in which Christians must *not* defend themselves? These are tough questions that require more than just knee-jerk or cavalier responses. Indeed, a lot is riding on the doctrine of self-defense. For instance, if self-defense against other human beings were not justified under any circumstances, then women with tubal pregnancies would have to perish with their unborn children (on account of bleeding from a ruptured fallopian tube), criminals would have free course over the goods that believers have "stored up" (Proverbs 13:22; Ecclesiastes 11:1; Matthew 25:16-21), and revolution would always be wrong.

If self-defense is wrong then we ought all to be anarchists—not "anarchy" in the sense of *chaos* but rather in its scientific sense of a civilization without any central and organized civil government. The dictionary defines anarchy as: "Absence of any form of political authority." The fundamental reason why government exists ultimately rests on the conviction that self-defense is right. Pure pacifists neither need nor want a government. They are apolitical and should be, logically, anarchists. Why then are Christians not anarchists? Only if the Bible supports the doctrine of self-defense would the principle of Christians using limited government for purposes of creating a common defense be justified.

In the same vein we may ask: "Why do Americans have (or even want) a political authority?" According to the doctrine of Jefferson in the Declaration of Independence, "Governments are established among Men" to secure our rights of life, liberty, and property. The Constitution sets forth the role of civil government as well: "to form a more perfect Union, establish Justice, insure domestic Tranquility, provide for the common defense, promote the general Welfare, and secure the Blessings of Liberty to ourselves and our Posterity." The third article of the (sadly) forgotten Articles of Confederation states: "The said States hereby severally enter into a firm league of friendship with each other, for their common defense, the security of their liberties, and their mutual and general welfare, binding themselves to assist each other, against all force offered to, or attacks made upon them, or any of them, on account of religion, sovereignty, trade, or any other pretense whatever."

In other words, in the most fundamental sense, the Founders wanted a government (but not a *state*) in order to protect them from predators. Politically, Americans covenanted together for a "common defense" because at some level self-defense is not practicable. Civil government becomes an extension of our right of self-defense and our desire for self-preservation. Nevertheless, regardless of what American political philosophy may have been, should those who adhere to biblical Christianity adopt it today?

Several New Testament passages can be used to support the doctrine of self-defense for a Christian. First,

John the Baptist did not condemn soldiers for doing their job, part of which included killing people, but only warned against abusing their office. "Likewise the soldiers asked him, saying, 'And what shall we do?' So he said to them, 'Do not intimidate anyone or accuse falsely, and be content with your wages'" (Luke 3:14). Second, Christ directed that Christians take up arms useful in self-defense: "he who has a money bag, let him take it, and likewise a knapsack; and he who has no sword, let him sell his garment and buy one" (Luke 22:36).

Third, the Apostle Paul at least implies that Christian men ought to defend their families as part of their provision: "But if anyone does not provide for his own, and especially for those of his household, he has denied the faith and is worse than an unbeliever" (1 Timothy 5:8). Note that Moses was not condemned for killing an Egyptian while defending and avenging one of his brethren (Acts 7:24, 28). Finally, although we cannot generate any conclusive argument from silence, it is notable—taking the preceding passages into account—that Christ did not condemn prudent planning for (and use of) warfare as a proper function of a wise king (Luke 14:31). Moreover, there are plenty of examples in the Old Testament of God condoning warfare and men going to battle. And God does not change, even if the administration of His kingdom does.

Clearly there is a sense in which Christians are to turn the other cheek (Matthew 5:39), suffer, and show forth the glory of God in doing so rather than defending themselves. There is a time in which we must suffer and die (Matthew 5:11; Philippians 1:29; 2 Timothy 2:3). Nevertheless, the New Testament does not indicate that Christians are called upon to be the world's doormats. Thus, in the current administration of God's kingdom, there seems to be room for Christians to pursue liberty and at times defend themselves against tyranny. In the final analysis,

Christians can bring glory to God either by suffering or through promoting liberty.

Aggression is not an inescapable cost of discipleship

In his famous work *The Cost of Discipleship*, Dietrich Bonhoeffer commended Christian suffering under tyranny and oppression as a means of demonstrating Christian faith and commitment.

> "It would be equally wrong to suppose that St. Paul imagines that the fulfillment of our secular calling is itself the living of the Christian life. No, his real meaning is that to renounce rebellion and revolution is the most appropriate way of expressing our conviction that the Christian hope is not set on this world, but on Christ and his kingdom. And so—let the slave remain a slave! It is not reform that the world needs, for it is already ripe for destruction. And so—let the slave remain a slave! [Christ took on the form of a slave too (Philippians 2:7)]...The Christian must not be drawn to the bearers of high office: his calling is to stay below."[87]

Was Bonhoeffer right? Should American Christians *not* run for "high office"? Should they be content with their "slavery" imposed upon them by a tyrannical state that confiscates more than half of their earnings in taxes, proactively regulates their behavior as a big brother would, and maintains a threat against their homes for nonpayment of property taxes?

If self-defense by Christians is biblical, why did Christ and the Apostles not defend themselves against the

---

[87] Dietrich Bonhoeffer (1995 [1959]), *The Cost of Discipleship*, New York: Simon & Schuster (Touchstone), p. 260. Apparently, Bonhoeffer modified his views on political action, cultural engagement and assassination later in life. Unfortunately, this widely-read book reflecting his initial, errant thinking continues to influence many Christians.

147

Roman state? Well, Christ had to die for the sake of His church. He said that He could have had "more than twelve legions of angels" (Matthew 26:53) to defend Him, but He chose not to defend Himself out of love for His people. (Note too that He never said that defending Himself would have been wrong.)[88] Earlier in His earthly ministry, Christ divinely avoided His persecutors since "His hour had not yet come" (John 7:30) and He warned Christians to "flee" coming persecutions and the destruction of Jerusalem (Matthew 10:23; 24:16; Luke 21:21). Fleeing is a form of self-preservation, which is a subset of self-defense.

Likewise, the Apostle Paul defended himself in court (Acts 22:1 [Jews]; 26:1*ff* [Festus]) and Paul went so far as to hope that Alexander the Coppersmith would be temporally castigated by God (2 Timothy 4:14)—perhaps even to further his self-preservation before the trial that would soon lead to his execution. Paul also instructs that those who are enslaved should take the opportunity to become free if they can do so: "Were you called while a slave? Do not be concerned about it; but if you can be made free, rather use it" (1 Corinthians 7:21).

Therefore, we see that Bonhoeffer, although well-intentioned, was mistaken. Christians should try to be free from slavery and tyranny when possible. If God opens the door, freedom might allow them to bring greater glory to God in their lives than would come from demonstrating their piety and service while living under oppression. It could be that the Apostles and early disciples were just be-

---

[88] There are instances in which self-defense is not appropriate. Peter was not condemned for the act of defending Christ but was admonished for forestalling His redemptive purpose. "Then Simon Peter, having a sword, drew it and struck the high priest's servant, and cut off his right ear. The servant's name was Malchus. So Jesus said to Peter, 'Put your sword into the sheath. Shall I not drink the cup which My Father has given Me?'" (John 18:10-11; cf. John 18:26; Matthew 26:51-53—"Put your sword in its place"; Mark 14:47; Luke 22:50-51—"Permit even this"). Likewise, David would not defend himself against Saul, whom He considered the Lord's anointed, since he thought it would have been inappropriate to do so (1 Samuel 24:6, 10; 26:9, 11, 16, 23; 2 Samuel 1:14, 16). David obviously defended himself on many other occasions.

148

ing expedient in not taking up arms. Just because a Christian has a right to defend himself does not mean that he should always do so. The early Christians had little hope of overpowering the brutal Romans.

Let's reason through when it is appropriate for Christians to forcibly resist tyrants and predators—even with deadly force. Consider: (1) an angry Christian brother attacking you with a knife; (2) an armed robber or other predator who enters your home in the middle of the night; (3) the local mafia organization that wants to shake you down for monthly contributions; (4) a criminal in public (e.g., as you pass by a small group of thugs who are gang raping a woman outside of a bar, they turn their attention towards you in a menacing way); (5) the invading army of another country; (6) the invading army of a country that your people just declared their independence from (but they refuse to acknowledge your independence from them, e.g. England in 1776); and (7) your own state which is extorting money from people "legally" and in other ways has become a predator—maybe even violating God's law.

The truth is that Christians may properly resist in *any* of the above cases. The logic appears incontrovertible. The fact that the predator in case #7 above was elected by the people makes no difference. It also makes no difference that representative government is producing tyranny. Resisting tyrants is just, whether they are elected or monarchs like King George III (meaning that the American "Revolution" was just).

We would not condone abortion or slavery just because elected state leaders sanction it. If state leaders behave as criminals then they become exposed to being justly killed by those who choose to defend themselves. The Founders agreed with this premise and thus approved the Second Amendment to ensure that citizens could defend themselves against the state. Killing thugs, repulsing criminals, and resisting tyrants (and states) are potentially ap-

149

propriate activities for a Christian—depending on the circumstances. Accordingly, Edmund Optiz describes the process by which the state undermines natural rights and thus becomes ripe for overthrow:

> If the state sets itself up as the supreme arbiter of human affairs, it must domesticate the individual lest any lingering remnants of self-reliance weaken the state's authority. The state must restrict the individual's effort to follow the dictates of his conscience, lest they conflict with the decrees of Caesar. In the interests of its own safety the state must eventually deny that the individual is a person, for the individual can be a person only when he puts his obligation to God ahead of his obligation to Caesar.[89]

Sadly, many Christians today have muddled thinking, having forsaken the ideals of the Founders and the premises of the New Testament. They wrongly support the predatory, proactive state. Instead, Christians should work against their enemy the *state* and its proactive policies. While many Christians think that self-defense against the state is *always* an unwelcome distraction from their primary mission, there are times when the purposes of Christians in the world can be served through self-defense. Therefore, Christians should defend themselves against the state, just as they would against any other criminal or crime organization. At the same time, Christians can and should support a limited *government*, established to protect them from predators and thus indirectly benefit the church and its primary mission.

---

[89] Rev. Edmund Opitz (1999), *The Libertarian Theology of Freedom*, Tampa, Florida: Hallberg Publishing Co., p. 145.

[A]ll are by nature equally free and independent, and have certain inherent natural rights, of which when they enter into a state of society, they cannot, by any compact, divide or divest their posterity.
    —George Mason (1725-1792)

Let the pulpit resound with the doctrine and sentiments of religious liberty. Let us hear of the dignity of man's nature, and the noble rank he holds among the works of God...Let it be known that...liberties are not the grants of princes and parliaments.
    — President John Adams (1735-1826)

Life, liberty, and property do not exist because men have made laws. On the contrary, it was the fact that life, liberty, and property existed beforehand that caused men to make laws in the first place.
    —Frederic Bastiat (1801-1850)

8 Rights, Just War, Torture, Capital Punishment, and Public Policy Theology

The challenging issue of inalienable rights

In the Declaration of Independence, Thomas Jefferson stated: "We hold these truths to be self-evident, that all men are created equal, that they are endowed by their Creator with certain unalienable Rights; that among these are Life, Liberty, and the Pursuit of Happiness [or property]." However, this assertion must be supported—if not by theological premise then at least by social custom. If the vast majority of the members of society do not "hold these truths" then the rights to life, liberty and property will *not* be respected. A "self-evident" right or truth is one which is, according to the dictionary, "evident without proof or reasoning; producing certainty or conviction upon a bare presentation to the mind."

Nonetheless, the idea that human beings have such fundamental or "natural" rights is not evident to many people. For instance, the Marxists are myriad who deny that human beings possess a right to property. An even greater number of people believe that only certain *classes* of human beings have rights to life or liberty. Unborn human beings are not considered to have rights until at least twenty weeks after conception—if not up until the point of birth (or beyond)—by many intelligent people. In some places, people regard those classified as incapacitated or economically unproductive as not being rights-bearers.

Still others find it perfectly acceptable to enslave certain classes of human beings—even the author of the Declaration of Independence owned black slaves! One need only consider the treatment of Indians and the Chinese Coolies to see that thinking regarding the abridgment of rights for certain classes of human beings extended far beyond the Founding Fathers. Furthermore, confiscation of income and wealth from certain classes of human beings by progressive and other kinds of taxation is not only commonplace but is widely considered to be civilized and just behavior.

So in what sense is the veracity of fundamental rights of life, liberty and property self-evident? Apparently, such rights were self-evident to the Founders, at least insofar as they were the province of Caucasians (and perhaps only Christian ones). For them, their rights were evident without proof or reasoning, producing certainty or conviction upon a bare presentation to the mind. It was *obvious* that they held natural rights to life, liberty, and property. It also made no difference whether savages or uncivilized human beings (like Indians, Negroes, Turks or Chinese) agreed with the self-evident nature of their rights.

The Founders knew that in order for society to be civil, and for men to be able to have effective social cooperation, some ground rules must be set down and agreed upon. If there would be no mutual and diligent respect for fundamental rights, then all their work in forming a civil government and its laws would be in vain. Setting aside the agendas and personal preferences of any members, they boiled down the rights to be respected to life, liberty, and property—the same three "natural" rights that philosopher John Locke had set forth in his *Second Treatise of Government* (1690).

Locke based much of his thinking in the Bible, particularly the Old Testament, and developed three premises. First, man, being created in the image of God, was not to be killed by other men except for a capital offense (Genesis 1:26-27; 9:6), implementing and confirming man's right to life. Second, permanent, involuntary slavery has always been an abomination for God's people (Leviticus 25:39; Nehemiah 5:5; John 8:32, 35; 1 Corinthians 7:21; Galatians 5:1). Third, the ownership and use of property to sustain a man's life, as well as for his family and heirs and the people of God, is clearly expressed and its integrity is not questioned (Genesis 13:2; 23:9; 50:13; Numbers 27:8-11; 2 Samuel 19:32; 1 Kings 21:1-19; 1 Chronicles 27:31; 2 Chronicles 17:13; 32:29; Proverbs 13:22; 22:28; 23:10; Jeremiah 37:12; Matthew 25:14-30; Acts 5:4; 1 Timothy 6:17-19).

As time rolled on, the classes of human beings whose fundamental rights are self-evident has expanded to include all races. Chattel slavery is now outlawed in nearly every country. The only classes currently excluded from being full rights-bearers are those who suffer from a physical, mental, or developmental defect (including being unborn). However, another important element has entered in: these rights are no longer natural but are instead considered to be *granted and held at the pleasure of the state.* And even though human beings are rarely property, they are still routinely conscripted and have their labor or property extorted from them under color of law, effectively rendering them slaves—at least in an abstract sense.

Unlike the vision of the Founders, one class of human beings has now taken charge of deciding if and when other classes of human beings will enjoy the exalted level of being rights-bearers. Politicians, judges, and other rulers, acting upon the lead of savant philosophers, have taken the chief role in determining which human beings have rights, effectively rendering void the ideals of Jefferson and the other Founders. In America, this fact is evinced in court rulings and decrees regarding abortion policy, the so-called right to die policy, euthanasia and assisted suicide policies, military conscription, and direct taxes on labor. In a sobering sense, history is the record of how wide or how narrow has been the class of human beings who are afforded rights.

Christian rights?

Do Christians have rights? Is it proper for them to assert their rights as Americans? If so, to what extent should they be asserted? The Bible teaches that Christians are not to claim their rights against each other, but rather to be defrauded if necessary (1 Corinthians 6:7-8; 1 Thessalonians 4:6). It is part and parcel of being a Christian to prefer others and to esteem others better than themselves (Romans 12:10; Philippians 2:3-4). They are even called upon to suffer abuse from unbelievers when they can bear testimony of Christ to them and promote peace (Matthew 5:38-42; Romans 12:17-21). The Christian life is, in reality, one of cross-bearing and suffering (Mark 8:34; Philippians 1:29). Therefore, in a sense, Christians have no rights—or at least they are commanded to not exercise them in most circumstances—for the sake of God's glory, the love of God's people, or for the purpose of bearing testimony to God's grace in them.

Nevertheless, if Christians are called to live in civil society and participate in its trade and institutions, then they must adhere to social customs. The Bible gives every indication that Christians are to work, buy, sell, give of their earnings, hold property, pass on an inheritance, and enter into commercial agreements with others. Thus, Christians need to both assert and comply with social customs for economic cooperation. Those customs include establishing and maintaining political and personal rights and liberties, assigning duties to government to protect rights and obligations on each other to respect them.

When Christians have a say in determining what rights will be concluded as "self-evident" it makes sense for them to base their recommendations on God's Word. Accordingly, the Founders originated a basis for claiming rights to life, liberty, and property in God's revelation to man as a means by which sinful men would be able to dwell together in peaceful cooperation in economic and social spheres. By establishing the civil rights of men, and limiting the scope of government to protect those rights against predators, the Founders (and Christians) became peacemakers in the world. They fulfilled the mandate of love toward one another (as outlined in the New Testament) and to the society in general (Galatians 6:10). "Now the fruit of righteousness is sown in peace by those who make peace" (James 3:18).

Although no civilization is without its imperfections, it is clear that the most peaceful, generous, and cooperative civilizations have been those which exalt private property rights, esteem life highly, and prize liberty. Christian commitment does not preclude the use of law and order in business or social behavior. Christians understand the sinful nature of men and thus understand, in the words of Jefferson, "that to secure these rights, governments are instituted among men, deriving their just powers from the consent of the governed." Absent private property rights, liberty, and the rule of law, history bears witness of the tragedy that will ensue under collectivist and totalitarian systems: war, chaos, destruction of property, murder, mayhem, poverty, and environmental degradation. By asserting fundamental rights to life, liberty, and property, Christians demonstrate the goodness of God in the world and sow peace and prosperity for men. To do the opposite would be to sin—harming their neighbors by worsening their terrestrial misery (Romans 13:10). Conceptually, being "stewards of the mysteries of God" (1 Corinthians 4:1) and being "good stewards of the manifold grace of God" (1 Peter 4:10) includes not only the Gospel itself but also in caring for all of the works of God that promote His kingdom and peace in the world.

But should Christians *forever* advocate the same set of rights promulgated by the Founders? Yes, they should! Those rights are derived from the unchanging precepts of God's Word and His attributes. But does the existence of democratic processes alter the *nature* of the action of government agents? In other words, can popularly elected rulers violate fundamental rights with immunity? For example, are extortion and abortion cleansed (i.e., no longer wrong) because they have been approved by a referendum or decreed by a ruler elected under democratic processes? After all, since we have representative government in America, some claim that Christians are precluded from chafing against legislation or decrees by disobeying edicts. Yet, clearly, for the Christian it is "self-evident" that the precepts of God's Word trump any of the political and social concoctions of men. A society based on adherence to His principles will lead to the "great society" rather than the failed proactive policies of rulers whose philosophy vies against such principles. At the end of the day, the opinions of all the rulers and philosophers of the world regarding rights and morality are of little worth compared to the decrees of the God of the universe.

Were our American Christian forefathers, such as the strong and devout Christian Stonewall Jackson, wrong in asserting their rights to self-defense of life, liberty, and property? They certainly were not. They were not merely fighting for "their" rights. They were fighting to preserve a system of social cooperation. Many endeavored to engender peace and prosperity "to them and their posterity", for the glory of God, for the benefit of the church, and for the expansion of the testimony of Jesus Christ in the world.

Our Christian forefathers were not wrong in performing acts of love and sowing the seeds of peace. On the contrary, Christians today do wrong by refusing to stand up to tyrants and by allowing this world's system to dominate their hearts, minds, and social or economic interactions.

Christian self-defense and just warfare

Standing for truth or civil rights is a scary business with dire consequences at times. It may even lead to war. But what is a "just war"?[90] When may Christians participate in war? Who are the biggest beneficiaries of war? May Christians kill each other in self-defense at home or when in combat?

Christians have been about this question ever since Augustine, and the majority consensus is that Christians may only participate in *just* wars (i.e., wars of self-defense rather than aggression). What ultimately determines whether a war is just is the believer's conscience after apprehending a candid understanding of the facts— notwithstanding claims of rulers that declare a conflict to be just. The reason Christians can participate in a collective defense effort is little different than the reason why they can undertake self-defense against predators individually. They are called upon to promote peace by preserving life, liberty, and property. And sometimes that call leads them to repel predators by force.

One implication of justifiable self-defense is the sad reality that Christians might end up killing some of their brethren when they engage in collective action (i.e., war).

---

[90] Laurence Vance notes: "[A]ll wars are not created equal. The vast majority of wars in the world's history have been destructive, unjust, and immoral...Obviously, an aggressive, preemptive war against a country with no navy or air force, an economy in ruins after a decade of sanctions, and that was no threat to the United States is not a just war [of self-defense]" Laurence M. Vance (2005), *Christianity and War and Other Essays Against the Warfare State*, Pensacola, Florida: Vance Publications, p. 26.

There are always those who will try to increase chaos and misery in society by abridging fundamental rights, and Christians who cherish peace will be right to stand up for life, liberty, and property—even by force of arms. Yet, Christians must take special care to minimize or eliminate bloodshed, especially when some of their brethren's lives may be in jeopardy. Sometimes this objective is difficult to achieve, with sinful choices of assailants leading to personal disaster at the hand of a brother defending his fundamental rights.

It is not sinful for a Christian to kill a brother who is attacking him either by robbing him or firing at him in an opposing army. A Christian can hardly check the Christian credentials of an unknown assailant prior to defending himself. Consider that there were undoubtedly professing believers on both sides in both the American War for Independence and the War Between the States. While the reprehensible circumstances are an abomination to God, there are often deadly consequences from sin (Galatians 6:7)—particularly in the case of aggressive behavior (Jeremiah 19:7; 21:9; 38:2; Matthew 26:52; Luke 21:24). So the brother-turned-assailant may end up dying on account of his sinful choice.

What special obligation does a Christian have to know about the spiritual condition of his assailant? Building on the premise of Christians in combat being accepted, the righteous brother will surely be troubled by the thought of killing his sinning brother in the opposing army as a matter of collective self-defense. The rule of thumb must be that a Christian prefers his brother, meaning that he should do whatever he can to know the status of a potential menace prior to confronting him. If he can ascertain that his opponent is a believer then he must try to avoid conflict, which can be especially difficult if the opponent speaks a different language or communication is otherwise unfeasible. In most wartime cases, it will be impossible to avoid conflict or find out the spiritual status of an adversary. Thus, a Christian must rely upon prayer to protect his brethren and Providence to direct all things justly. Of course, a Christian can avoid this problem altogether simply by refusing to enlist, even if he is conscripted. When in doubt, this tactic may be best. However, in the case of a just war, a Christian must be left to his liberty to take up arms and fight for the glory of God and peace among men if he wishes.

Nevertheless, there will be occasions when a Christian's conscience will not permit him to fight. Should Christians resist the draft? At times they should. They cannot support aggressive warfare. They are to undertake actions which ultimately promote peace and prosperity for their families and the church, as well as the glory of God and the expansion of His kingdom (see chapter 11). But what about resisting the draft in just wars of national defense too? Well, ordinarily this concern is moot since Christians will spontaneously rally to support a just cause. But they could in theory still justly resist the draft as a violation of individual liberty, becoming a *de facto* form of enslavement. Let us remember the biblical premise: "Let each be fully convinced in his own mind" (Romans 14:5).

What can be said with confidence is that Christians may only enlist to defend their homes and country—and may never attack another country in a war of aggression. It is hard to see, therefore, how a Christian could have rightfully been part of either the British loyalists or Northern (Lincolnite) armies. The same thing could be said of the more recent conflicts in Iraq and Vietnam (and perhaps others).[91]

---

[91] Congruently, Laurence Vance astutely remarks: "[T]he greatest threat to freedoms of the American people is not Iraq. The greatest threat to the freedoms of the American people is not some country six thousand miles away; it is our own government." Laurence M. Vance (2005), *Christianity and War and Other Essays Against the Warfare State*, Pensacola, Florida: Vance Publications, p. 71.

Furthermore, we can confidently assert that Christians should not favor or implement the use of weapons of mass destruction, knowing that innocent people—including many Christians—will *unavoidably* be killed. Christians are to sow peace in the world and to not do harm to a neighbor (Psalm 34:14; Matthew 5:9; Romans 13:10; 14:19; 2 Timothy 2:22; Hebrews 12:14; 1 Peter 3:1). Further, one's theology of warfare must be reconciled with passages like Galatians 6:10: "As we have therefore opportunity, let us do good unto all men, especially unto them who are of the household of faith." The notion of nuclear, chemical, or biological obliteration is repugnant to such biblical doctrine.

Remember that states and rulers are the greatest beneficiaries of war, along with certain business interests that profit from trade during wartime—or that manufacture weapons and harness energy for the war machine. Christians must not participate in evil but overcome it with good (Romans 12:21). So let us not be accomplices of wickedness, or of the vile deeds and unjust wars of the "kings of the earth" (Isaiah 24:1; Revelation 16:14; 18:3, 9) and the contemporary rulers of America.

Christianity and torture

Contemporary Christians face many ethical dilemmas regarding Christian reaction to public policies of self-defense, capital punishment and, especially, the use of torture. Jesus Christ was tortured by the state. He was scourged, humiliated, had his beard plucked out, was forced to bear his own cross, and was ultimately cruelly executed by crucifixion.[92] Yet was such state practice some-

---

[92] Rough interaction with the state is part of the Christian life: "But take heed to yourselves: for they shall deliver you up to councils; and in the synagogues ye shall be beaten: and ye shall be brought before rulers and kings for my sake, for a testimony

thing to be emulated by Christians or a practice that they should condone? While torture is part of God's overall plan for the ages, it does not seem to be part of His plan for the present age. One day, Christ will return and deliver all the workers of iniquity to the torturers for eternity in hell (Matthew 18:34). But on earth neither He nor his followers practiced retribution in the form of torturing other men for any reason. Indeed, at least in terms of earthly retribution and vengeance, the Apostle Paul exhorts Christians: "Do not be overcome by evil, but overcome evil with good" (Romans 12:29).

The exclusion of torture as part of God's plan when Christ walked the earth was evident. God was even merciful to the demons: "And suddenly they [the demons] cried out, saying, 'What have we to do with You, Jesus, You Son of God? Have You come here to torment us before the time?'" (Matthew 8:29). Jesus did not torment them immediately. In a similar passage: "And he [a demon] cried out with a loud voice and said, "What have I to do with You, Jesus, Son of the Most High God? I implore You by God that You do not torment me" (Mark 5:7). Why Jesus was so merciful to demons may be somewhat of a mystery. But given the way that He treated His enemies, should not Christians also take their cue from Christ? How can Christians back state policies that deal with other men's lives in such a cavalier manner?

Here is the Christian's calling: "Let your light so shine before men, that they may see your good works and glorify your Father in heaven" (Matthew 5:16). There is no mention of either cruelty or torture as part of those good works or shining light. Remember the golden rule: "And just as you want men to do to you, you also do to them like-

---

against them" (Mark 13:9 KJV). Also: "Then shall they deliver you up to be afflicted, and shall kill you: and ye shall be hated of all nations for my name's sake" (Matthew 24:9 KJV). Such was the lot of all of the Apostles and countless Christians, along with the Old Testament prophets.

wise" (Luke 6:31). Self-defense is both necessary and justifiable in a fallen world (Luke 22:36, etc.). But there is no indication in Scripture that Christians may be cruel or use torture in order to find out about potential threats or to gather other information—especially not information to promote the state's proactive policies and wars.

Information gathering may be part of warfare but wartime conditions are no excuse for acting unethically or sinfully. For example, General Sherman's soldiers were not exonerated from their crimes of raping Southern women by virtue of the fact that a state of war existed. Christians must not condone cruel, vindictive, barbaric, humiliating, or sadistic practices. Biblical principles stand against cruelty: "A righteous man regards the life of his animal, but the tender mercies of the wicked are cruel" (Proverbs 12:10). So then are captured soldiers or suspected terrorists—even if they are proven aggressors—deserving of worse treatment than farm animals? Christians are called to a higher standard of behavior—even in exercising self-defense, conducting war, and carrying out capital punishment.

Accordingly, the Founders were wise and biblical when they prescribed in the Eighth Amendment: "Excessive bail shall not be required, nor excessive fines imposed, *nor cruel and unusual punishments inflicted.*" Likewise, the *Geneva Convention Relative to the Treatment of Prisoners of War* (1949) correctly censured torture (in Articles 3, 17, 87 and 130). "Persons taking no active part in the hostilities, including members of armed forces who have laid down their arms and those placed hors de combat by sickness, wounds, detention, or any other cause, shall in all circumstances be treated humanely, without any adverse distinction founded on race, colour, religion or faith, sex, birth or wealth, or any other similar criteria. To this end the following acts are and shall remain prohibited at any time and in any place whatsoever with respect to the abovementioned persons: (a) Violence to life and person, in particular murder of all kinds, mutilation, *cruel treatment and torture*; (b) Taking of hostages; (c) Outrages upon personal dignity, in particular, *humiliating and degrading treatment*; (d) The passing of sentences and the carrying out of executions without previous judgment pronounced by a regularly constituted court affording all the judicial guarantees which are recognized as indispensable by civilized peoples" (Article 3, emphasis added). *"No physical or mental torture*, nor any other form of coercion, may be inflicted on prisoners of war to secure from them information of any kind whatever. Prisoners of war who refuse to answer may not be threatened, insulted, or *exposed to any unpleasant or disadvantageous treatment of any kind"* (Article 17, emphasis added). Christians should be active advocates of biblical principles in reactive public policies, rejecting torture, and heralding the virtues of the Eighth Amendment and the Geneva Convention.

If someone is attacking you then you may kill or disable him. Self-defense is a biblical principle. However, you may not toy with him as with a spider dangled over a candle's flame. Sadism is not a biblical ideal for Christian practice. All men—even captured soldiers in aggressing armies, criminals, and terrorists—are created in the image of God and must be respected.

Thus, captured soldiers should not be tortured. Once an aggressor is captured then he is no longer a threat. He may be executed when doing so is the just penalty for his crimes but he must not be tortured. Do unto him as you would have him do unto you if you were the one captured. As well, remember that most soldiers in aggressive actions are conscripted by states and may not share the philosophical goals of their rulers. They may not want to fight but are doing so to save their lives from state tyranny. This fact should at least be a mitigating circumstance in many cases that gives us further reason to shun the practice of torturing captives.

Terrorists and men who commit capital crimes should be executed without cruelty. Capital punishment for murder could be an acceptable practice (Genesis 9:6), although its administration by the wayward state must always be suspect. Indeed, Christians should be wary of public policies promoting the death penalty—especially when administered by states rather than local judges with local jury trials. Why should Christians trust the state to do justice? States have been the greatest distorters of justice in history! Nevertheless, if capital punishment is to be advocated by Christians, execution by torture or cruelty must not be condoned.

Remember that the enemies of Christ—rather than Christians—practice cruelty and torture. "Consider my enemies, for they are many; and they hate me with cruel hatred" (Psalm 25:19). Cruelty is a sign of an unrighteous and unregenerate heart. "Deliver me, O my God, out of the hand of the wicked, out of the hand of the unrighteous and cruel man" (Psalm 71:4).[93] Cruelty and torture are distinctives of unbelievers. "Then she [Delilah] lulled him [Samson] to sleep on her knees, and called for a man and had him shave off the seven locks of his head. Then she began to torment him, and his strength left him" (Judges 16:19). Yes, Delilah tortured Samson. Is Delilah a good example for Christians to follow?

Where in the Bible do we find examples of Jesus, the Prophets, or the Apostles being cruel? Evil men were cruel to them but consider what the Apostle Peter stated about the proper manifestation of Christian character in response: Remember Jesus "who, when He was reviled, did not revile in return; when He suffered, He did not threaten, but committed Himself to Him who judges righteously" (1

---

[93] God complained about His covenant people being cruel: "Even the jackals present their breasts to nurse their young; but the daughter of my people is cruel, like ostriches in the wilderness" (Lamentations 4:3). In other words, they were wayward. Since when is cruelty part of the fruit of the Spirit?

Peter 2:23). And "having a good conscience, that when they defame you as evildoers, those who revile your good conduct in Christ may be ashamed" (1 Peter 3:16). Accordingly, Christians should be *marked as merciful.* "The merciful man does good for his own soul, but he who is cruel troubles his own flesh" (Proverbs 11:27). Men marked by cruelty are hated by men and they are often abhorred by God. But a Christian's character should be marked by "love, joy, peace, longsuffering, kindness, goodness, faithfulness", as well as by "righteousness and truth" (Galatians 5:22; Ephesians 5:9). Cruelty simply does not fit in the list.

Therefore, Christians should not be characteristically cruel. Cruelty is opposed to their new nature. "There is no fear in love; but perfect love casts out fear, because fear involves torment. But he who fears has not been made perfect in love" (1 John 4:18). Following the apostolic logic, perfect love (coming from God) casts out fear (being separated from God) which necessitates torment (in this life and later in hell). Think of some cruel men: Nero, the many Papal Inquisitors, Attila the Hun, General William T. Sherman, Stalin, Mao Tse-Tung, Pol Pot, and Robert Mugabe. Were they Christians? Was God's way shown through their actions? No, they exemplified the opposite. Cruelty and torment are reserved for hell when God concludes "this present evil age" (Galatians 1:4). Until then, Christians should loathe to advocate bringing any aspect of hell to earth—including torture.

Christians should defend themselves but they should not be brutal, pitiless, or malicious. If they advocate capital punishment then they should also advocate that it be carried out in a genial manner. They should not enshrine torture as good and reasonable conduct—whether in America, or as practiced by U.S. forces in Guantanamo Bay, or by the out-sourcing of torture of enemy combatants and alleged terrorists in Uzbekistan. American public policy at home or abroad should not mimic that of Stalin or Pol Pot.

The cruel and brutal scourge of General Sherman must be shunned. Moreover, Christians should not monger over war. War is a horrible thing, even when necessary and just. It is neither to be desired nor glorified. And neither should torture and cruelty be part of a Christian's personal course of action or any public policy which he backs.

The people never give up their liberties but under
some delusion.
—*Edmund Burke (1729-1797)*

World War is the second worst activity of mankind,
the worst being acquiescence in slavery.
—*William F. Buckley Jr. (1925-)*

Contemplate the mangled bodies of your countrymen,
and then say, "What should be the reward of such
sacrifices?"...If ye love wealth better than liberty, the
tranquility of servitude than the animating contest of
freedom, go from us in peace. We ask not your coun-
sels or arms. Crouch down and lick the hands which
feed you. May your chains sit lightly upon you, and
may posterity forget that ye were our countrymen!
—*Samuel Adams (1722-1803)*

9 The Theology of Public Policies of Enslavement

Are modern Americans enslaved?

According to the dictionary, a *slave* is "a person who is owned by someone" or "one who is abjectly subservient to a specified person or influence". Many libertarians, constitutionalists, and patriots claim that modern Americans are slaves—or at least trapped in a system of peonage. They reckon that Americans are not truly free.

In order to work, Americans often need to get a permit, credential, or license from the state. If they own their own business, such regulation is even more egregious. They are further compelled to forfeit roughly half of their earnings to the state through various taxes—which are then spent to support the welfare state, pagan seminaries (public schools), and many other objectionable policies. They can be conscripted into military service against their wills, forced to expend their labor for the state and risking their lives by fighting the aggressive wars it sanctions. They do not truly own their lands and homes but merely have the *privilege* to use and possess them—so long as the "fee" (property tax) is paid and the state's rules are complied with fully. Americans are also compelled to use a *fiat* currency—which singularly enjoys legal tender status—

instead of privately-issued notes or commodity money (i.e., gold or silver), forcing them to participate in the welfare state debt and funding racket. The state even requires couples to obtain its permission prior to marrying. While the War Between the States was not primarily a conflict to end Negro slavery, it did mark the beginning of the part-time enslavement of all Americans.

In the starkest terms, an American actually differs little from a feudal serf in his legal standing, economic freedoms, and personal liberties. Sure, technology and knowledge have significantly changed since AD1300, rendering slave life more convenient. But an onerous tax system tantamount to the feudal tenement and fee system remains—along with myriad manorial (state) rules to govern serf behavior and living. Most areas of life are regulated by the state: education, medicine, finance, business, fishing, gun ownership, house building, driving, safety standards, emergency preparedness, and so on. While Americans are told that they are "free", the reality is quite the opposite. It might be more accurate to say that Americans are slaves who are allowed to obtain periods of freedom by paying bribes, rendering service to the state, and being compliant. (Note that such free time encourages peaceful compliance as it helps most American slaves or peons "feel" free.) Perhaps more than half of an American's life and labor is spent in either indirect or direct service to the state. So, at the very least, Americans are part-time involuntary servants. The fact that Americans voted themselves into slavery does not make their condition less deplorable. Accordingly, the bondage decried by libertarians, constitutionalists, and patriots is plausible—at least in the abstract.

However, from America's inception, the idea of involuntary servitude has been repugnant. Slavery is the antithesis of the principles of the Founding Fathers. John Quincy Adams wrote: "The inconsistency of the institution of domestic slavery with the principles of the Declaration of Independence was seen and lamented by all the Southern patriots of the Revolution; by no one with deeper and more unalterable conviction than by the author of the Declaration himself [Thomas Jefferson]. No charge of insincerity or hypocrisy can be fairly laid to their charge. Never from their lips was heard one syllable of attempt to justify the institution of slavery. They universally considered it as a reproach fastened upon them by the unnatural step-mother country and they saw that before the principles of the Declaration of Independence, slavery, in common with every other mode of oppression, was destined sooner or later to be banished from the earth. Such was the undoubting conviction of Jefferson to his dying day."[94] Benjamin Franklin said: "Slavery is...an atrocious debasement of human nature."[95]

In his excellent article, "The Bible, Slavery, and America's Founders" (2003), Stephen McDowell remarks: "As the Founders worked to free themselves from enslavement to Britain, based upon laws of God and nature, they also spoke against slavery and took steps to stop it. Abolition grew as principled resistance to the tyranny of England grew, since both were based upon the same ideas."[96] The Declaration of Independence says: "all men are created equal, that they are endowed by their Creator with certain unalienable Rights; that among these are Life, Liberty, and the Pursuit of Happiness." Even though many people scorn this political doctrine, American Christians can stand firm for the truth and the principles of liberty. Surely in America we have a legal rationale for revolting against enslavement!

---

[94] John Quincy Adams (1837), *An Oration Delivered Before the Inhabitants of the Town of Newburyport, at Their Request, on the Sixty-First Anniversary of the Declaration of Independence, July 4th, 1837*, Newburyport: Charles Whipple, p. 50.

[95] Benjamin Franklin (1987 [1789]), "An Address to the Public from the Pennsylvania Society for Promoting the Abolition of Slavery", in Franklin, *Writings*, New York: Library of America, p. 1154.

[96] Stephen McDowell (2003), "The Bible, Slavery, and America's Founders", online text: http://www.wallbuilders.com/resources/search/detail.php?ResourceID=94.

The ethics of slavery

Is slavery wrong? McDowell outlines the biblical view of slavery. The Old Testament *prohibited* involuntary servitude by means of abduction. "He who kidnaps a man, whether he sells him or he is found in his possession, shall surely be put to death" (Exodus 21:16). "If a man is caught kidnapping any of his countrymen of the sons of Israel, and he deals with him violently, or sells him, then that thief shall die; so you shall purge the evil from among you" (Deuteronomy 24:7; confirmed by 1 Timothy 1:10). However, voluntary servitude was permitted with qualifications (Exodus 21:2-6; Deuteronomy 15:12-18). The Old Testament prohibited returning runaway slaves as well (Deuteronomy 23:15-16), which would seem to defy America's Fugitive Slave Law (1850). Paul discussed how slaves and masters were to act (Ephesians 6:5-9; Colossians 3:22-25; 4:1; 1 Timothy 6:1-2; Titus 2:9-10) but he did not endorse involuntary slavery or the Roman slave system. As McDowell notes, "God's desire for any who are enslaved is freedom (Luke 4:18; Galatians 5:1). Those who are set free in Christ then need to be prepared to walk in liberty."

Slavery was an accepted way of life in the Roman world (consider the matter-of-fact mention of slavery in Matthew 10:25, Mark 10:44, 1 Corinthians 7:21-24, Galatians 3:28, Ephesians 6:5-9, Colossians 3:11, Revelation 6:15, and Philemon 1:10-17). About one-third of the population in Roman times was enslaved, but not all slaves were brought into their condition in the same manner. Theonomist R.J. Rushdoony provides a thesis that distinguishes "a slave by nature and by choice", particularly "where debt and theft were concerned" (Deuteronomy 23:15-16). Some people in the first century were enslaved as a result of committing a crime, attempting to pay off a debt, or by voluntarily election. Enslavement for such reasons would hardly be wrong, and revolt against one's master would

172

hardly be justified under such circumstances. This idea was confirmed in the Old Testament: "If a man steals...he shall surely make restitution; if he owns nothing, then he shall be sold for his theft" (Exodus 22:1, 3).

Note that the peculiar circumstances of many instances of Roman slavery, such as being "sold for his theft", is probably why the Apostle Paul exhorted Christian slaveholders to be good masters instead of letting their slaves go (Ephesians 6:9; Colossians 4:1; 1 Timothy 6:2). The slaves whom those believers owned were probably justly enslaved for debt, chose to be in voluntary servitude, or had become slaves as punishment for a crime. We have no reason to believe that Paul was altering the principles prohibiting slavery-by-kidnapping in Exodus and Deuteronomy by telling Christian masters to treat their slaves obtained by piracy and kidnapping with equity (but without setting them free).

Most slaves during the Roman Empire were kidnapped foreigners: prisoners of war, sailors captured and sold by pirates, and people bought outside the Roman territory, although impoverished Roman citizens often resorted to selling their children into slavery. Such slaves faced harsh lives subject to the whims of their owners, often being whipped, branded, or cruelly mistreated. Yet the prospect of manumission—the act of being freed from servitude—encouraged slaves to be obedient and efficient. Under these circumstances, slavery would be wrong. Would not revolt against one's master thus be justified?

How should Christians respond when they are enslaved or abused against their will? Should Christians care that they are in bondage—even part-time bondage in America? The Apostle Paul implied that they *should* care, observing that a freeman will have more opportunities to serve the Lord in this life. The Apostle Paul indicates that slaves should be content, but if they can become free to do so (1 Corinthians 7:20-24).

This doctrine means that Christian slaves who find the possibility of becoming free should endeavor to obtain freedom. The Bible does not specify whether only legal and peaceful means, or even illegal means, of obtaining freedom may be utilized. Indeed, apostolic doctrine proposes that that Christians should avoid being enslaved in the first place. "You were bought at a price; do not become slaves of men" (1 Corinthians 7:23). It implies that they may repulse enslavers by force as an act of self-defense when they have the means to do so—including, apparently, using force against both unbelieving and professing Christian masters. It does not forbid a slave from assaulting a sinning brother in Christ (who has abducted and enslaved him) in order to make his escape. The Apostle simply says: "if you can gain your freedom, avail yourself of the opportunity" (1 Corinthians 7:21 *ESV*). Escaping such enslavement is not so much the exercise of one's rights over a brother's wishes; it is an act of obedience to God over against the sinful whims of men. Likewise, American Christians would not be wrong to avail themselves of any means of escaping their slavery to wayward rulers whenever possible.

Perhaps the Apostle Paul was encouraging Christian slaves in the Roman Empire to vie for manumission. But a slave had no "opportunity" to be manumitted unilaterally. It was not a choice or action of which he could "avail" himself independently. Thus, the action of availing oneself of the opportunity to be free, which Paul expressed, must be akin to using other means over which the slave had at least some degree of control—perhaps including disabling his master or "running away".

Biblical principles regarding the institution of slavery in whatever form, and in whatever country, still have relevance today. The biblical passages pertaining to slavery might have to be interpreted differently in each country according to local custom and circumstance, but the principle remains that Christians must avail themselves of becoming free from involuntary servitude when possible.

Reckoning with slavery

The New Testament gives us some clues about dealing with slavery—including the part-time slavery of modern Americans. For instance, the Apostle Paul informs us that Onesimus, once enslaved for unknown reasons, "departed for a while" from his master Philemon (Philemon 1:15), a Christian slaveholder living in Asia Minor (probably Colosse). He had been an "unprofitable" servant to Philemon (Philemon 1:10). We do not know if Onesimus became free of bondage legally or illegally. Paul simply stated that he was "sending him back" (Philemon 1:12) from Rome, and we do not know the reason why. The most common understanding of the event is that Paul confronted Onesimus about his rebellion and, after repenting, he was being returned to his lawful master and owner. Accordingly, Paul and Onesimus were glorifying God by obeying Roman law. Yet Paul was hoping all along that Philemon would do a good deed and free his dear friend Onesimus, thus granting permission for him to work further with Paul.

However, there are a few better, alternative interpretations. First, it could be that Onesimus had become legally free but had defrauded his former master (Philemon 1:18), requiring him to now make amends before Paul in good conscience could continue to associate with him. Perhaps Onesimus did not run away, as John Gill notes, but simply *departed* after surreptitiously embezzling something from Philemon. Second, it could be that Onesimus was enslaved on account of some debt that he owed Philemon and had unjustly rebelled, running away. But upon conversion, both Paul and Onesimus realized the need to make amends with Philemon, and Paul was hoping that Philemon would forgive Onesimus' debt so that he could work with Paul's ministry.

Third, it could also be that Onesimus had been unjustly enslaved (perhaps by abduction) before Philemon was converted, but Onesimus had escaped, and was subsequently converted under Paul's ministry. After being discipled, Onesimus became "profitable" in the faith (Philemon 1:11) and became very close to Paul. Thus, Paul was sending him back (with considerable regret) as a forerunner to his own planned visit (Philemon 1:22). Or perhaps Paul had some special encouragement to send to a church in the area and Onesimus, knowing the way, was a logical choice as a messenger. Either way, Paul, wanting to avoid any grief arising from the former relationship, wrote Philemon a letter to guarantee Onesimus' security. Rather than the most common explanation of the event, one of these three interpretations seems more plausible given the principles taught elsewhere in the New Testament—especially where Paul tells slaves to avail themselves of the opportunity to be free when possible (1 Corinthians 7:21).

And this principle of Scripture applies to Americans. While some specific biblical premises must apply only to certain ages or cultures—just as buying swords or giving holy kisses have given way to buying guns and shaking hands—the general principles derived from Scripture must be applicable to all ages and cultures, regardless of any newfangled technology or policy. In the case of slavery, even if the nature and conditions of servitude changes, the principle laid down by the Apostle still applies: *Christians should avail themselves of opportunities to be free when possible.* Only when there is no apparent possibility for liberty should Christians be "content" in earthly slavery.

For example, if a black person was either kidnapped or born into servitude without hope of escape then he should be content (1 Corinthians 7:20, 22). But if he could have availed himself of the opportunity to be free by any means then he should have done so. Moreover, Paul's mandate applies to modern American "slaves" in the same way. Why would the principle of the Bible apply to only one case and not the other?[97] Christians should try to be free even if it means breaking the rules to do so.[98]

The Scriptures make it clear that involuntary slavery is foul, and that Americans should try to escape their part-time slavery. There is never a qualification attached like "escape only if it is legal", unless we force an interpretive bias onto the circumstances of Onesimus and Philemon to generate such a doctrine. Further, the Old Testament makes clear the revealed will of God regarding slavery for that people and none of these commands would chafe against the idea of escaping involuntary servitude by *any* means.[99]

So how does a proper, biblical understanding of slavery affect one's view of revolution or disobedience to the state? It makes all the difference in the world! Modern American Christians find themselves in a condition of part-time involuntary servitude to the state. Thus, they have Scriptural warrant to free themselves from those shackles

---

[97] Even though the circumstances of American bondage have been different than those under the Roman Empire, the biblical principles of slavery must still be applicable.

[98] Of course, becoming free or running away might involve breaking the law. For instance, Negro slaves in America violated the Fugitive Slave Law (1850) and other state laws by running away. They were considered chattels under state law and were thus covered under the common law of property. Given this fact, would the Apostle Paul have advocated that Christian Negroes compelled into involuntary servitude try to become free by "illegal" means—or only by legal means? Would Paul have spoken differently to slaves under the Roman system than he would to those under the American system in the 17th through 19th centuries? What counsel would he have given regarding escaping the part-time involuntary slavery of modern America—even by breaking the rules? It seems clear that contentment was to be the proper posture when freedom was impossible but otherwise the pursuit of one's freedom by any means was to be undertaken.

[99] In ante-bellum America, a Negro slave would have been right to run away from his master. Conversely, it would not be right for a voluntary servant to run away in order to avoid an indentured servitude contract. It would also be wrong for a person in the condition of involuntary servitude for the punishment of a crime (as noted in the U.S. Constitution, Thirteenth Amendment) to runaway.

177

by whatever means possible: rebuffing conscription, avoiding paying taxes that support the welfare state (and never overpaying on account of ignorance of what one truly owes), voting consistently pro-liberty, and serving on a jury as a detractor against state abuses.

The spirit of resistance to government is so valuable on certain occasions, that I wish it to be always kept alive.
    —President Thomas Jefferson (1743-1826)

Civilization is the progress toward a society of privacy. The savage's whole existence is public, ruled by the laws of his tribe. Civilization is the process of setting man free from men.
    —Ayn Rand (1905-1982)

Liberty has never come from the government. Liberty has always come from the subjects of it. The history of liberty is a history of resistance.
    —President Woodrow Wilson (1856-1924)

The consolidation of the States into one vast empire, sure to be aggressive abroad and despotic at home, will be the certain precursor of ruin which has overwhelmed all that preceded it.
    —General Robert E. Lee (1866)

10 A Christian "Rebellion" —The War for American Independence

Resisting the state

In a contemporary Evangelical church, a preacher recently proclaimed: "Rebellion against authority is rebellion against God." Another Evangelical pastor has said: "If it's illegal, it's sinful." (He must be thankful for much grace to cover his sins of disobedience to the state—in light of all the legislation he inadvertently violates.) And a recent caller to a radio show said something like: "Once a proposal becomes the law a Christian must obey it," implying that disobedience is sin. These Tory principles are widely-held by American Christians. But is such sentiment correct? Is *resistance* to tyrants, which they call "rebellion", necessarily sinful?

Rebellion against God is certainly always wrong. It is condemned in Scripture as being analogous to "witchcraft" (1 Samuel 15:23). Having a rebellious attitude or to "despise authority" is likewise unacceptable Christian practice (2 Peter 2:10; Jude 1:8). The Bible teaches that Christians are to "be subject to the governing authorities" which are "appointed by God" (Romans 13:1) and to submit "to every ordinance of man for the Lord's sake"—both in the case of kings and lower magistrates or governors (1 Peter

2:13). Nevertheless, the doctrine of submitting to civil rulers is surely *qualified*. As noted earlier, no Christian theologian has ever held that the New Testament requires absolute submission to *every* civil government decree. Even the Apostles disobeyed civil authority when they believed obedience to it would cause disobedience to God. They resisted tyranny by obeying God and were thus wrongly considered "rebels".[100]

Christians must not consider the commands in Romans 13:1-7, 1 Peter 2:13-17, and Titus 3:1 to be *absolute*. Indeed, taking into account the "whole counsel of God", it is clear that God's people have *not* and should *not* submit themselves to "*every* ordinance of man" (1 Peter 2:13) in an absolute sense. As illustrated in the book's introduction, the civil disobedience of the Egyptian midwives, Ehud, Daniel, Shadrach, Meshach, Abed-Nego, the Magi, and Peter and John exemplify the appropriateness of resistance at times.

Judging from these biblical premises, therefore, the foremost doctrinal issue for a Christian theology of public policy is apparently *not* whether Christians may ever disobey state decrees, but rather *when* civil disobedience by Christians becomes mandatory—or, further, when obedience becomes optional or discretionary for a Christian who must be free to act within the parameters of his conscience. Indeed, the core question boils down to when (or at what point) civil disobedience is justified, and what test must be applied to determine when such rebellion is righteous. Remember, *civil disobedience* and *rebellion* to the state are

---

[100] Even a century later, commentator David Brown noted that the principles of Jefferson and the Founders were not proscribed by Romans 13:1: "[T]he statement applies equally to all forms of government, from an unchecked despotism—such as flourished when this was written, under the Emperor Nero—to a pure democracy. The inalienable right of all subjects to endeavor to alter or improve the form of government under which they live is left untouched here." Robert Jamieson, A. R. Fausset and David Brown (1871), *Commentary Critical and Explanatory on the Whole Bible*, Grand Rapids, Michigan: Christian Classics Ethereal Library (e-book reprint).

synonymous terms, the former being the patriot's perspective and the latter the tyrant's.

At many points over the course of history, rebellion has been widely held to be a good thing and has thus been proclaimed by church leaders. Their message has been simple and straightforward: to disobey tyrants is to obey God. So it was at the founding of the United States of America. Accurately depicting the mindset of the Christian Founders, James Willson discusses the implications of civil disobedience or "revolution" in light of the fact that the state is empowered by God (viz., the state has been ordained by God along with all things—including Satan).

> Does Paul [in Romans 13:1] mean no more than this [that we submit to rulers merely because they have power]? Assuredly he means something far different. This clause assigns a reason for that hearty subjection which the apostle had just enjoined. But, surely, the mere fact that one possesses "power," can be no reason why his claims should be acknowledged, and his laws conscientiously obeyed. If so, the slave—ay, the slave who has been stolen from his own land and ignominiously held as a chattel—would be required to admit, as from God, the validity of his master's claims. To throw off his chains, and make his way to his native home as a freeman, would be rebellion against God. No doctrine could be more agreeable than this to tyrants, and to all that panders to unholy power; for, if this be Paul's meaning, there is no despot, no usurper, no bloody conqueror, but could plead the divine sanction, and, more than this, the devil himself could lay the teachings of Paul under contribution to enforce his pre-eminently unholy authority. An interpretation which leads to such monstrous conclusions—that would bind the nations to the footstool of power with iron

chains, and utterly crush every free aspiration—
that would invest with the sanctions of the divine name the most flagrant usurpation and the
most unrelenting despotism—stands self-
condemned.[101]

In the 1770s, American Christians viewed British
public policies as grounds for armed resistance. The colonists not only believed that they had a right to resist British
"tyranny", they held that submission (or not rebelling)
would have been sinful. Thus, preachers *incited* revolution
by advancing biblical rationale. Preachers' arguments in
support of civil disobedience were manifold: (1) Parliament
had set itself up in an idolatrous manner by claiming sovereignty "in all cases whatsoever" over the colonies (and it
was blasphemy to think that mere human beings could ever
have such authority); indeed, Reformed colonists wanted to
preserve their identity as a covenant people, and Parliament's claims represented both tyranny and idolatry, because honoring the claims of the king would be tantamount
to forsaking God who says to "have no other gods" before
Him; (2) the vibrant church in the "wilderness" of America
represented the "New Israel", while the King and his cronies represented a satanic onslaught aimed at harming
God's chosen people, thus giving Christians a rationale for
self-defense against the civil authority; (3) Christians had a
right to be free from tyranny (citing Galatians 5:1) along
with the means to redress grievances regarding unfulfilled
expectations in (or violations of) colonial charters and basic
human rights; and, more implicitly, (4) self-defense was
justified on account of the abuses of life and property
which emanated from King George III and Parliament—
including their undertaking of legal plunder in the colonies.
The civil authority could be resisted in the same way that a

[101] James M. Willson (1853), *Civil Government: An Exposition of Romans xiii. 1-7*, Philadelphia: William S. Young.

homeowner resists a robber or a businessman withstands a thug.

This chapter highlights the actions of the American Founders—Christian ones in particular—in endeavoring to showcase the various historical Christian theologies of public policy. While many of us believe that the Founders were right in "rebelling", many other Christians disagree. Thus, it is worthwhile to discuss the interaction (and intersection) of faith and civil disobedience, especially in light of the rising onslaught of modern public policies against Christians.

Christians and revolution

The Bible indicates that being a revolutionary can bring temporal trouble. "My son, fear the Lord and the king; do not associate with those given to change [via revolution]; for their calamity will rise suddenly, and who knows the ruin those two can bring?" (Proverbs 24:21-22). When the Jewish religious leaders were "furious" with the Apostles for preaching the Gospel, Gamaliel reminded his Council about the failed revolutionary attempts of Theudas and Judas of Galilee (and their men)—most of whom were executed by the civil authorities (Acts 5:33-39). Not all revolutionary attempts fail of course, but the probability of success is low and the likelihood of imprisonment or death for treason is high. As Gamaliel said, if a revolutionary movement "is of God" it will stand; otherwise it will fail. And the general counsel of the Bible is that if one wants to preserve his life he had better think twice about being a revolutionary.

The Founding Fathers knew what they were getting into by opposing the world's most powerful empire. Their commitment was summed up in the closing language of the Declaration of Independence: "And for the support of this

Declaration with a firm reliance on the protection of divine providence, we mutually pledge to each other our lives, our fortunes, and our sacred honor." The Founders who read Proverbs 24:21 evidently viewed it as sobering practical advice about avoiding temporal consequences rather than as a general directive to be obeyed in all cases. And their resulting successful revolt was extraordinary, being aided by many symbiotic cultural dynamics of the time. Still, Proverbs 24:21-22 and Acts 5:33-39 provide a constant reminder to Christians to beware of participating in revolution. Let us be reminded of the fact that what was practical for the Founders might not be prudent for us today.

Moreover, the Bible indicates that the motive for submitting to civil authority is to glorify God, to avoid worldly distractions that detract from the church's main mission, and that Christians may lead "a quiet and peaceable life" (1 Timothy 2:2). At least in the short term, revolution would seem to be counter-productive to evangelism and building the church.

In order to meet such biblically-based objectives, Christians may have to be practical or expedient when confronted by the civil authority. The Bible counsels that when eating with a ruler, "put a knife to your throat if you are a man given to appetite" (Proverbs 23:2). Jesus told Peter to fetch a coin from the mouth of a fish—not because he had been worried about His unpaid tax liability but because He did not want to "offend" the civil authorities (Matthew 17:27). Jesus knew that the tax had not been paid and yet had apparently expressed no concern about breaking the rules. Perhaps this event formed part of the rationale that led the Pharisees to accuse Jesus of "forbidding to pay taxes to Caesar" (Luke 23:2). At any rate, avoiding confrontation in general is important for a Christian. This ideal is the driving force behind the Apostle Peter's wide admonition: "Honor all people. Love the brotherhood. Fear God. Honor the king" (1 Peter 2:17).

The American Founders sought to avoid confrontation with King George III, and only after what Thomas Jefferson called a "long train of abuses and usurpations" did they choose to "rebel" against him. Would the Apostles have rebelled against Rome at some point too? Surely, Nero was every bit as evil and defiant as King George III, and yet the Apostles did not rebel against Nero. Perhaps they would have done so—at least if they had the arms and soldiers to pull it off (cf. Luke 14:31). The War for American Independence was fought over a fundamental issue of authority: specifically, the place where "the consent of the governed" rested and who was entitled to rule. In 1775, there was widespread doubt about the legitimacy of centralized power exercised from London.

Apparently the Christians in the 1770s believed that civil disobedience and armed revolution were justified and prudent so long as a good or godly reason could be found for such revolt and as long as the insurgents were backed with sufficient firepower to have a decent shot at success. The Scripture is silent (or at least not conclusive) on whether Christians can revolt against the state when they have the means to do so. We do not know what Paul and Peter would have done or taught if pro-Christian forces were able to muster sufficient resources to defy Nero. Yet the Scriptures seem to indicate that Christians have a right of self-defense (Luke 22:36), which could be taken as the right of defense against both criminals and state plunderers like King George III—or George W. Bush for that matter. Or should we simply believe that apostolic teaching regarding submission to (and honoring of) civil rulers prohibits Christians from ever defending themselves against them? Must Christians never attack civil rulers—no matter how tyrannical the state becomes or how much it plunders its citizenry? A well-grounded Christian should not think so. As James Willson correctly contends:

But we may go further, and assert that Paul [in Romans 13:2] did not intend, by the language before us, to forbid even the forcible resistance of unjust and tyrannical civil magistrates, not even when that resistance is made with the avowed design of displacing offending rulers, or, it may be, the change of the very form of the government itself. There are few in this land, or in any free country, to deny the right of a nation to rid itself of oppressive power—whether foreign or domestic. The right of revolution, for the purpose of throwing off usurping or tyrannical rule, need not, now and here, be defended. That question was settled in England by the Revolution of 1688, when the nation, rising in its might, expelled James II as an enemy to the constitutional rights and liberties of the people. The separate national and independent existence of these United States is the fruit of successful revolution. And where is the American—the American Christian—who does not rejoice in the hope that the principles of liberty will spread and prevail, even though they be ultimately established upon the wreck of thrones demolished or overturned?[102]

The Tory preacher's view, "Rebellion against authority is rebellion against God", is wrong while the Founders' actions were right. King George III was an overbearing thief and a depriver of civil liberties. Since the colonists had the power to resist, they were rightly exhorted to do so—especially considering the implications of 1 Corinthians 7:21-24. For some of us, no further justification is needed to attack a wayward, tyrannical, and predatory state beyond the fact that is plundering us or depriving us of our

---

[102] James M. Willson (1853), *Civil Government: An Exposition of Romans xiii. 1-7*, section 2 (re verses 1 and 2), Philadelphia: William S. Young.

liberties. Like a robber or other criminal, the state can be opposed when it is prudent and possible to do so.

Other willing Christian insurgents, however, need further validation. For instance, many preachers and theologians in the 1770s proclaimed that Romans 13:1-7 and 1 Peter 2:13-17 were only binding insofar as government honors its "moral and religious" obligations. Otherwise, the duty of submission was nullified. Indeed, rulers had no authority from God to do mischief; it was blasphemous to call tyrants and oppressors the ministers of God. And each individual was left to decide when a ruler crossed the line.

In the final analysis, using either of these methods to justify civil disobedience leads to the conclusion that state tyranny can be properly resisted by Christians. Indeed, Christians are remiss who do not oppose tyrants.

The American Revolution

According to a public policy theology popular among modern Evangelicals, the American Founders sinned greatly by rebelling against their earthly sovereign King George III. Why? Let's consider a few of the "sins" committed by the American Founders and their associates.

On June 9, 1772, the British revenue cutter *Gaspee* ran aground near Providence, Rhode Island. The hated and feared anti-smuggler Lt. William Dudingston was put ashore along with his crew, and on the next morning the *Gaspee* was burned by a group of patriots led by Abraham Whipple. Rhode Island chief justice Stephen Hopkins refused to bring the men to justice. Even though the Crown offered a reward for the names of the culprits, no one would turn in Whipple and his men. There was overwhelming public (and Christian) support for the revolutionary action.

Similarly, on October 12, 2000 the *USS Cole* was bombed by several Arabs who thought that they were fighting for the right cause, killing seventeen American servicemen. But should the Arab insurgents be deemed criminals or patriots for their cause? Our tendency is to justify the American insurgents and condemn the Arabian ones, although in the abstract there is not that much difference between the actions of the two bands (other than the important fact that no one was killed aboard the *Gaspee*). Would our view change if the *USS Cole* had been attacked by Christians in New Zealand instead? The usual American response is that anyone who attacks American interests is wrong. What about the Christian response—irrespective of nationality or politics? For whatever reason, it seems that there is an underlying (moot) assumption that what is against America must also be against Christianity. Indeed, it seems that American Christians in 2005 have a more confused public policy theology than their predecessors did some 230 years earlier.

By January 1773, dozens of "Committees of Correspondence"—political communication conduits that spread news that fostered the revolutionary movement—had been formed in Massachusetts and other places, including Virginia and the Carolinas. These groups actively utilized lively political meetings and printed materials to incite a spirit of rebellion against the king. British governors viewed their actions as treason. But were these colonial Englishmen really criminals and rebellious sinners against the king and God, or were they courageous and righteous believers defending themselves against a tyrant and thus glorifying God in the process? If Christians have the means and power to rebel against evil, then why shouldn't they do so—to the glory of God?

On December 16, 1773, the British ships *Dartmouth, Eleanor,* and *Beaver* (laden with tea belonging to the East India Tea Company) were anchored in Boston harbor. They were boarded by about 150 patriots (a.k.a. rebels) disguised as Mohawk Indians. Recalcitrant local merchants were unwilling to accept the cargo since they did not want to pay the import duty imposed on the tea. Congregationalist Christian John Hancock, Boston's richest resident, reportedly led the raiding party that emptied 342 chests of tax-tainted tea (worth 18,000 pounds sterling) into the sea. The raiders did not destroy any other property on the ships. Were these British subjects—mainly Christian men who knew what the Bible said about submission to the king—sinning by committing crimes of destroying private property and disobeying the civil authority? If a Boston Tea Party was justifiable Christian action in 1773, why would it not be today?

On September 5, 1774, the first Continental Congress was firmly established, being comprised largely of professing Christians. Since the assembly had no basis in English law, and could have been held as illegal by the king, its very existence was an act of revolution. May a Christian in good conscience be part of a movement that is considered "revolutionary" and "treasonous" by the civil authority?

On December 14, 1774, Continental Congressman and attorney John Sullivan led the first military action by 400 Colonial Minutemen against the British in Portsmouth. Without casualties, they captured Fort William and Mary, seizing the military hardware that the militia would use in future military actions. In January 1775, King George III made clear that he considered such activities rebellious: "The new England governments are in a state of rebellion. Blows must decide whether they are to be subject to this country or independent." Parliament responded by ordering troops against the largely Christian residents of Massachusetts. Later, on August 23, 1775, the king issued "A Proclamation for Suppressing Rebellion and Sedition" whereby he accused the colonists of proceeding "to open and avowed rebellion, by arraying themselves in a hostile manner, to withstand the execution of the law, and traitorously preparing, ordering and levying war against us." Do Christians have a right to defend themselves against a king that the Sovereign Lord has placed over them? What about Christians in 1993 or 2006 rising up with arms against President Bill Clinton or President George W. Bush and their cronies? Is there a difference? Does the existence of democratic processes debilitate just revolt?

On April 19, 1775, Christians fought against the British in church courtyards in Lexington, and on the road to Concord, Massachusetts. In this overt rebellion against civil authority, 49 (mostly Christian) patriots were killed and another 46 were wounded or missing, while 73 British troops were killed and another 200 were wounded or missing. On June 17, 1775, the Battle of Bunker Hill took place. British forces attacked Patriots on Breed's Hill overlooking the sea approach to Boston Harbor. Nearly half of the British troops (1,054 of 2,400) were killed or wounded. American Colonel William Prescott told his troops: "Don't fire till you see the whites of their eyes!"

Using this example, is it proper for Christians to take aggressive action against legitimate civil authority?[103] What would we think of a group of Christians led by a modern-day Prescott pointing at a group of ATF agents about to assail them? Does anyone remember the government-led massacres in Ruby Ridge, Idaho in 1992 and in Waco, Texas in 1993? May Christians fight back against the oppressive state? Is martyrdom the *only* righteous option in the face of state cruelty?

On September 22, 1776, a few months after America declared independence—and despite not being recognized by Britain as an independent country—Capt. Nathan Hale said "I only regret that I have but one life to lose for

---

[103] James Willson reminds us: "God alone is the source of legitimate authority. He is sovereign. Man is His. Power, not derived from God, is ever illegitimate. It is mere usurpation." James M. Willson (1853), *Civil Government: An Exposition of Romans xiii. 1-7*, section 2 (re verses 1 and 2), Philadelphia: William S. Young.

my country." At the age of 21, he was about to be executed by the British for espionage. Hale was a devout Christian in the Puritan tradition. The king considered him a rebel regardless of whether or not Hale considered his allegiance changed on account of the Declaration of Independence. Did that Declaration free Hale and other Christians from their duty to obey the previous civil authority? Even though that authority did not recognize the new country's independence? Who should a Christian obey when two sovereigns are vying for recognition over him as citizen?

These questions may be difficult to answer but serious Christians must strive to do so. Revolution is never legal. If Christians really want to change the world they will probably have to break the law at some point. Those who want to be patriots and hope to promote liberty within the political process are living in a fantasy world. States do not yield power voluntarily. Citizens must take rulers to Runnymede in order to have any hope of securing greater liberty. The American Founders realized this truth and pursued it with unflinching vigor. We enjoy the benefits of their labors and sacrifices. Let's be bold in likewise defending those liberties just as our valiant forefathers did, putting aside the torpid Tory mindset that would torpedo our freedoms.

Our Christian forefathers living during the 1770s were revolutionaries. Preachers and theologians of the day actively advocated rebellion against the civil authority and Christians complied—participating in the social and political upheaval that resulted in a new, unique country.[104]

---

[104] Similarly, consider the deportment of the persecuted first century Roman believers: "Let us not forget why the Christians were killed. They were *not* killed because they worshipped Jesus. Various religions covered the whole Roman world...Nobody cared who worshipped whom so long as the worshipper did not disrupt the unity of the state, centered in the formal worship of Caesar. The reason the Christians were killed was because they were rebels." Francis A. Schaeffer (1982), *The Complete Works of Francis Schaeffer*, vol. 1, Westchester, Illinois: Crossway Books, p. 88.

We should also consider that the position of Christians in England might have been different. Did English preachers condemn the activities of the colonists in their sermons? No doubt many would have remarked that the American colonists who were rebelling against their king were (sinfully) violating Romans 13:1-7 and 1 Peter 2:13-17. Tory pastors in America—Anglican or otherwise—also thought that the rebels (patriots) were in sin. Since the king had a divine right to rule, Christians must therefore maintain their allegiance to him. However, these loyalist Anglicans lost their influence in America, being assailed intellectually and otherwise—primarily by Baptists, Presbyterians, German Reformed, Dutch Reformed, French Huguenots, Lutherans, and Congregationalists.

Furthermore, during the War for American Independence, to whom should these divine right Tories have been loyal: a colonial government body or King George III? Looking back, one would be tempted to say 'to the colonial government' because we know the outcome of the war. But the outcome was hardly clear to Nathan Hale or to King George III. It was not clear to General Benedict Arnold either. He was considered both a patriot and a traitor by both sides during the war. Clearly, Colonial victories in upstate New York were achieved by this brilliant general, who later proved helpful to the British.

On May 10, 1775, Arnold and Ethan Allen led 200 Green Mountain Boys to capture Fort Ticonderoga on Lake Champlain, confiscating 50 cannon, 2,300 pounds of lead and a barrel of flints for muskets from the king in order to supply the militia in Boston. He led tremendous military campaigns in New York and Quebec. Yet he was mocked by the Continental Congress, and on September 21, 1780, he offered to exchange West Point for 20,000 pounds and a commission as major general in the British army. Now here's the tough question: "Was Arnold in sin when he joined the Americans, when he joined the British, or on both occasions?" He obeyed the civil authority of King George III but disobeyed American authorities. If the Apostles Paul and Peter were Arnold's contemporaries, to whom would they tell him to "submit" and to "honor"? Given his duplicity and bad character, was Arnold a Christian? Could he have been righteous in following his conscience at both junctures?

The case of Benedict Arnold illustrates the significance of the liberty of conscience perspective. Each Christian must determine whether or not to obey the civil authority with respect to the public policy that he faces. Each Christian must do what he can to free himself from slavery to the state—reflecting again on the Apostle Paul's authorization: "if you can gain your freedom, avail yourself of the opportunity" (1 Corinthians 7:21 *ESV*). Each Christian has to continually evaluate his earthly political commitments. A Southerner who stood with the Northern Patriots against the British could rightly (if he lived long enough) stand against his former Northern comrades when the circumstances changed after the North invaded the South. Likewise, a modern patriotic Christian can rightly oppose the wayward American state.

The key point is that Christians must be on their guard against evil, be ready to engage their culture in whatever way God leads them, and be willing to resist the state when possible—even when such "rebellion" is illegal. The security-loving Tory mindset may be popular in modern America's mealy-mouthed pulpits but it is useless in encouraging Christians to fulfill their proper activist calling or to be good stewards of their American heritage of freedom.

I am in love and my sweetheart is LIBERTY. I walk the soil that gave me birth and exult in the thought that I am not unworthy of it...And when I look forward to the long ages of posterity, I glory in the thought that I am fighting their battles. The children of distant generations may never hear my name but still it gladdens my heart to think that I am now contending for their freedom and all its countless blessings.
—Brig. Gen. Francis Marion (1834-1915)

That we are to stand by the president, right or wrong is not only unpatriotic and servile, but is morally treasonable to the American public.
—President Theodore Roosevelt (1858-1919)

11 The Christian Fight for Peace

Fighting for Peace

Some things are worth fighting for and at times struggling for peace forms a part of our civic duty. Christians may justly fight, when prudent, either by rhetoric and diplomacy or by political power and arms—especially when their purpose is to quell the evil intrusions of the interventionist state. In order to establish sanctuary in a fallen world, Christians may thus forcibly oppose tyrants or other criminals who attempt to undermine fundamental rights through destroying life and property.

Sometimes Christian resistance will entail taking up arms against the state oppressor, but it should not entail primary aggression. When it comes to use of force, Christians may only act in self-defense. They fight tyrants to promote peace only after they have been egregiously assailed or oppressed. Correspondingly, Christians should not support policy that authorizes the state to police the world in a proactive, constabulary function. All Christian action, including their "rules of engagement", must be bounded by the principles of God' Word.

In chapters 7–9 of *A Christian Manifesto*, Dr. Francis A. Schaeffer argues that there is a point at which a

Christian must take up arms against the state. He maintains that resisting tyrants is ultimately part of a Christian's civic duty. Following the feisty preacher John Knox and Samuel Rutherford in *Lex, Rex* (1644), Schaeffer states that prior to violent action, a Christian must take certain steps as his civic duty: (1) petition elected officials, (2) utilize the courts to establish precedent that favor Christian values, and (3) flee when persecuted (if possible). He notes that the actions of the American Founders were justified because they followed this prescription, having petitioned the Crown and finding nowhere to flee (or perhaps having no need to flee given that the Crown was already so remote from them), observing that the Crown had lost its legitimacy when it became a lawbreaker. Thus, not doing one's civic duty by forcefully resisting the King would have been *sin*. For a Christian to do nothing in the face of collectivist or interventionist tyranny is to permit injustice and violence in society—clearly a sinful action for those who are commanded to "pursue peace" (2 Timothy 2:22; Hebrews 12:14; 1 Peter 3:11).[105]

How can Schaeffer's doctrine of civil disobedience be reconciled with biblical teaching? After all, Jesus clearly says: "My kingdom is not of this world. If My kingdom were of this world, My servants would fight, so that I should not be delivered to the Jews; but now My kingdom is not from here" (John 18:36). The apparent contradiction is resolved once the *redemptive purpose* of Christ's earthly ministry is taken into consideration. "For the Son of Man did not come to be served, but to serve, and to give His life a ransom for many" (Mark 10:45). When Jesus walked on the earth, neither He nor His disciples defended themselves, realizing that His "time is not yet come" (Luke

---

[105] 2 Timothy 2:22: "Flee also youthful lusts; but pursue righteousness, faith, love, peace with those who call on the Lord out of a pure heart." Hebrews 12:14: "Pursue peace with all people, and holiness, without which no one will see the Lord." 1 Peter 3:11: "Let him turn away from evil and do good; Let him seek peace and pursue it."

4:30; 9:51; John 7:6; 8:59). Jesus meant that although He came to die for His people it was not yet the *right* time for Him to die according to the Father's predetermined plan (Acts 2:23). After His redemptive purpose had been accomplished, however, the dissemination of the Gospel of peace began through Christian transformational action bounded by different criteria. Jesus had wrought peace with God for His people. Now His people were to promulgate peace by engaging their culture.

On the one hand, the people of this world often do not know what makes for true peace (Luke 19:42).[106] There is a peace that the world gives, often granted through state "magistrates" and rulers like Felix (Acts 16:36; 24:2). But this peace is fleeting, as the Apostle Paul warns: "For when they say, 'Peace and safety!' then sudden destruction comes upon them, as labor pains upon a pregnant woman. And they shall not escape" (1 Thessalonians 5:3). When God judges the nations and the kingdoms of this world, He will "take peace from the earth" so "that people should kill one another" (Revelation 6:4).[107] So not only is the "peace" of earthly states characteristically fleeting, but also God Himself will remove any peace established by states when He comes in judgment. Thus, man-produced peace is vain.

On the other hand, Jesus Christ brings another message to His people: "These things I have spoken to you, that in Me you may have peace. In the world you will have tribulation; but be of good cheer, I have overcome the world" (John 16:33). Peace is part of the "fruit of the Spirit" (Galatians 5:22) and peacemakers are blessed, being called "sons of God" (Matthew 5:9). "Now the fruit of righteousness is sown in peace by those who make peace"

---

[106] Luke 19:42: "If you had known, even you, especially in this your day, the things that make for your peace! But now they are hidden from your eyes."

[107] The Lamb opening the second resulted in: "Another horse, fiery red, went out. And it was granted to the one who sat on it to take peace from the earth, and that people should kill one another; and there was given to him a great sword" (Revelation 6:4).

(James 3:18). Christians are to bring peace both spiritually by the Gospel and socially by engaging their culture, although the Bible teaches that the peace they convey does not always "remain" where they go (Matthew 10:13; Luke 10:5-6).[108] One of the greatest benefits of Christ's advent was that it brought the way of peace to men (Luke 1:79; 2:14) through the Gospel, both "with God"—"in believing" (Romans 5:1; 15:13) and "always in every way"—as Christians live their lives (2 Thessalonians 3:16). And therefore Christians are called to be at peace with one another, providing a good testimony to those who do not believe (Mark 9:50; 2 Corinthians 13:11; 1 Thessalonians 5:13).[109]

The invasion of the kingdom of God into the world has not come by force of arms but by the suffering Servant who casts out Satan and makes peace between God and men. If Christ wanted to conquer the Romans militarily He could have done so (cf. Matthew 26:53). But that was not God's plan. Nevertheless, since the resurrection and ascension, the Gospel is spreading and the dominion mandate (Genesis 1:26-27) is being implemented by peacemaking Christians who are called to transform their culture. And defending themselves against predators so that men may live in peace becomes part of their civic duty.

Considering the spiritual battle raging between God and Satan, it should come as little surprise that the spread of God's kingdom often does not occur peaceably. Paradoxically, the Lord is both the "God of peace" and the God who assails the kingdom of Satan: "And the God of peace will crush Satan under your feet shortly" (Romans 16:20),

---

[108] Matthew 10:13: "If the household is worthy, let your peace come upon it. But if it is not worthy, let your peace return to you." Luke 10:5-6: "But whatever house you enter, first say, 'Peace to this house.' And if a son of peace is there, your peace will rest on it; if not, it will return to you."

[109] Mark 9:50: "Salt is good, but if the salt loses its flavor, how will you season it? Have salt in yourselves, and have peace with one another." 2 Corinthians 13:11: "Finally, brethren, farewell. Become complete. Be of good comfort, be of one mind, live in peace; and the God of love and peace will be with you." 1 Thessalonians 5:13: "Be at peace among yourselves."

implying that His judgment will come upon Satan's kingdom in both the spiritual and temporal realms. The Christian's civic duty should be similarly directed. Jesus is called the Prince of Peace (Isaiah 9:6) and yet He tells us: "Do not think that I came to bring peace on earth. I did not come to bring peace but a sword" (Matthew 10:34). The reason is simply that even though a battle rages in the spiritual world between principalities and powers (2 Corinthians 10:4-6, Revelation 12:7; Jude 1:9; Daniel 10:13), this battle spills over into time and space, being manifested principally through conflicts between Christians and false religion or the state. However, God's kingdom has invaded the world, casting out Satan's kingdom and disrupting the false "peace" that Satan gives (Luke 11:21).

Surely, the preaching of the Gospel and its transformation of hearers brings men peace with God. But the preaching of the Gospel also yields a threat to Satan's kingdom, resulting in social rancor and violence as Satan seeks to defend his turf. The church is to neither be the initiator of violence nor use force to create converts. Yet the Bible indicates that individual Christians may use force to defend themselves against attacks from criminals—even state criminals. Martyrdom is not their only choice. Indeed, the threat of force is the only deterrent that keeps a state in line and Christians must be ready to use their might to that end. Of course, prudence would direct that using force should only be considered for egregious, ongoing violations of civil liberties. The civil disobedience and resistance doctrine of Dr. Francis A. Schaeffer thus has no quarrel with the Scriptures and rightly concurs with Jefferson's caution in the Declaration of Independence.[110] Christians may serve

---

[110] "Prudence, indeed, will dictate that governments long established should not be changed for light and transient causes; and accordingly, all experience hath shown, that mankind are more disposed to suffer, while evils are sufferable, than to right themselves by abolishing the forms to which they are accustomed. But, when a long train of abuses and usurpations, pursuing invariably the same object, evinces a design

God by fleeing, by diplomatically securing secession to obtain political independence, or by fighting in self-defense.

Ironically, Christians must *fight* for peace, and their greatest achievement and objective should be to promote *peace*. As Benjamin Franklin reminds us, "there was never a good war or a bad peace."[111]

Conversely, let us recall that the great "achievements" of modern man—unbelief, totalitarianism, secular humanism, Darwinism, and socialism, just to name a few—have brought poverty, misery, hatred, and war to human civilizations. But Christians should have the opposite record. They can promote peace with God by preaching the Gospel and they will promote peace and goodwill among men by advocating limited government and free markets.[112] They may also promote earthly peace by engaging their culture politically: by voting, by signing petitions, by writing to congressmen, and by serving on juries in order to establish and secure fundamental rights for all people equally (and utilizing civil government as a means to defend these rights).

If we remember that the state is humanity's foe, how can Christians justly use it to be their henchman? The state has wrought the antithesis of peace on earth. It has brought terrestrial hell to millions of people: shortening lives, extorting funds, degrading the environment, and destroying property. Therefore, Christians should not endeavor to recruit the state into God's service. They should not try to take over the evil state and use it, even after some

---

to reduce them under absolute despotism, it is their right, it is their duty, to throw off such government, and to provide new guards for their future security."

[111] Benjamin Franklin, *Letter to Josiah Quincy* (September 11, 1783).

[112] Laurence Vance prudently notes: "The 9/11 attacks were just the beginning of a worldwide revolt against the current U.S. foreign policy of a global empire. Only a Jeffersonian foreign policy of peace, commerce, friendship, and no entangling alliances can arrest the menacing U.S. Empire." Indeed, "The current U.S. foreign policy of belligerency, intervention, hegemony, and subjugation is a far cry from the example of Jefferson." Laurence M. Vance (2005), *Christianity and War and Other Essays Against the Warfare State*, Pensacola, Florida: Vance Publications, pp 116, 61.

vain process of purification, to promote virtue in society. Instead, they should be active in transforming their culture through cultural engagement (including civil disobedience on occasion) and Gospel preaching, thus reducing the impact of evil and the grief that comes from the state.

For this reason, it is important for American Christians to be informed and vote for candidates who will stand by the principles of liberty. They should not cop out and vote pragmatically, viz. for "the lesser of two evils". Christians must overcome evil with good and that feat cannot be achieved by pragmatism. A Christian's vote is never "wasted" when it is cast for someone or some policy backing good principles. But it is always wasted when it is cast for evil—even the lesser of two evils.

Some Christians might go beyond merely voting and even venture to get involved with politics. They may do so when they believe that running for office will allow them to pursue peace by encouraging the recognition of fundamental rights, the maintenance of free markets, and the rule of law.[113] Furthermore, all Christians should be eager to sit on a jury in order to be ready to free any captive of the state who is having his fundamental rights violated. They can do this by nullifying an unjust or stupid decree (i.e., the procedure known as "jury nullification").

Freedom is neither free nor cheap and Christians who want to enjoy political freedom need to be prepared to pay the price of keeping it. Professor Richard Beeman reminds us: "There is a story, often told, that upon exiting the Constitutional Convention Benjamin Franklin was approached by a group of citizens asking what sort of gov-

---

[113] Dietrich Bonhoeffer was simply mistaken when he wrote in *The Cost of Discipleship* that Christians should never aspire to high political office. Some peacemaking Christians might be effective in government office that promotes proactive policy. In remarking on the humility that a disciple must display he did not take into account the role a disciple has in engaging his culture and being a peacemaker. Whether or not they pursue a *legitimate* political office (i.e., one based in reactive policy) ought to be left to the liberty of each Christian's conscience.

ernment the delegates had created. His answer was: 'A re-public, if you can keep it.' The brevity of that response should not cause us to under-value its essential meaning: democratic republics are not merely founded upon the consent of the people, they are also absolutely dependent upon the active and informed involvement of the people for their continued good health."[114] Accordingly, American Christians fighting for peace now face the challenge of trying to *keep* the republican form of government that the Founders entrusted to them.

---

[114] Richard R. Beeman (2005), "A republic, if you can keep it", *National Constitution Center*, http://www.constitutioncenter.org/explore/ThreePerspectivesontheConstitution/ARepublic,IfYouCanKeepIt.shtml.

A patriot must always be ready to defend his country against his government.
    —Edward Abbey (1927-1989)

Americans, indeed all free men, remember that in the final choice a soldier's pack is not so heavy a burden as a prisoner's chains.
    —President Dwight D. Eisenhower (1953)

Every normal man must be tempted at times to spit on his hands, hoist the black flag, and begin to slit throats.
    —H.L. Mencken (1880-1956)

12 The Second Amendment and Public Policy Theology

The right to keep and bear arms

The Second Amendment to the American Constitution is familiar to many of us: "A well regulated Militia, being necessary to the security of a free State, the right of the people to keep and bear Arms, shall not be infringed." Along with the other nine initial amendments, collectively known as the Bill of Rights, the Second Amendment was ratified by ten of the original thirteen States on December 15, 1791.[115]

The words "well regulated" mean well-equipped in terms of uniform and armament. The militia's armament should be fully manned, sighted-in and ready. According to the U.S. Code, the word "Militia" means what is now called the "unorganized militia", i.e., "all able-bodied males at least 17 years of age and…under 45 years of age…who are not members of the National Guard or the Naval Militia".[116] During Virginia's ratification convention in 1788, Founding Father George Mason said: "I

---

[115] *Pro forma* ratification of the Bill of Rights was given by Vermont after it became a state in 1791 (about a year and a half after the proposed amendments were sent to the states for ratification), and by Georgia, Connecticut, and Massachusetts in 1939.
[116] 10 U.S.C. 311(2)

ask, Who are the militia? They consist now of the whole people, except a few public officers."[117] (Similar statements were made by Founders James Madison and Richard Henry Lee.) Mason worried that some day only a privileged class of men would bear arms, resulting in tyranny. Mason also said: "the best and most effectual way to enslave" a country is "to disarm the people".[118]

The Second Amendment was intended to be the ultimate check against a tyrannical state. In a real sense, it is the right of revolution built into the Constitution—becoming the foremost guarantor of all other rights and the Constitution itself. Neither the legislature nor the executive may abridge its effect. (Accordingly, the United States Supreme Court has ruled: "All laws which are repugnant to the Constitution are null and void."[119]) Thomas Jefferson highly prized an armed citizenry,[120] and wanted to instill a permanent spirit of resistance within the American people. In his letter to William S. Smith on November 13, 1787, Jefferson wrote: "What country before ever existed a century & half without a rebellion? & what country can preserve it's [sic] liberties if their rulers are not warned from time to time that their people preserve the spirit of resistance? Let them take arms. The remedy is to set them right as to facts, pardon & pacify them. What signify a few lives lost in a century or two? The tree of liberty must be refreshed from time to time with the blood of patriots & tyrants. It is it's [sic] natural manure."

---

[117] 3 Elliot's Debates 425

[118] Ibid. 380

[119] *Marbury vs. Madison*, 5 U.S. (2 Cranch) 137, 174, 176, (1803).

[120] "Laws that forbid the carrying of arms...disarm only those who are neither inclined nor determined to commit crimes...Such laws make things worse for the assaulted and better for the assailants; they serve rather to encourage than to prevent homicides, for an unarmed man may be attacked with greater confidence than an armed man." (Thomas Jefferson, *Commonplace Book*, 1774-1776 [quoting from Cesare Beccaria's *On Crime and Punishment* (1764)]).

Tench Coxe, an active political figure before and after the American Revolution, was clear regarding the intentions of the Founders with respect to bearing arms. He wrote in the *Philadelphia Federal Gazette* on June 18, 1789: "As civil rulers, not having their duty to the people duly before them, may attempt to tyrannize, and as the military forces which must be occasionally raised to defend our country, might pervert their powers to the injury of their fellow-citizens, the people are confirmed by the next article [the Second Amendment] in their right to keep and bear their private arms."[121]

In his proposed Virginia constitution (June 1776), Jefferson wrote: "No free man shall ever be debarred the use of arms." Samuel Adams and other Founders agreed. Richard Henry Lee, a signer of the Declaration of Independence, stated: "To preserve liberty, it is essential that the whole body of people always possess arms."[122] Alexander Hamilton agreed in *The Federalist Papers* (no. 29) that a well-trained and well-armed citizenry would provide a check against tyranny. "[I]f circumstances should at any time oblige the government to form an army of any magnitude that army can never be formidable to the liberties of the people while there is a large body of citizens, little if at all inferior to them in discipline and the use of arms, who stand ready to defend their own rights and those of their fellow-citizens."

It is clear what the Founders had in mind by the Second Amendment. The question that remains for Christians is whether or not they can apply it to their activities

---

[121] Tench Coxe (1789), "Remarks on the First Part of the Amendments to the Federal Constitution" (writing under the pseudonym "A Pennsylvanian"), *Philadelphia Federal Gazette*, June 18, 1789, page 2, col. 1. Coxe also said: "Congress has no power to disarm the militia. Their swords, and every other terrible implement of the soldier, are the birthright of an American...The unlimited power of the sword is not in the hands of either the federal or state government, but, where I trust in God it will ever remain, in the hands of the people" (*Pennsylvania Gazette*, Feb. 20, 1788).

[122] Walter Bennett, ed. (1975), *Letters from the Federal Farmer to the Republican*, Tuscaloosa: University of Alabama Press, pp. 21, 22, 124.

and still be righteous. May a Christian join in resisting the state (1) generally or (2) particularly in America because the Second Amendment allows him to do so? A well-grounded Christian should answer both questions with the affirmative. One reason that the Apostles did not attack the Roman state was because they lacked the wherewithal to do so. Unlike the American Founders, they did not have the military strength to attempt such an overthrow. They also did not have a Second Amendment to back them up. Christians may "rebel" against tyrannical states when it is wise, prudent, and feasible to do so. And this fact is further enhanced by the existence of the Second Amendment.

The Bible is the Christian's final authority for faith and practice. It says that Christians must passively submit to "rulers", "kings", and "governors" (Romans 13:3; 1 Peter 2:13-14). However, what happens when lower rulers are traitors to the highest ruler and supreme authority of the land? Regardless of whether or not a strong case can be made for Christian resistance against tyrants without the Constitution and Declaration of Independence, surely a case can be made for Christian resistance with them.

The Second Amendment injects a form of built-in "rebellion" into the American system, which the Apostles did not enjoy while living under Roman rule. Indeed, the Declaration of Independence and the Bill of Rights have imbued all Americans (including Christians) with the hallowed right of revolution. If Christian obedience to the civil authority entails primary obedience to the American Constitution, then this fact ought to have far-reaching ramifications for the way believers interact with their culture.

The unique situation of the American Christian

The establishment of the unusual system of governance in America changed the strict application of Romans

208

13:1-7, Titus 3:1, and 1 Peter 2:13-17 for American Chris-tians—even if application of the passages to Christians in other countries may differ. For us Americans, being "subject to the governing authorities" could rightly entail armed resistance against the tyrannical state. Since "the governing authorities" in America are the Constitution and the Declaration of Independence, a Christian could be obedient to them and still attack wayward rulers with the support of the Second Amendment.

Yet the tenor of the New Testament outlines the normal course of affairs for Christians as makers, propagators, pursuers of peace (Matthew 5:9; Romans 14:19; Hebrews 12:14; James 3:18; 1 Peter 3:11). , The Christian's priority must be to disseminate serenity, even though Christ said that He would bring division rather than peace on earth through the expansion of His kingdom (Luke 12:51, cf. John 16:33).

But Christians are not to pursue peace (or compromise) at *any* cost. When it comes to political activism, Christians need to be particularly careful to not align themselves with the wrong side. Recall that the Jews wickedly and maliciously called for Christ to be crucified, claiming that they had "no king but Caesar" (John 19:15). In so doing, they aligned themselves with an evil ruler—whether to Caesar, a king or Roman governor—rather than "the King of kings" (1 Timothy 6:15; Revelation 17:14; 19:16). Caesar's dominion notwithstanding, Jesus Christ has authority over all earthly rulers.

The Jews ignored this fact and made their position clear with their mind-set: "We will not have this man to reign over us" (Luke 19:14). They chose to submit to and obey wayward lower authorities and reject the Supreme Authority. In the same manner, American Christians suffer temporal loss—and may even displease the Lord—by choosing to submit to wayward elected officials and bureaucrats instead of the supreme law of the land. They also disobey it by following the lead of rulers who promote partaking in redistributive public looting through welfare programs and adorning "big brother" policies that allow the state to overstep its bounds.

There is no doubt about it: Christians will have some interaction with the state. Jesus said, "You will be brought before governors and kings for My sake, as a testimony to them and to the Gentiles" (Matthew 10:18; cf. Mark 13:9; Luke 21:12). And rulers tend to be oppressors who "lord it over" their people (Ecclesiastes 5:8; Matthew 20:25). Normal Christian experience has been to stand trial before oppressors, just as the Apostles Peter and Paul did, and to testify of Christ (Acts 4:8-12; 5:29-33; 26:1-32). The interface of Christians with the state is frequently unpleasant, oppressive, or even fatal, as was the case when rulers attempted to "abuse and stone" the Apostle Paul and Barnabas (Acts 14:5).

Just how do Christians who are pursuing peace become entangled with the state? Well, the Bible indicates that Satan himself, being "enraged" with Christians, will "make war" with them, casting some "into prison" by means of the state (Revelation 2:10; 12:17–13:1, 7). Thus, under the Providence of God, Christians are likely to become embroiled with the state. And so it has been since the first century (beginning with Christ and the Apostles). In America, however, the rules of engagement have changed and Satan's successes have been mitigated. Christians enjoy the reality of the Second Amendment and are remiss when they do not join together and use it to refresh the tree of liberty from time to time with the blood of patriots and tyrants—as Jefferson said.

When do Christians know that it is the right time to resist? Answering this question takes some careful thought and consideration of many variables. Surely, the reason for resistance has existed since the 1860s, having been redoubled by events of the 1870s, the 1910s, and the 1930s. Given the principles of America's founding, the South was right both in seceding and in defending its homeland against the northern aggressors. But the South was not prudent in its strategy on many political and economic fronts. Even with the two greatest generals in American history they were not able to overcome the invader. Southerners probably did not choose the right time or strategy to resist the tyrant, even though their Jeffersonian passion for secession was laudable—and still would be in modern America.

A prudent and holistic plan must be put into place before any coordinated action against the state should be undertaken (cf. Luke 14:31). But until the fight begins, Christians should make use of peaceful means—the political process—even though there is little hope for real success. They should stay active, "do business" (Luke 19:13), engage their culture, and keep a good collection of arms handy with wicked rulers in their sights.[123]

Collective action against tyranny

The Founders primarily envisioned collective action of a militia under the Second Amendment. Generally, no call for vigilantism or for independent assassination plots exists, such as the one Israelite judge Ehud undertook against king Eglon—a wicked ruler that God had raised up to chastise His rebellious people (Judges 3:12-23). That is not to say that a Christian would necessarily sin by assassinating a wicked ruler like Nero, Domitian, Hitler, Stalin, Lincoln, Pol Pot, Castro, or Idi Amin. Killing them would instill peace by delivering many people from misery and

---

[123] Of course, there are other kinds of Christian action that can help to debilitate a tyrannical state. Some examples include depriving the state of resources by avoiding taxes when possible (or by refusing to pay taxes not owed), refusing to serve in the military, or temporary emigration (exiles have proven to provide good support for a revolution).

suffering—a suitable task for Christians (cf. Proverbs 24:11-12, Galatians 6:10). The Bible teaches that the overthrow and death of wicked rulers causes social "jubilation" and that their name "will rot" (Proverbs 11:10; 10:7). Indeed, why would slaying an evil ruler, when possible, differ from killing a serial killer, a common thug, or another criminal in self-defense?

Since the Bible teaches that people shout, rejoice, and have jubilee over the death of a wicked ruler, should Christians refrain from rejoicing along with their countrymen? Should they mourn when a Stalin is assassinated and rejoice only when such an evil ruler dies of natural causes? The Bible makes no such distinction. Surely, God takes no pleasure in the death of the wicked (Ezekiel 33:11) and neither should we. However, this truth does not undermine the reality taught in Proverbs 11:10: people have a feeling of relief, excitement, and joy as a result of an evil ruler's demise. (Just ask any older Ukrainian.)

Yet Christians cringe at the notion of assassination of an evil ruler. Why is assassination less shocking or repugnant to them when the military performs it? Why would private militias, mercenaries, or pastors like Dietrich Bonhoeffer be wrong for accomplishing such military operations? Some might worry that severe ramifications could ensue from the state's reaction against Christians who espouse such a "radical" idea. Such a threat should not matter if we are promoting the truth, realizing the importance of developing a biblical theology of public policy, so long as Christians enjoy some measure of free speech and it is expedient to exercise that right. Are we not commanded to "buy the truth", along with wisdom, instruction, and understanding, and to not sell it (Proverbs 23:23)?

The logic of a theology of public policy pertaining to assassination of evil rulers is fairly straightforward.

Given that (1) there is a right of self defense, that (2) there is no amnesty afforded to any assailant on account of his office or profession, and (3) provided that one is the potential victim, an eyewitness of a crime, or a member of a group which has definite knowledge about the notorious nature of the crimes that have been and will be committed by a predator (the connection between an evil ruler and his crimes should be evident to all), then (4) the predator may be stopped by force—even lethal force. There is one further qualification: (5) those methods which expose innocent people to the least jeopardy (as is the case with assassination) must be preferred,[124] since Christians highly respect human life as "the image of God" (Genesis 1:27; 9:6) and must not trammel it recklessly.

Accordingly, Bonhoeffer did not sin by participating in the plot to assassinate Hitler.[125] How can Christians claim otherwise? (Whether his methods were prudent is a different question.) If Hitler had instead died while facing Bonhoeffer on the battlefield, no one would question the rightness Bonhoeffer's actions. Christians are inconsistent if they approve of a military operation against Hitler's headquarters but find fault with a stealth assassination attempt by Bonhoeffer at the same place.

Nevertheless, the fact that assassination could be the right action does not mean that Christians have to frequently practice it or even advocate it.[126] Surely, it must be

---

[124] As opposed to massive military campaigns that lead to the loss of innocent lives (nowadays euphemistically called "collateral damage").

[125] Bonhoeffer's sister-in-law, Emmi Bonhoeffer, is puported to have said that Bonhoeffer's rationale for assassinating Hitler was: "If I see a madman driving a car into a group of innocent bystanders, then I can't, as a Christian, simply wait for the catastrophe and then comfort the wounded and bury the dead. I must try to wrestle the steering wheel out of the hands of the driver."

[126] The whole matter of assassination must be considered deductively in order to derive the appropriate biblical principles regarding it, beginning with two parameters. First, it is important to note that setting the bounds for a public policy theology is not the same as advocating a particular action. For instance, a woman *may* have the right to divorce her husband if he commits adultery just one time (even if he repents), but that right does not mean that she *should* do so. So it is with the matter of assassination. Just be-

used as a last resort in our own country. To avoid problems of passion and vigilantism, assassination of evil rulers is best carried out by a collective force or a "well-regulated militia". The Founding Fathers saw the prudence in patience: "Prudence, indeed, will dictate that Governments long established should not be changed for light and transient causes."[127] Such patience does not preclude assassination under the proper circumstances, especially when assassination is accomplished through a Second Amendment militia operation.

However, Christians should accredit the merits of assassination for foreign policy. How many American and Iraqi lives would have been saved if the United States military would have simply assassinated Saddam Hussein and his top cronies? Remember that Ehud, living prior to the

---

cause assassination of an evil ruler is considered to be a righteous event does not mean that a Christian should necessarily become an assassin. While establishing the ultimate bounds of right Christian conduct is valuable, doing so does not produce an outcome with a *prescriptive* character. Second, if government agents are predators and criminals, they become exposed to violence just as other lawbreakers. Notwithstanding those who espouse a revitalized or reshaped divine right of kings view, modern rulers simply do not enjoy special immunity or amnesty card on account of their office that would preclude any defensive action by Christians against them. Likewise, the fact that American congressmen enjoy limited freedom from arrest and prosecution while on the job does not imply that they enjoy the same immunity in a private home. (The American Constitution, Article 1, Section 6 says: "They [congressmen] shall in all Cases, except Treason, Felony and Breach of the Peace, be privileged from Arrest during their Attendance at the Session of their respective Houses, and in going to and returning from the same; and for any Speech or Debate in either House, they shall not be questioned in any other Place.") If one may shoot a robber or a rapist caught in the act, one may also shoot a felonious government agent. It makes no difference that they are kings, senators, or bureaucrats. However, the fact that one *may* do so does not mean that he *should* do so. And a Christian exercising his right to resist authority does not necessarily mean that he will avoid the consequences of such action.

[127] Even divine righters like John McGarvey and Philip Pendleton agree: "When it becomes apparent to the populace that the government has fallen into this state of aberrance [where righteousness is put down and evil is exalted], revolution is inevitable; but till the information becomes general, the individual must submit, for slight mistakes do not justify momentous changes and vast social upheavals, and peace for the many may well be purchased at the discomfiture of the few. But if armed or physical resistance is forbidden, *moral* resistance is strictly and unequivocally enjoined." John W. McGarvey and Philip Y. Pendleton (1916), *Thessalonians, Corinthians, Galatians and Romans*, vol. 3, ch. IV, "The faith-life discharging civil duties, and recognizing the divine ordination of governments", Cincinnati: The Standard Publishing Company, pp.508-509.

establishment of the Old Testament theocracy, was an assassin. Yet he was evidently commended by God for his work. The godly general Stonewall Jackson was ready and willing to cross the Potomac River in order to hang Lincoln after the first battle of Manassas. Hundreds of thousands of lives would have been saved. Would he have been wrong if he had done so? Was John Wilkes Booth wrong for assassinating Lincoln after the war? What is ultimately the moral difference between Ehud, Jackson, and Booth—if anything?

Providence has often directed collective action (rather than assassinations) as the means to overthrow evil rulers, and the rationale of the Founders seems to follow this premise concerning domestic tyranny. It is difficult, apart from a miracle, for one man or even a small group to pull off a revolution. It is also unclear that attempting to do so will bring glory to God—which is the foremost goal of a Christian. The Bible records the fatal failure of some who revolted against tyrants (see Acts 5:36-37).[128] Instead, the collective courage and stamina of principled men has prevailed at providential moments, including climactic events like Runnymede and Yorktown. Accordingly, the Founders realized that liberty would best be preserved by a collective force, which they termed "a well regulated militia".

---

[128] Absalom was killed while trying to overthrow David (Samuel 18:14–19:10), but David is not normally regarded as being an "evil" ruler and Absalom was not righteous or godly in his motives or conduct. Furthermore, the uprightness of assassination was apparently curtailed under the theocracy since David would not kill Saul when he had him cornered in a cave (1 Samuel 24:3-8) and David condemned the soldier who killed "the Lord's anointed" (2 Samuel 1:9-16). Of course, being divinely "ordained" or "appointed" (Romans 13:1-2) after the theocratic era has not made subsequent rulers "the Lord's anointed".

PART IV

PUBLIC POLICY AND CHRISTIAN DUTY

I am not well versed in history, but I will submit to your recollection, whether liberty has been destroyed most often by the licentiousness of the people, or by the tyranny of rulers? I imagine, Sir, you will find the balance on the side of tyranny: Happy will you be if you miss the fate of those nations, who, omitting to resist their oppressors, or negligently suffering their liberty to be wrested from them, have groaned under intolerable despotism. Most of the human race are [sic] now in this deplorable condition...
   —Patrick Henry (1788)

As nations cannot be rewarded or punished in the next world, they must be in this...by an inevitable chain of causes and effects, Providence punishes national sins by national calamities.
   —George Mason (1788), [mistaken, sadly]

The life of the nation is secure only while the nation is honest, truthful, and virtuous.
   —Frederick Douglass (1818-1895)

13 The Theology of Nations and Nationalism

The biblical idea of "nation"

The biblical idea of a *nation* is not analogous to the modern concept of a state. Yet many preachers have erred by forcing the modern scheme of states into passages dealing with nations (or peoples). It is quite impossible for preachers to square the spurious notions—(1) that Americans are the "people of God", (2) that the territory of the United States is the "land" of God's people, or (3) that America as a nation can "repent" and be "healed"—with what the Bible teaches. Indeed, to comprehend the United States of America as a "nation" in a biblical sense is to distort the teaching of the Word of God.

If God is not bound by political boundaries, then how does He deal with nations? What is a nation in a biblical sense? Generally, a nation is an ethnic aggregate or a race. It is the swelling of the extended family over generations; an ethnic group identified by lineage, language, and culture—typically taking the namesake of a patriarch (e.g., the "nation of Israel"). Thus, a nation is a group of related people headed by single man (e.g., Abraham), composed of tribes, which are composed of clans, which are composed of families. A tribe becomes a nation when it grows sufficiently to have large subdivisions.

Accordingly, in Genesis 10:5 the Bible says "the coastland peoples of the Gentiles were separated into their lands, everyone according to his language, according to their families, into their nations." In Genesis 25:16 we read that "the sons of Ishmael...[had] towns and their settlements [named after them], twelve princes according to their nations." A man named Tidal was called the "king of nations" (Genesis 14:1, 9), probably referring to his rule over several undesignated peoples, as opposed to the kings of specified nations like Shinar, Ellasar, and Elam. Ethnic groups like the Geshurites, Girzites, Amalekites, Edomites, Moabites, Ammonites, Philistines, and Amalekites are called "nations" too (1 Samuel 27:8; 1 Chronicles 18:11), and some of these nations are mentioned as having controlled territory (denoted as their "country") throughout the Old Testament. Abraham was told that he would become "a father of many nations", "a great and mighty nation" that would bless other nations, and that "kings" would come from him (Genesis 17:4-5; 18:18; 17:16).

Sometimes in Scripture the word *nations* is used in a pejorative sense. It can be used to allude to the embodiment of evil represented by ungodly Gentile practices, or the place where evil kings arise to do mischief against God's people, such as those arrayed against the Lord in battle (Lamentations 1:10; Isaiah 14:9; Revelation 14:8; Psalm 83:4; Isaiah 13:4).[129] Jesus tells us that "nation will

---

[129] The Greek words translated "nation" or "nations" in the New Testament also support the ethnic group understanding of the terms rather than the mistaken modern understanding based on the common vernacular. The roots of these words come through in English (using the King James Version New Testament) in a similar way to their usage in Greek: (1) ἔθνος (ethnos)—underlies the translation of nation or nations sixty-one times (or 93.9 percent of the occurrences)—from which are derived the English words ethnic and ethnicity; (2) γένος and γενεά (genos and genea)—underlies the translation of nation or nations three times (or 4.6 percent of the occurrences)—from which are derived the English words genus, group and class (even genealogy); and (3) ἀλλόφυλος (allophulos)—underlies the translation of nation or nations once (or 1.5

rise against nation" (Matthew 24:7; Mark 13:8; Luke 21:10). However, ethnic groups are infrequently identified solely for a political attribute of aggression or by a trait of immorality. Their ethnic character remains paramount.

In Scripture, the word *country* is more analogous to the modern idea of nation or political jurisdiction of a government or a state. There are many such cases in Scripture: (1) Abraham was told by God: "get out of your country" and dwell in a "foreign country" (Genesis 12:1; Acts 7:3; Hebrews 11:9); (2) Joseph cannily accused his brothers of spying out the "country" of Egypt (Genesis 42:30); (3) the Israelites dwelt in the "country of Goshen" (Genesis 47:27); (4) the children of Israel "searched out" and conquered Canaan—also known as the "country which the Lord swore to our fathers to give us" (Deuteronomy 26:3; Joshua 2:2; 7:2) and to three tribes were given the "country of Gilead" (Joshua 22:9); (5) the Magi "departed for their own country another way" (Matthew 2:12); (6) a prophet is honored everywhere "except in his own country, among his own relatives, and in his own house" (Mark 6:4; Matthew 21:33; John 4:44); (7) businessmen and noblemen traveling abroad to other countries (Matthew 21:33; 25:14; Mark 12:1; 13:34; Luke 19:12; 20:9); (8) Mary "went into the hill country with haste" (Luke 1:39), and (9) the multitudes listening to Jesus sought lodging and provisions in "the surrounding towns and country" (Luke 9:12).

Further, the political significance of the word country is perhaps most plainly set forth by: (10) the prodigal son who "journeyed to a far country... and joined himself to

---

percent of the occurrences)—meaning a foreign people or nation (e.g., a Gentile one). Accordingly, these words imply that people groups or ethnic aggregates are embodied in the words nation and nations. They certainly do not refer to the group of people living within the political confines of countries like America. Similarly, the few Hebrew words translated as nation or nations in the King James Version Old Testament refer to people groups according to ethnicity rather than cohorts confined inside political boundaries or classified by political allegiance. Thus, it is evident that the idea of nation in the Bible does not carry the same significance as the word in our English vernacular.

a citizen of that country" (Luke 15:13, 15); and (11) Joses "a Levite of the country of Cyprus" (Acts 4:36), who was obviously of the nation of Israel. The word country usually refers to the political confines of some place.[130] Regrettably, many preachers have been misinformed and confused, assuming that the modern usage of "nation" is analogous to the biblical concept of *nation* rather than only being analogous to the biblical concept of *country*. As we will see, they have erred by transposing their vernacular onto the Scriptures, causing their hearers to stumble with them.

Ethnic aggregates rather than political boundaries

In the Bible, a *nation* simply does not refer to a political apparatus demarcated by territory. When the Bible says, "Let all the nations be gathered together, and let the people be assembled" (Isaiah 43:9), it does not refer to the inhabitants of the various political boundaries set by men throughout history but to the ethnic lineage of people groups and cultures. The Lord told Rebekah that, "Two nations are in your womb, two peoples shall be separated from your body; one people shall be stronger than the other, and the older shall serve the younger" (Genesis 25:23)—showing that one nation can become divided into many. Her son Jacob (Israel) was to become "the one nation on the earth whom God went to redeem for Himself as a people" (2 Samuel 7:23), as opposed to other ethnic groups and peoples.

Human rather than political attributes are ascribed to nations. More than metaphorically, nations have "eyes", "mouths", and "ears". They can "drink" or be "drunk", can "hear", can bear a "yoke of iron", can "shake" from fear,

---

[130] The word *country* can also mean "the countryside" as was the case when Jesus went "into the country near the wilderness" to avoid the Jews (John 11:54), or for Simon the Cyrenian who was coming "from the country" (Mark 15:21; Luke 23:26).

can "know" God, can be enraged, can "abhor" or "hate" others, and can "be ashamed" (Isaiah 52:10; Micah 7:16; Revelation 14:8; 18:3; Jeremiah 6:18; 25:15; 28:14; Ezekiel 31:16; 36:23; 38:23; Psalm 2:1; Acts 4:25; Proverbs 24:24; Matthew 24:9; Micah 7:16). They can "assemble and come" and "gather together all around". They can be "deceived" and become "ungodly" (Joel 3:11; Revelation 18:23; 20:8; Psalm 43:1).[131] Such traits can hardly be applied even figuratively to states.

In Daniel, the phrase "peoples, nations, and languages" is repeated five times (Daniel 3:4, 7; 4:1; 5:19; 6:25; 7:14). Similar phrases are engaged seven times in the book of Revelation—combining the words tribes, tongues, peoples, multitudes, and nations (Revelation 5:9; 7:9; 10:11; 11:9; 13:7; 14:6; 17:15).[132] The Apostle John is likely alluding to the prophet Daniel, and both writers make clear that people groups rather than political constituencies are signified by the word "nations". The other words in these phrases also refer to individual human beings classified according to their ethnicity or culture, rendering any understanding of nation as a political structure incongruent with the immediate context.[133] Accordingly, when the Bible states that, "men of all nations, from all the kings of the earth who had heard of his wisdom, came to hear the wisdom of Solomon" (1 Kings 4:34), it means that men from all races and ethnic groups, including those of high political office, learned from Solomon.

---

[131] The Israelites desired that Samuel would give them "a king to judge [them] like all the nations" so that they would be "like all the nations" (1 Samuel 8:5, 20)—not because they lacked the political boundaries that other nations had but because they wanted a territorial ruler akin to theirs.

[132] These are: "tribe and tongue and people and nation"; "all nations, tribes, peoples, and tongues"; "many peoples, nations, tongues, and kings"; "peoples, tribes, tongues, and nations"; "every tribe, tongue, and nation"; "every nation, tribe, tongue, and people"; or "peoples, multitudes, nations, and tongues".

[133] It might seem curious that the political word "kings" is once included in Revelation 10:11 except that the word also refers to an individual's profession, making it congruent with the other synonyms in the set.

Such biblical usage of the word nation is exemplified elsewhere. First century Jewish elders acclaimed a Roman centurion as being one who "loves our nation, and has built us a synagogue" (Luke 7:5). They did not use "our nation" to signify that the centurion built it because he loved the political boundaries, citizenship rules, or dominion of the Roman authorities over Palestine. They meant that the centurion loved the Jewish people and therefore built them a synagogue. Likewise, when the Jews accused Jesus of "perverting the nation, and forbidding to pay taxes to Caesar" (Luke 23:2; cf. John 7:12), they did not mean that Jesus perverted the Roman political system or its constituency. They meant that He stirred up the Jewish people to disobey Caesar and not pay Roman taxes.

Similarly, the first century high priest had "prophesied that Jesus would die for the nation, and not for that nation only, but also that He would gather together in one the children of God who were scattered abroad" (John 11:51-52). This prophecy did not indicate that Jesus was going to die for all the people within chosen political jurisdictions. Instead, it meant that Jesus would die for all of "His people", from His "chosen generation" (Matthew 1:21; 1 Peter 2:9), snatched from every ethnic group on earth. Pilate also demonstrated this understanding when he said "Your own nation and the chief priests have delivered You to me" (John 18:35), indicating that Jesus' ethnic group—what Luke calls "the nation of the Jews" (Acts 10:22)—had delivered Him up. Jesus' nation was neither Rome nor any Roman province. He was of the nation of Israel, in the country of Palestine, which was then being subjugated by the Roman civil authority. Paul too admitted his ethnic alignment with the Jews, twice calling them "my own nation" (Acts 26:4; Galatians 1:14). Thus, a biblical nation has *everything* to do with ethnicity and *nothing* to do with territory or political boundaries.

223

National sins and national repentance

God is not concerned about the repentance and salvation of America *as* a nation-state but rather the salvation of the nations *within* America. Jesus Christ used the term *nation* to mean His chosen people—the spiritual "seed" of Abraham (Galatians 3:29)—as opposed to Abraham's physical lineage. "Therefore I say to you, the kingdom of God will be taken from you and given to a nation bearing the fruits of it (Matthew 21:43). The Apostle Peter makes it clear that the church of Jesus Christ is now God's "holy nation" and His "special people" rather than ethnic Israel. "But you are a chosen generation, a royal priesthood, a holy nation, His own special people, that you may proclaim the praises of Him who called you out of darkness into His marvelous light" (1 Peter 2:9). And the Apostle John similarly esteems the work of Christ in redeeming His church from all racial and cultural groups: "For You were slain, and have redeemed us to God by Your blood out of every tribe and tongue and people and nation" (Revelation 5:9).

Accordingly, Jesus "shall inherit all nations", not in some political sense but in terms of gaining a people from all ethnic groups.[134] The Psalms declare that Jesus Christ has "the nations" for His "inheritance", and has become the "head of the nations", where "all the families of the nations shall worship before" Him. God's salvation is known "among all nations",[135] so that "all nations shall serve Him" and "all nations shall call Him blessed" (Psalms 82:8; 2:8; 18:43; 22:27; 67:2; 72:11, 17). Now "all nations shall flow to" the Lord's house, "a house of prayer for all nations", where "all the nations shall be blessed" (Isaiah 2:2; Mark

---

[134] This idea is likely implied in the apostolic discussion of the "firstfruits" from Achaia in Romans 16:15 and 1 Corinthians 16:15.

[135] Under this blessed existence, "men from every language of the nations shall grasp the sleeve of a Jewish man, saying, 'Let us go with you, for we have heard that God is with you'" (Zechariah 8:23).

11:17; Galatians 3:8). The gospel is at the present "a witness unto all nations" that "repentance and remission of sins should be preached in His name among all nations", "for obedience to the faith among all nations for His name" (Matthew 24:14; Luke 24:47; Romans 1:5). Thus, Christians are called to "make disciples of all the nations" via the gospel which must "be preached to all the nations" (Matthew 28:19; Mark 13:10). As a result, "the glory and the honor of the nations" will be present in heaven (Revelation 21:26).

Clearly, God is interested in forming His church from the remnant of nations now confined in all countries worldwide. Capricious political boundaries are not in view in these verses—Roman or otherwise. The Bible is speaking of reaching all ethnic groups. In the end, Jesus will gather "all the nations" before Him for judgment (Matthew 25:32), speaking not of judging political authorities or constituencies but rather ethnic aggregates.

While "the nations rage", it is the Lord that "makes nations great, and destroys them; He enlarges nations, and guides them" (Psalm 2:1; Acts 4:25; Job 12:23; cf. Psalm 118:10). God "destroyed seven nations in the land of Canaan"; "the nations have perished out of His land" (Acts 13:19; Psalm 10:16). Indeed, "All nations before Him are as nothing, and they are counted by Him less than nothing and worthless" (Isaiah 40:17). God is speaking about the insignificance of people groups, not of political covenants.

Just think about the blessings that have been bestowed upon ethnic groups within Western Europe and America in recent centuries, stemming from revivals and widespread acceptance of the Gospel for many generations. Sometimes God will "grant...repentance" to masses of people (2 Timothy 2:25), such as He did in the case of Nineveh, Macedonia, and Corinth (Jonah 3:5; 4:2, 11; Matthew 12:41; Luke 11:42; Acts 16:9-10; 18:10). These good people, God's elect, were not so much identified by their political allegiances as by their ethnic and cultural attributes. They retained their godly character even after being exiled to new political jurisdictions, as with the Puritans fleeing to America.[136] Hence, the blessings of America are not the result of God favoring its political organization but rather the godly culture of the nations which have flowed into it.

Individuals repent and believe; political entities do not. Only individuals or ethnic groups are said to be judged in the Bible: "The wicked shall be turned into hell, and all the nations that forget God" and "Let the nations be judged in Your sight" (Psalm 9:17, 19). "When He gives quietness, who then can make trouble? And when He hides His face, who then can see Him, whether it is against a nation or a man alone?" (Job 34:29). The idea of national repentance defined by non-ethnic, political boundaries is bogus.

America is *not* a nation in the biblical sense

It is error to comprehend the United States of America as a *nation* in a biblical sense. America's territory contains people from many nations, all falling under the political authority of the Constitution. Even though many of God's people are also Americans it is incorrect to equate the American people with God's people. Moreover, the territory of the United States is *not* the special or promised "land" of the people of God. Territory does not become sacred on account of some Christians inhabiting it.

Regrettably, many modern preachers have failed to grasp these facts. Two passages of Scripture commonly twisted in contemporary sermons are: "If My people who are called by My name will humble themselves, and pray

---

[136] Many other examples could be cited: the Huguenots fleeing from French papists, the Baptists fleeing from persecution in central Europe to the New World, or the early Christians being exiled by Nero to the southern shores of the Black Sea (1 Peter 1:1).

and seek My face, and turn from their wicked ways, then I will hear from heaven, and will forgive their sin and heal their land" (2 Chronicles 7:14) and "Blessed is the nation whose God is the Lord, the people He has chosen as His own inheritance" (Psalm 33:12). These verses are inappropriately preached or interpreted as follows: "If Americans will humble themselves, and pray and seek God's face, and turn from their wicked ways, then God will hear from heaven, and will forgive America's national sins and heal the country." Further, the God of the Bible is purported to be America's God and, as a result, many Americans presume that the American people have been chosen as God's inheritance. From these errors emerge the underlying specious idea that certain "national sins"—which occur within arbitrary and variable political boundaries (e.g., the United States)—will lead to divine judgment. Nonetheless, "national repentance" is possible when sought in earnest.

However, there are no such national sins, and no national repentance. The Bible does not indicate that God any longer deals with nations as He did under the Old Covenant. He used to deal uniquely with the nation of Israel (i.e., the "people" and the "inheritance" referred to in 2 Chronicles 7:14 and Psalm 33:12), often violently opposing and dispossessing the Gentile nations. For instance, it was said that "the Lord strikes the nations who do not come up to keep the Feast of Tabernacles" (Zechariah 14:18). Certainly, Gentiles could abandon their pagan ways and join Israel, as was the case with Rahab the Canaanite, Ruth the Moabitess, and those Jews who heard Peter preach in Jerusalem described as "devout men, from every nation under heaven" (Joshua 6:25; Hebrews 11:31; Ruth 1:22; Acts 2:5). But these individuals were the exception rather than the rule under the Old Covenant.

Now God deals with nations by calling out his elect from every nation—forming a new and holy nation called the church—and abandoning the rest to eternal condemna-

227

tion. Thus, passages like 2 Chronicles 7:14 and Psalm 33:12 have no more application to the political constituents of America than they do to political constituents of largely Muslim Indonesia, largely pagan New Guinea and Madagascar, or largely Roman Catholic Paraguay and Argentina.

A similar critique may be leveled at the abuse of the infamously mistreated verse: "Righteousness exalts a nation, but sin is a reproach to any people" (Proverbs 14:34). This verse should *not* be interpreted that the political realm America will be exalted when its decrees are righteous. It means that blessing will follow when a family is converted to Christ, and then a clan follows suit, and finally over time (perhaps encompassing several generations), an entire tribe or larger ethnic aggregate "nation" may be depicted as faithful. At that point, the righteousness of those people exalts them both temporally and eternally. One may see examples of this blessing (or imperfect tendencies toward it) in the people of Judah under Josiah and the people of Nineveh, as well as the households of Moses, Samuel, David, Lydia, and the Philippian jailor (2 Kings 23:4-24; Jonah 3:5-10; Hebrews 3:2, 5; 1 Samuel 2:35; 22:14; Acts 16:15, 34). Widespread good character and habits among any ethnic group have an uplifting effect.

Conversely, sinful habits and proclivities are a snare to any ethnic group: "Do not be deceived: 'Evil company corrupts good habits'" (1 Corinthians 15:33). Remember how Paul warned Titus about the character of the people of Crete: "Cretans are always liars, evil beasts, lazy gluttons" (Titus 1:12), and how God debilitated Pharaoh on account of Sarai: "But the Lord plagued Pharaoh and his house with great plagues because of Sarai, Abram's wife" (Genesis 12:17). Modern America contains many ethnic groups— nations—which have many bad habits. But the true Christian nation in America is no more implicated by the evils of its neighbors than Lot was in Sodom, Israel was in Egypt, Judah was in Babylon, or Christians were in Rome. It is not the fault of Christians that their neighbors practice sin. Of course, individual Christians may fall into the sins of the nations around them (2 Kings 17:15), but they can and should remain holy (Romans 6:1; 1 Corinthians 10:13; Hebrews 12:14).

Nationalism and Christian emigration or immigration

If the Christian "nation" is comprised of every nation, how can it be right for Christians to be *nationalists* in the common sense of the term? Regrettably, modern cultural dynamics have led many Christians to embrace the sin of nationalism. The dictionary defines nationalism as "a sense of national consciousness exalting one nation above all others and placing primary emphasis on promotion of its culture and interests as opposed to those of other nations".[137] Absent a theocracy, the New Testament clearly stands out against nationalism. Christians are "strangers and pilgrims" in this world and include brethren from "every tribe and tongue and people and nation" (Hebrews 11:13; Revelation 5:9b).

The Christian's King is Jesus and his "country" is a heavenly one where ethnicity is not important and all speak the same, delightful language of "Beulah" (Hebrews 11:16b; Isaiah 62:4b). That fact implies, in short, that nationalism is a prideful sin that is deleterious to Christian thinking, to missionary endeavors, and to personal sanctification. Indeed, the tightest loyalty a Christian should have in this world is to other believers—no matter what political realm they belong to. The moment a believer is more American, British, Argentine, Peruvian, Chilean, Chinese, Czech, etc. than he is Christian, he is guilty of nationalism.

---

[137] That is, "nations" in the modern sense of the word. Issues regarding the sin of nationalism are also covered more extensively in Dr. Cobin's *Bible and Government: Public Policy from a Christian Perspective*, pp. 41-48.

At any time a Christian favors the people of "his country" (e.g., fellow Americans) more than Christians in other countries he is guilty of the sin of nationalism. Are we loyal to Jesus and His church first and to our fellow citizens only secondarily? Or have we succumbed to nationalism?

One indication might be right in our church sanctuaries. Do we publicly recognize and applaud soldiers involved in aggressive wars? Jesus met with Roman military men (e.g. the Roman centurion), and John the Baptist met with soldiers (Luke 3:14), but neither one applauded them for their profession or work. While they did not condemn the profession, they did not praise it either. Such soldiers were part of an occupying force during the "pax Romana" rather than part of an aggressing army. While we can be supportive of individual soldiers, it makes no sense for pastors to imply the body's approval of Christians who aggress other people. We would not, of course, give special recognition and applause to thugs, rapists, murderers and pillagers who might be in the congregation. But pastors are often willing to give such recognition to members of the state's aggressive military forces that effectively do much of the same things (legally and without social reprisals from the community). What reason do we have, other than the assertions of rulers and other protagonists of war, that the U.S. military is engaging in a defensive rather than aggressive war effort? Laurence Vance offers some candid commentary on the realities of modern American military service:

> For far too long Christians have turned a blind eye to the U.S. Global Empire of troops and bases that encircles the world. Many Christians have willingly served as cannon fodder for the state and its wars and military interventions. Christians who haven't died (wasted their life) for their country in some overseas desert or jungle increasingly perpetuate the myth that being a

soldier in the U.S. Military is a noble occupation that one can wholeheartedly perform as a Christian.[138]

The state has historically been the greatest enemy of Christianity. Yet, many Christians in the military have made the state their god. Members of the military are totally dependent on the state for their food, clothing, shelter, recreation, and medical care. They are conditioned to look to the state for their every need. But the state demands unconditional obedience. Shoot this person, bomb this city, blow up this building—don't ask why, just do it because the state tells you to... The state will tolerate God and religion as long as He and it can be used to legitimize the state.[139]

The U.S. Military, although officially called the Department of Defense, is the state's arm of aggression. If it limited itself to controlling our borders, patrolling our coasts, and protecting our citizens instead of intervening around the world and leaving death and destruction in its wake then perhaps it might be a noble occupation for a Christian. But as it is now, the military is no place for a Christian.[140]

Do we ask for the state's blessing for our existence as a church corporation or for tax-exempt 501(c)(3) status? Jesus gives us our charter, not the state. Christians should give regardless of tax-favored status, and limited liability can be achieved by using common law trusts or foundations instead of corporations.

---

[138] Laurence M. Vance (2005), *Christianity and War and Other Essays Against the Warfare State*, Pensacola, Florida: Vance Publications, p. 13.
[139] Ibid., pp. 16-17, 18.
[140] Ibid., pp. 22-23.

Do we prominently display the American (or state) flag, indicating our body's support for the state and compliance with its edicts? Moreover, "the Pledge [of Allegiance to the U.S. flag] is an allegiance oath to the omnipotent, omniscient state."[141] If our primary allegiance is to Christ and secondarily to His people, then why would we ever want to conflate the message of the Gospel and the equipping of the saints with statecraft? The state has nothing to do with the church or salvation and therefore the state's flag has no place in our church sanctuaries. In other countries around the world the state flag rarely appears in church sanctuaries.[142] Why are American church sanctuaries different? Can we honestly imagine the first century Christians hoisting a Roman eagle in their places of worship? Nationalism can indeed be manifested in many ways but it is always an egregious idolatry that Christians must learn to shun.

How about support of nationalism through public policy? Is it right for Christians to oppose immigration of foreigners through public policies? Legal immigration is probably not a concern for Christians, but what about *illegal* immigration? By now it should be clear that the only true outsiders to a Christian are the unbelieving "dogs" of this age—especially those political and wealthy figures who revel in ungodliness (Matthew 7:6; Philippians 3:2; Revelation 22:15). Christians around the world are superficially separated by language and political boundaries but are unified by the Holy Spirit—even though many Christians apparently ignore this fact.

Sadly, at times they enthusiastically advocate the bombing of other countries, adversely impacting other

---

[141] Ibid., p. 18.

[142] From the author and his wife's personal traveling experiences, churches visited in Italy, Guatemala, Chile (at least generally), Peru, Argentina, Kenya, Montenegro, Jamaica, Honduras, Czech Republic, England, Tahiti, Israel, Jordan, Switzerland, France, and Turkey did not have a state flag in the sanctuary (although some churches in these countries might admittedly have one).

Christians. How many Christians were killed or injured by the American bombings of Tokyo, Hiroshima and Baghdad? Consider again the insight of Laurence Vance:

> No one wakes up in the morning with the desire to drop bombs on people in foreign countries that he does not know, have never injured him in any way, and are no threat to him or his family. This desire is always government [i.e., state] induced and government [i.e., state] sponsored. When it comes to mass murder, the state takes a back seat to no one.[143]

> To get a war to work—to get men to kill other men that have never aggressed against them and that they don't even know—the state must do two things: convince men to love the state and to hate the members of other states. The first is always cloaked in patriotism, and leads to acceptance of interventionism. The second is always cloaked in nationalism, and leads to hatred toward foreigners within one's country.[144]

Does the perceived necessity of bombing a country override our obligation to protect innocent human life—especially the lives of our brethren, the poor, and the oppressed? A Christian foreign policy will necessarily be distinct from that of unbelievers because it is influenced by biblical principles. Christians should not be duped by state propaganda.

Christians are pilgrims in this world who seek a heavenly country (Hebrews 11:6). They are told by Christ to "flee" persecution (Matthew 10:23; 24:16; Mark 13:14; Luke 21:21), as Joseph and Mary did (Matthew 2:13)—along with countless other believers throughout history. Such obedient fleeing might entail a Christian having to

---

[143] Ibid., p. 60.
[144] Ibid., p. 88.

enter another country, perhaps violating the country's immigration policies.[145] But so what? Christians are remiss if they make the well-being of their country the primary focal point for deciding the veracity of immigration policy rather than the well-being of God's beloved people.

On the one hand, a Christian's nationality is irrelevant and Christians should welcome believing immigrants with open arms—whether they are legal or illegal in the state's eyes. For Christians, borders and the legality of migration are trivial or extraneous when it comes to obeying Christ's command to flee persecution or to love and prefer one another in Christ (Philippians 2:2). How can Christians who financially and prayerfully support national pastors and church members living under tyrannical regimes hinder those same people from fleeing to America (or freer countries) by any means? The sanctimonious divine right notion that Christians may only flee when it is legal to do so—and then only immigrate to America after they have clearance from state bureaucrats—is fallacious, hypocritical, and unbiblical.

On the other hand, a Christian may support the limited government where he lives, procuring better self-defense of life and liberty. As well, a Christian is called to steward his private property (Proverbs 27:23-24).[146] To those ends, Christians may justly back *reactive* public policy to safeguard national borders, oppose any migration that undermines the common defense of life, liberty, and property, and even (by default rule) oppose the illegal immigration of ordinary unbelievers. Such reactive immigra-

---

[145] The divine righter may argue that Christ's command is made obsolete or irrelevant by the edicts of men—through the modern state (the oracle of God)—since, they presume, those who fled in biblical times were not disobeying public policy. Since we have the state's decree today prohibiting illegal immigration then Christ's words have been superseded by men. But this dubious eisegesis is much harder to accept than to simply say that what Christ commanded is still valid and binding on believers today.

[146] "Be diligent to know the state of your flocks, and attend to your herds; for riches are not forever, nor does a crown endure to all generations" (Proverbs 27:23-24)—along with many other verses promoting good stewardship.

tion policy will be most efficiently and effectively carried out through market-based solutions rather than clumsy and venal attempts by government enforcement.

But an American Christian must always be a Christian first and an American second. He must *think* and consider each issue on its own merits before supporting or rejecting any particular migration policy. He must avoid jumping on an absolutist bandwagon that opposes *any and all* illegal immigration *out-of-hand* that would cause him to shirk his biblical responsibilities toward his brethren.[147] How could a believer in good conscience obliquely pummel or trammel his Christian brother by endorsing a proactive policy that adversely affects him? He must prefer Christians of any nationality over unbelieving Americans. And he should "do good" to poor or oppressed unbelievers when possible too (as Galatians 6:10 mandates) by facilitating their migration. Thus, in the final analysis, a Christian should oppose any *proactive* immigration or foreign policy that curtails his biblical obligations, and only support proper reactive immigration and foreign policies.

---

[147] A biblical understanding of nations leads us to embrace a theology of public policy that differs widely from that advocated by many Christians—especially in America. Christians should not *absolutely* oppose illegal immigration. Christians should not obey men rather than God.

The only difference between a tax man and a taxidermist is that the taxidermist leaves the skin.
        —Mark Twain (1835-1910)

They have the usual socialist disease; they have run out of other people's money.
        —Margaret Thatcher (1975)

A friend of mine was asked to a costume ball a short time ago. He slapped some egg on his face and went as a liberal economist.
        —President Ronald Reagan (1988)

If taxation without consent is not robbery, then any band of robbers have only to declare themselves a government, and all their robberies are legalized.
        —Lysander Spooner (1856)

14 Public Finance Using State Lotteries

Are state lotteries immoral?

"Don't smoke, chew, or run with girls that do" is a popular adage in some Christian circles today. Christians are concerned about what God thinks about their behavior. They are also concerned about what men think.

Of course, any true Christian who struggles with a contemptuous sin like pornography will not herald his addiction, but in many places Christians will seek to cover up arguably less egregious activities like drinking alcohol, smoking cigars, or even gambling now and then. These practices are often viewed as taboo—even when used in moderation. Paradoxically, Christians are able to openly indulge in overeating or overspending on cars, clothing, and entertainment devices without chagrin. Gluttony and profligate spending seem to be more acceptable sins among believers than other excesses, creating (widespread) inconsistency of thought among Evangelicals about what is appropriate Christian behavior.

In order to resolve the inconsistency of thought, let us consider a classification of Christian action and practice highlighting four items: pornography, wine, Milky Way candy bars, and prayer. The broad headings of this arrangement (assigning a letter to each of the four items) would be: [A] "never permissible" (e.g., pornography) and [B] "permissible". Category B could be further divided into three sub-classifications: [1] "permissible in moderation" (e.g., wine), [2] "always permissible unless there are extenuating circumstances" (e.g., Milky Way candy bars), [3] "always permissible without qualification" (e.g., praying to the true God or preaching the gospel). These categories are especially apropos in terms of our entertainment choices, and in terms of helping us identify the public policies we would support or criticize.

Impermissible behaviors

Category A practices, such as viewing pornography, are relatively easy for Christians to identify and eschew. They are, obviously, always sinful. A Christian would be  hard-pressed to think of any general, legitimate use for something like pornography (although he might be willing to entertain an argument to the contrary if someone wanted to make one). In a word, Category A items are *intrinsically* evil themselves or are part and parcel of an institution that is intrinsically evil. The scriptural rule regarding such practices would seem to be summed up in 1 Thessalonians 5:22, 1 Peter 2:11 and Romans 12:21: "Abstain from every form of evil", "Beloved, I beg you as sojourners and pilgrims, abstain from fleshly lusts which war against the soul" and "Do not be overcome by evil, but overcome evil with good."

In his January 11, 2003 article in *World*, "Wages from Sin", Pastor John Piper seems to place playing the lottery under category A. He is mistaken. There is nothing intrinsically evil about either the purchase or the entertainment provided by the lottery ticket. Whether or not the lottery as an institution is evil is more intriguing, but to condemn any voluntary action that is not specifically condemned by the Scriptures (such as gambling or lotteries) is probably imprudent and may well be an encroachment upon Christian liberty. Indeed, the institution of the lottery, at least insofar as it is by nature a game based on probability like the casting of lots, is mentioned in the Bible without condemnation (see Leviticus 16:8; Joshua 18:6-10; 1 Samuel 14:42; 1 Chronicles 24:31; 25:8; 26:13-14; Nehemiah 10:34, 11:1; Jonah 1:7; Proverbs 16:33; and Acts 1:26). The casting of lots was even used by godly men (apparently) to determine the will of God.

Behaviors permissible in moderation

The Scriptures seem to indicate that Christians may use alcoholic beverages like wine and beer in moderation (e.g., John 2:1-11; 4:46; 1 Timothy 5:23, etc.). Thus, Category B1 practices would be permitted up to a point, beyond which (e.g., one's inebriation) the practice becomes sinful. Although there might be some people who abstain from Category B1 practices because of past excesses or because it would cause another to stumble (cf. Romans 14:13-21), they would not be considered evil in general but are essentially *amoral*. Buying lottery tickets should be included among the many Category B1 practices, which may provide genuine enjoyment or entertainment value when used in moderation. As Schansberg rightly notes, when gambling with a small amount of money is treated purely as entertainment, concerns about greed and materialism, getting something for nothing, poor stewardship, reliance on luck instead of Providence, and addiction fade away.[148]

Certainly, a family that spends $5 per month on lottery tickets is not going to harm itself financially any more

---

[148] D. Eric Schansberg (2003), *Turn Neither to the Right nor to the Left*, Greenville, South Carolina: Alertness Books, pp. 117.

than a family that spends $5 per month at Blockbuster Video. Like any form of entertainment, the value of which is always determined by subjective individual preferences, Category B1 practices provide some value to the participants. Just because a man is not very entertained by renting and viewing *Mary Poppins* or by playing skee-ball in an arcade does not mean that these activities do not entertain others.

Is there a point at which expenditures for entertainment for a Christian turn into excess? Of course there is, but that point is *not* usually a bright line that can be objectively determined by onlookers. The scriptural rule regarding such practices (or Christian liberties) would seem to be summed up in 1 Corinthians 6:12 and Romans 14:4: "All things are lawful for me, but all things are not helpful. All things are lawful for me, but I will not be brought under the power of any" and "Who are you to judge another's servant? To his own master he stands or falls. Indeed, he will be made to stand, for God is able to make him stand."

Behaviors always permissible unless there are extenuating circumstances

Category B2 practices are never sinful in and of themselves. It is not wrong to buy candy bars—Baby Ruth, Milky Way or otherwise—in general. However, if a person is overweight, buying candy might be sinful because it compounds his gluttony and lack of self-control. It might also be sinful for cavity-prone people to buy candy. In either of these cases, issues arise involving caring for our bodies (cf. 1 Corinthians 6:19-20). Moreover, in large enough quantities, partaking of Category B2 practices could entail poor stewardship, lack of wisdom, or defective priorities. How much of God's money should we waste? The scriptural rule regarding such practices would seem to be summed up in (among other places) 1 Corinthians 4:2,

9:27 and 10:23: "Moreover it is required in stewards that one be found faithful", "But I discipline my body and bring it into subjection, lest, when I have preached to others, I myself should become disqualified" and "All things are lawful for me, but not all things are helpful; all things are lawful for me, but not all things edify".

Social ramifications of playing the state lottery

Piper's condemnation of greed and covetousness among state lottery players is accurate. Paul said that, "those who desire to be rich fall into temptation and a snare and into many foolish and harmful lusts which drown men in destruction and perdition" (1 Timothy 6:9). Jesus said, "Take heed and beware of covetousness, for one's life does not consist in the abundance of the things he possesses" (Luke 12:15).

However, Piper's notion that playing the lottery harms the poor is debatable. Even if poor people are worse off because state lotteries or other gambling exists, that fact does not mean that the participation by relatively wealthier individuals exacerbates poverty. Moreover, there is no good reason to assume that public policy outlawing lotteries would reduce poverty or gambling, any more than Prohibition in the 1920s reduced alcohol use. Indeed, Piper's notion smacks of the sentiment that is commonly found in modern American liberals, who blame big business or big government for bad individual behavior and its outcome. But such sentiment is false.

Is it not said that lung cancer and smoking addiction are not the fault of the individuals who choose to smoke but rather the fault of greedy, manipulative firms like Phillip Morris and R. J. Reynolds, along with advertising firms and the media which make commercials that impel people to smoke? They are supposedly profiting at the expense of the weak and poor and the federal government compounds the problem by issuing subsidies to tobacco farmers.

This sort of drivel, although commonplace, is simply not true. People choose actions, and expend scarce resources for them, because they expect to benefit. Voluntary individual choice is never someone else's fault. Adam had no right to alleviate his guilt by blaming Eve, nor did Eve by blaming Satan. As the Scripture says in Galatians 6:5 and 2 Corinthians 5:20, "each one shall bear his own load" and "we must all appear before the judgment seat of Christ, that each one may receive the things done in the body, according to what he has done, whether good or bad".

Individuals will be judged according to what they have done in the body without appealing to the sins of others for mitigation of the consequences. State lottery winnings are not "plunder" (as Piper said), and playing the lottery in moderation does not necessitate "spiritual suicide". They are proceeds from an entertaining game (at least to some) with very poor odds, in which millions of individuals voluntarily choose to participate. Lottery tickets represent a tax on people who are bad at math.

Local church offerings made from state lottery winnings

Piper does not want his ministry or church to receive any of the filthy lucre of lottery winnings. Piper's reasoning would be sensible if his goal were to reduce the number of people in his church who are given to excess in the lottery. But Piper should be careful to not go beyond what the Bible says. After all, Jesus received a fragrant, expensive gift that was bought by a woman of ill repute. Consider Luke 7:36-39:

> *36* Then one of the Pharisees asked Him to eat with him. And He went to the Pharisee's house,

and sat down to eat. *37* And behold, a woman in the city who was a sinner, when she knew that Jesus sat at the table in the Pharisee's house, brought an alabaster flask of fragrant oil, *38* and stood at His feet behind Him weeping; and she began to wash His feet with her tears, and wiped them with the hair of her head; and she kissed His feet and anointed them with the fragrant oil. *39* Now when the Pharisee who had invited Him saw this, he spoke to himself, saying, "This man, if He were a prophet, would know who and what manner of woman this is who is touching Him, for she is a sinner."

On a similar occasion, the Apostle John records that the disciples too—Judas Iscariot in particular—complained about Mary's inefficient use of the valuable oil. "But Jesus said, 'Let her alone; she has kept this for the day of My burial. For the poor you have with you always, but Me you do not have always'" (John 12:7-8). It was Judas Iscariot who raised concerns about the poor being harmed. If Jesus Christ was willing to receive benefits from apparently wasteful means, or even from ill-gotten gains, then why should the church reject them? Surely, Piper does not want to align himself with Iscariot in inaccurately or even disingenuously pleading the case of the poor!

Furthermore, one might argue that the doctrine of Proverbs 13:22b would reach the epitome of fulfillment in the giving of lottery winnings to the church. It says, "The wealth of the sinner is stored up for the righteous". Why is it wrong for the saints to benefit by the undoing of the wicked? Accordingly, the Bible records many instances where the wealth of the unsaved is rightly received by God's people and used for righteous purposes.

The Queen of Sheba—not necessarily a believer— and Hiram's ships brought exotic treasures to Solomon that augmented the glory of the Temple and wealth of God's people (1 Kings 10:1, 10-12; 2 Chronicles 9:1, 9-11). The unbelieving king Artaxerxes granted Nehemiah's request for safe passage and timber to rebuild the Temple, Jerusalem's wall, and houses in Judea (Nehemiah 2:4-8). The wise men from the East (or Magi)—astrologers that interpreted dreams and performed magic—were probably not truly converted men and yet Christ received their gifts by Joseph and Mary (Matthew 2:1-2,9-12). Ananias and Sapphira were slain for lying to the Holy Spirit but there is no indication that their offering was refused by the church (Acts 5:1-11).

Gambling in the Bible

The Bible does not condemn gambling *per se*. It only condemns the excesses that might devolve from gambling. Therefore, the lottery is permissible in moderation (a Category B1 activity), like using wine or beer, which the godly may use with restraint. This statement concurs with the *Westminster Confession of Faith* too—in its application of the eighth commandment against fraud and lying. Its *Larger Catechism* (question 142) condemns "wasteful gaming; and all other ways whereby we do unduly prejudice our own outward estate, and defrauding ourselves of the due use and comfort of that estate which God hath given us." Excessive gambling is sin, just as excessive use of alcohol (drunkenness) is sin.

Moreover, we must also affirm a commitment to the providential understanding of life. There is nothing that is outside of the control of a sovereign God. Yet God has set forth certain random processes to serve His purposes in the world, as Ecclesiastes 9:11 affirms: "I returned and saw under the sun that—the race is not to the swift, nor the battle to the strong, nor bread to the wise, nor riches to men of understanding, nor favor to men of skill; but time and chance happen to them all." In this life, God permits the

lottery to work just as He permits random number generators to work, but always under His permissive decree.

Even if most Christians do not play the lottery, they
should leave those who do to their liberty. And there is no
reason for churches to abstain from receiving gifts derived
from state lottery winnings that will help them further the
Gospel, edify the church, and assist the poor, widows, and
orphans. Regrettably, the state lottery has been a significant
bone of contention among Evangelicals and conservatives.

The lottery is the best tax

The state lottery is one of those things which divide
men of good will on the political and social right. On the
one hand, staunch conservatives despise state lotteries. For
instance, the platform of the Constitution Party says:
"Gambling promotes an increase in crime, destruction of
family values, and a decline in the moral fiber of our country. We are opposed to government sponsorship, involvement in, or promotion of gambling, such as lotteries, or
subsidization of Native American casinos in the name of
economic development." On the other hand, a state lottery
policy is refreshing for many pro-life libertarians.

Why would libertarians like the lottery? The reason
has nothing to do with the morality of gambling but everything to do with the nature and propriety of the *tax*. Yes,
the lottery is a tax. State lottery revenues fund functions of
civil government just like coercive taxes. The difference is
that lotteries are *voluntary*—unlike any other significant
tax source.

In fact, enthusiastic and greedy people rush to play
the lottery. The author once spoke to the South Carolina
Lottery director, who stated that during a recent $100+ mil-
lion "Powerball" game, sales exceeded 15,000 tickets per

hour—a rate faster than the tickets could be printed. Can you think of any other tax that people rush to pay?

By contrast, the state extorts money from people by taxing income, sales, gasoline, real property, luxury, and various "sins", along with requiring licenses, permits, registration fees, and traffic fines, all of which go to the general budget of the state. Then the state doles out paltry welfare benefits. Yet receiving these benefits is nowhere near as exhilarating as having the television station's cameraman at a winner's front door. Somehow, buying a pile of lottery tickets (albeit with a remote chance of winning) is much more fun than "contributing" 12.4 percent of one's earnings for his Social Security "program"? Given the prognostications of some, lottery ticket accumulation might also be rational since the odds of winning the lottery are likely greater than a young man's chances of ever collecting Social Security benefits.

The "stupid" tax

Let's face it: the state lottery is a "stupid tax". Like other monopolized "public enterprises", the lottery does not produce the high quality, low-priced, innovative, and consumer-friendly product that would be offered in a free market. For instance, Las Vegas and Atlantic City casinos compete by advertising the highest payouts (e.g., slot machines paying 98.3 percent in one casino versus only 97.8 percent in others), and people flock to consume the services provided. The South Carolina Lottery's payout is a measly 58 percent[149]—rather meager compared to Las Vegas casino rates. Hence, one could make the case that playing the state lottery is a pursuit of fatuous or ignorant people.

---

[149] In South Carolina, lottery administration costs are 12 percent. About 30 percent of revenues fund scholarships—or slide into the state's coffers. And 58 percent are paid out in prizes.

Of course, not all lottery players are dolts or idiots. For instance, the author's brother-in-law once stated that—as a Calvinist—he need buy only one ticket. If the sovereign Lord wants him to win the jackpot, then only one ticket is required. Perhaps one could argue that the Calvinist-lottery thesis provides a basis for a man buying five $1 lottery tickets per year. The opportunity cost imposed on his family from buying these tickets corresponds to ordering one medium pizza instead of one large one—not much of a concern.

While thinking Christians will likely choose to not play the lottery—not so much on account of their scruples but because they do not want to pay the "stupid tax"—such choices should be left to the liberty of conscience of each individual believer. Buying a few lottery tickets per year is morally inconsequential for the typical Christian, and other Christians should be careful to reserve judgment about any Christian who has done so.

The ethics of public finance through state lotteries

Now someone will argue that we are forgetting about the fact that gambling is a social evil and that it supports wicked institutions. This point is well taken, at least in terms of *excessive* gambling. However, as far as the aforementioned example is concerned, no thinking Christian should be convinced that his $5 annual expense has any moral implications other than the reduction of a tenth of a pound from his waistline due eating a little less pizza.

Thinking Christians know wherein lies real evil in the world: false religion and the state are the wickedest institutions among men—far worse than any Mafia family in Atlantic City or Las Vegas, or any inefficient state-run lottery business. So we must keep our minds from becoming muddled by paying too much attention to relatively inconsequential institutions and practices, including casinos and state lotteries. But even if some Christians insist upon shunning state lotteries, why should they allow the ethical implications of their convictions block them from supporting the use of state lotteries as a voluntary taxation scheme?

The Bible says that "the wealth of the sinner is stored up for the righteous" (Proverbs 13:22) and "he who is filthy, let him be filthy still" (Revelation 22:11). We should prefer that obtuse people scurry to pay a voluntary "stupid tax" any day versus having state-organized crime units blitz us via extortionist tax policies. Somebody has to pay for the limited government we desire. Why not let the government be financed by voluntary taxes like lotteries? In fact, why not call for a general repeal of all income, sales, and real property taxes, replacing them with lotteries instead? That idea should at least catch the eye of the most zealous Constitution Party member, along with all libertarians and American Christians who love liberty!

The ethics of receiving educational grants from lotteries

One last practical item regards whether or not Christians should take lottery-financed education benefits which are prevalent in many states. For instance, the South Carolina Life Scholarship and Piedmont Fellows Scholarship programs are financed by the lottery. These educational grants are financed 100 percent by voluntary taxes. In this case, there is no moral problem with accepting such funds. The funds are not stolen. (The educational programs in other states may be different and should be scrutinized by principled Christians prior to participating in them.)

As noted in chapter 1 of this book and in *Bible and Government*, it is wrong and sinful for Christians (or anyone) to take any welfare state, proactive policy benefits. Doing so makes one complicit in receiving stolen funds and effectively robbing innocent people. However, the state lottery is categorically different than welfare because there is no extortion and thus no stolen funds. There is no Robin Hood role of robbing from one group and giving to another.

Plus, in South Carolina, the policy does not seem to be proactive, but rather a means for the state to pad its coffers and for politicians to garner votes. On the whole, South Carolina's lottery scheme is probably better characterized as a policy of inefficient provision. The educational grants are a means of making voters happy, creating government jobs to "boost" the economy, and a means for the state to skim off a small portion of the spoils. The same thing may be said of urban works projects and "internal improvements". Thus, if one has no scruples about choosing to use "public enterprises" like public libraries or state parks, then letting the ignorant fund his family's intellectual development should not be troublesome. A lottery-funded program in places like South Carolina is simply not morally repugnant like proactive redistributive welfare policy.

In certain rare or unusual circumstances, lottery-funded scholarships pose a moral dilemma. For instance, in South Carolina, when the number of students "entitled" to receive lottery money in a given year exceeds the lottery receipts available to fund their corresponding scholarships—an event which has never happened—the shortfall must be made up out of the state's general budget. In such a case the educational policy would become a redistributive genre of proactive policy. So it would behoove a person to confirm that no such unusual circumstances exist prior to applying for any lottery-based educational grant.

Do you have college-bound kids wanting to attend college in places like South Carolina? Have little fear of gathering what sinners have voluntarily stored up for your family. Christians may enthusiastically support state lottery policy—the great "stupid tax". The "sinners" who indulge will end up paying some of the expenses of government.

And perhaps one day Christian activists may help replace our extortive taxation system with a purely voluntary one utilizing lotteries.

You and I have a rendezvous with destiny. We will preserve for our children this, the last best hope of man on earth, or we will sentence them to take the first step into a thousand years of darkness. If we fail, at least let our children and our children's children say of us we justified our brief moment here. We did all that could be done.
    —*President Ronald Reagan (1911-2004)*

Private and public life are subject to the same rules; and truth and manliness are two qualities that will carry you through this world much better than policy, or tact, or expediency, or any other word that was ever devised to conceal or mystify a deviation from a straight line.
    —*Gen. Robert E. Lee (1807-1870)*

The only thing necessary for evil to triumph is for good men to do nothing.
    —*Edmund Burke (1729-1797)*

Those who do not take an interest in public affairs are doomed to be ruled by evil men.
    —*Plato (427BC-347BC)*

15 Christian Civic Duty in America

Christian Activism

All Christians should be activists, although the extent to which each individual Christian engages in political action should be left to the liberty of his conscience. Christians can assert political influence through many means: including petitioning the government for a redress of grievances, voting, participating in public meetings and informational lectures, writing to elected officials, and participating in jury duty. All of these activities are *costly* to Christians, not only in terms of incidental expenses incurred but also in terms of time. Accordingly, engaging in some political activities might seem to make no sense—at least theoretically—unless we begin to view them in a different light.

For example, voting is always futile in the sense that there is virtually no chance that any individual vote can change the outcome of a major election. The expected cost exceeds the expected benefit. Yet voting makes more sense for a Christian activist once other accrued benefits are considered. Economic efficiency is reached when the *benefits* of activism are elevated in our minds through exalting the importance of spreading the truth, standing up for principles, and transforming our society by heralding the fundamental rights that America's Founders held dear. To the extent that voting can help accomplish these things or encourage virtue it becomes a *net* benefit to a Christian (i.e., the benefit exceeds the cost).

Of course, some political action remains out-of-bounds. For instance, Christians should generally not be involved in working for immoral state bureaus including welfare redistribution, public education, and agencies that defy fundamental rights. By and large, Christians should not back any proactive policy either by working for a bureau that implements such policies or by voting for their creation or extension. The same restriction applies to working for or patronizing most public enterprises and state-run industries.

Nevertheless, Christians have warrant to exercise political rights when it is expedient to do so. The Apostle Paul used his political clout as a Roman citizen both when he employed his rights and when he "appealed to Caesar" (Acts 16:37-38; 22:25-26; 25:11; 28:19). Christians may thus likewise make use of political means to declare and affirm that the inalienable rights of life, liberty, and property (or the pursuit of happiness) are *fundamental rights*,[150] derived *antecedent* to the existence of the state.[151] They can advocate that the state does not *grant* such fundamental rights. On the contrary, the primary reason that government is formed is to protect these rights. The American Founders clearly understood that no man holds his fundamental rights at the pleasure of the state.

Christian activists should work to spell out these fundamental rights in particular. First, all human beings

---

[150] These rights are set forth in the Declaration of Independence and the Fifth Amendment (Bill of Rights) to the Constitution.

[151] Steven Yates notes: "We had developed a respect for the individual that existed nowhere else in the world, and established the idea that individual rights are natural; that is, they *antecede*, and are not granted by, governments [states]. What the government [state] *grants*, after all, it can just as easily *take away*." Steven Yates (2005), *Worldviews: Christian Theism versus Modern Materialism*, Greenville, South Carolina: The Worldviews Project, p. 83.

share equally in the right to life, and the state may not abridge the right to life of any particular human being (or class of human beings) "without due process of law" and subsequent conviction of a capital offense. Second, all human beings share equally in the right to liberty, and the state may not forcibly enslave, conscript, or incarcerate a human being "without due process of law" and subsequent conviction of a crime. Third, all human beings share equally in the right to hold and enjoy property, so long as their pursuit of happiness does not infringe upon the rights of others, and the Constitution prohibits government from taking private property "for public use, without just compensation".[152] To this end, we should activate the doctrine of Vicesimus Knox.

> Let us reject all Machiavelism [*sic*], all political ethics, that contradict the acknowledged principles of truth and moral honesty. There can be no legitimate government which is not founded and supported by systems of conduct favourable to the happiness of human creatures,—the great mass of the people. Good government cannot be formed on the basis of falsehood and chicanery.[153]

---

[152] Such public uses include highways, dams, bridges, government office buildings, military installations, and similar public projects. Other uses such as increasing local tax revenues, clearing urban blight, removing church buildings, promoting urban development, and similar proactive "public interest" or "public welfare" schemes are not contemplated in the phrase "for public use". The phrase "just compensation" refers to market value based on comparable properties, and would not preclude the government from paying relocation expenses. Of course, such loopholes are constitutional matters, but in terms of a Christian ideal there should be no eminent domain policy at all. If the government needs real property for some project then let its bureaucrats go to a realtor like other people do. Christian activists might shoot for the ideal of eliminating eminent domain. At the same time, they might fight to at least preserve the constitutional restrictions, in light of the dangerous popular "living interpretation" of modern courts.

[153] Vicesimus Knox (1824 [1795]), *The Works of Vicesimus Knox*, vol. VI, Section XXXII, "On Political Ethics; Their Chief Object Is to Throw Power into the Hands of the Worst Part of Mankind, and to Render Government an Institution Calculated to Enrich and Aggrandize a Few, at the Expense of the Liberty, Property, and Lives of the Many", London: J. Mawman, p. 121.

But as popular commotion is always to be dreaded, because bad men always arise to mislead its efforts, how desirable is it that it may be prevented, by conciliatory measures, by a timely concession of rights, by redress of grievances, by reformation of abuses, by convincing mankind that governments have no other object than faithfully to promote the comfort and security of individuals, without sacrificing the solid happiness of living men to national glory, or royal magnificence. True patriotism and true philosophy, unattached to names of particular men, or even to parties, consider the happiness of man as the first object of all rational governments; and, convinced that nothing is more injurious to the happiness of man than the spirit of despotism, endeavour to check its growth, at its first and slightest appearance.[154]

Since Christians are required to "overcome evil with good" (Romans 12:21), they should be at the forefront of the battle to save their fundamental rights from being taken away by the wayward state and its evil policies. Accordingly, American Christians might choose to organize or participate in First Amendment protests to that end. They might also "break the law" in order to preserve life. (A strong case can be made from Proverbs 24:11-12[155] that justifies abortion clinic protesting with groups like Operation Rescue.)

And here's another biblically-based maxim apropos to Christian social conduct: *The truth is never owed to a criminal.* Accordingly, any statute requiring the disclosure

---

[154] Vicesimus Knox (1824 [1795]), *The Works of Vicesimus Knox*, vol. VI, Section XXXIV, "Of Mr. Hume's idea, that absolute monarchy is the easiest death, the true euthanasia of the British constitution", London: J. Mawman, p. 125.

[155] Proverbs 24:11-12: "Deliver those who are drawn toward death, and hold back those stumbling to the slaughter. If you say, 'Surely we did not know this,' Does not He who weighs the hearts consider it? He who keeps your soul, does He not know it? And will He not render to each man according to his deeds?"

of privileged information may be violated by Christians in order to prevent the state from committing crimes. We have biblical examples of deceit being used to preserve higher values of personal security and good stewardship (i.e., protecting one's life, liberty or property from predators): the Hebrew midwives, Rahab, Ehud, and the Magi.

If a robber enters your home and demands to know if you have any gold you do *not* have to tell him the truth. If Hitler's men ask you if you have any Jews you do *not* have to tell them the truth. If a taxing authority that accomplishes evil policies by extortion desires voluntary disclosure of your earnings (that you can avoid by some means), you do *not* have a duty to tell them the whole "truth" about your earnings. If you can avoid being robbed then why would you place yourself in harm's way?

As noted in chapters 6 and 9, the taxpaying requirement set forth in Romans 13:6-7 refers to circumstances in which paying a tax is demanded by the state on-the-spot, and where noncompliance would inevitably expose a Christian to facing the state's "wrath"—not to mention cause him much anxiety. Jesus Christ was remarkably not worried about His unpaid tax liability (Matthew 17:27), even though, being omniscient, He knew it existed. He was accused of being opposed to paying taxes (Luke 23:2), and He clearly had no misgivings over circumventing them. The implication from Matthew 17:24-27 is that Jesus would have been content to avoid paying the Temple tax had Peter not blunderingly committed Him to pay it.

Christians overcome evil with good by proclaiming the truth and living a life that glorifies the Lord. On occasion, being valiant-for-truth involves exercising political rights or even breaking the state's rules. Yet God is honored as Christians spread goodness and expose or cast out evil state policies.

The objective of Christian civic duty

Active Christians need an objective in carrying out their civic duty. In America, Christians need to have a vision of what an ideal *republic* would look like, along with some specific objectives of social transformation in order to achieve that republic. A fallen world can be improved by a Christian's efforts, but his efforts need to be focused.

In terms of political activism, a useful starting point for thinking about ideals is facilitated by considering society without any political structure, as well as considering the actions of fallen men in establishing it. The natural state of society is *anarchy*—not in the sense of untrammeled chaos but in the sense of having no established civil authority. Yet the sinful tendencies of men have led them to create states—parasitic power structures that devour social order and bring chaotic social conditions. As bad as society under anarchy may be it is always preferable to life under a state. Edmund Optiz succinctly defines the ideal role of government that Christian activist should aim for:

> There is a place for government in the affairs of men, and our Declaration of Independence tells us precisely what that place is. The role of government is to protect individuals in their God-given individual rights. Freedom is the natural birthright of man, but all that government can do in behalf of freedom is to let the individual alone, and it should secure him in his rights by making others let him alone.[156]

Therefore, Christians must be active in promoting a limited government that improves the social conditions that exist under anarchy. But they must also help to develop the means to check the power of government so that this pre-

---

[156] Rev. Edmund Opitz (1999), *The Libertarian Theology of Freedom*, Tampa, Florida: Hallberg Publishing Co., p. 142.

dominant social apparatus is not transformed into a virulent and lethal state. They must establish institutions that secure and guarantee fundamental rights through the collective self defense of limited government, the strict application of the rule of law, and completely free markets.

Jury nullification is one such method for American Christians—from the ordinary to the most sophisticated— to work out a proper civic duty. Through jury nullification Christians can apply God's principles to criminal or civil cases and quash a wayward judge's penchant or defy a foul decree of the legislative or executive branches. To promote this concept, the American Jury Institute was founded.

Their website candidly and lucidly states:[157] "Juries protect society from dangerous individuals and also protect individuals from dangerous government. Jurors have a duty and responsibility to render a just verdict. They must take into account the facts of the case, mitigating circumstances, the merits of the law, and the fairness of its application in each case...Jurors, as the representatives of the people, hold no personal agenda during any trial and most certainly not the government's agenda[158]...and are, in fact, the only truly objective individuals in the courtroom. The role of our

---

[157] See http://www.fija.org/ and http://www.americanjuryinstitute.org. Their mission is: "to inform all Americans about their rights, powers, and responsibilities when serving as trial jurors. Jurors must know that they have the option and the responsibility to render a verdict based on their conscience and on their sense of justice as well as on the merits of the law."

[158] The site adds: "Let us not forget that the prosecutors, judges, arresting officers—and the forensic investigators in most cases—are all a part of and receive their paychecks from government, with personal power bases to build and personal careers to protect through the 'productivity' of successful prosecutions resulting in convictions. Jurors have no such stake in the outcome." Plus, "The recognition of the authority and right of jurors to weigh the merits of the law and to render a verdict based on conscience, dates from before the writing of our Constitution, in cases such as those of William Penn and Peter Zenger. Should this right ever be suppressed, the people will retain the right to resist, having an unalienable right to veto or nullify bad and oppressive laws, and in fact then would be morally compelled to do so." And "Many existing laws erode and deny the rights of the people. Jurors protect against tyranny by refusing to convict harmless people. Our country's founders planned and expected that we, the people, would exercise this power and authority to judge the law as well as the facts every time we serve as jurors. Juries are the last peaceful defense of our civil liberties."

jurors is to protect private citizens from dangerous, unconstitutional government laws and actions." By doing so, jurors react against tyrannical states.

The republic that Christians should vie for is one based on the need for *reactive* public policy.[159] As pointed out in chapter 1, reactive policies are those policies which pertain to limited government: protection from predators foreign and domestic, seen and unseen (including hazardous microorganisms), and the establishment of law and order. Conversely, *proactive* policies seek to change or restrict the behavior of people or to redistribute social wealth via welfare state programs or by granting monopoly privileges to business interests.

What exactly does it mean to have a republic limited to reactive public policy? Local criminal courts, along with an appeals system, a military and some police forces to protect us from predators, a health department to combat epidemics, a statistics and elections section, some apparatus for engaging foreign policy including a consular system, border control, and passport issuance would be all that is required. A federal court system would deal with constitutional and inter-jurisdictional matters. The sheriff and judges from each county would be the highest civil authorities to ensure domestic tranquility. All other modern state functions would be privatized.[160]

Having this kind of republic also means the elimination of proactive policies: welfare and poverty programs,

---

[159] Jury nullification is one of the main means that Christians have to achieve predominantly reactive public policy. Christians may also participate in voting, local political meetings, letter-writing to congressmen, liberty-advocating political action committees, and drives to petition government for a redress of grievances are other means of attaining and retaining reactive (rather than proactive) public policy.

[160] State functions to be privatized include: building inspections, public works projects (e.g., roadways, bridges, railroads, and dams), civil procedure, marriage and divorce, product safety, mining regulation, space exploration, transportation and occupational safety, securities and insurance markets oversight, central banking and currency emission, national parks, food and pharmaceutical grading, institutional accreditation, medical and disability insurance, small business development, postal services, firefighting and most policing services, and retirement plans (e.g., Social Security).

Social Security, federal grants, public education, agriculture, homeland security, borrowing, empire-building, foreign aggression, and wage and price controls. There would be no regulation of business whatsoever. There would be no state-granted monopoly privileges for business interests: tariffs, patents, copyrights, licenses, or permits. All welfare would be performed by private charities and churches.

Consequently, taxes would be very low, almost entirely indirect and voluntary through lotteries and use fees. There would be no need for payroll deductions or income taxes. Real property would be fully allodial[161] or absolute with no property taxes, regulation or eminent domain. Government would have few tasks and society would have greater peace and prosperity as a result of individuals enjoying more liberty. People would also have greater personal responsibility for their own actions and would be willing to ensure that the rights of others are not violated.

This ideal or vision of civil society, paring off some 90 percent of the current behemoth state (and the proportionate amount of taxes it requires), is what Christian activists should contend for as their proper civic duty.[162] And with such clear objectives in mind Christians can effectively work to improve this fallen world.

---

[161] For further discussion of allodial property and allodial policy, see John M. Cobin (1997), *Building Regulation, Market Alternatives, and Allodial Policy* (chapter 4, "An Overview of American Allodialism") and John M. Cobin (1999), *A Primer on Modern Themes in Free Market Economics and Policy* (chapter 15, "Allodialism as Economic Policy"), both published by Alertness Books, Greenville, South Carolina.

[162] 19th century Presbyterian theologian R.L. Dabney warned Christians against veering off a principled course in conservative activism: "American conservatism is merely the shadow that follows Radicalism as it moves forward to perdition. It remains behind it, but never retards it, and always advances near its leader. This pretended salt hath utterly lost its savor: wherewith shall it be salted? Its impotency is not hard, indeed, to explain. It is worthless because it is the conservatism of expediency only, and not of sturdy principle. It intends to risk nothing serious for the sake of the truth, and has no idea of being guilty of the folly of martyrdom." Robert L. Dabney (1979 [1897]), *Discussions, Secular*, Vallecito, California: Ross House Books, p. 496.

260

Suppose you were an idiot. And suppose you were a member of Congress. But I repeat myself.
    —*Mark Twain (1835-1910)*

A wise and frugal government, which shall restrain men from injuring one another, which shall leave them otherwise free to regulate their own pursuits of industry and improvement, and shall not take from the mouth of labor the bread it has earned. This is the sum of good government.
    —*President Thomas Jefferson (1801)*

One man with courage makes a majority.
    —*President Andrew Jackson (1767-1845)*

Every decent man is ashamed of the government he lives under.
    —*H.L. Mencken (1880-1956)*

16 Concluding Remarks

Summary of the key themes presented in this book

Several key themes discussed in this book—based in Scripture and informed by logic and knowledge from economics, history, and public policy—form the basis for a Christian theology of public policy. The most fundamental theses stem from a few key ideas.

First, God ordains *all* things: evil and good alike. Second, the spiritual clash between the kingdom of God and the kingdom of Satan is often manifested in earthly phenomena, including using the state and false religion, which are the two henchmen of Satan's unholy trinity, to persecute or revile Christians who are promoting the Gospel and God's principles.

Third, Christians are called to be peacemakers— which paradoxically involves fighting for peace at times. Christians are not to be aggressors but they may practice self-defense against predators (including state predators). Predators, such as socialists and totalitarians, take away peace and bring misery, war, poverty, and destruction. By opposing them with force, Christians serve as peacemakers.

Fourth, collective defense by means of the reactive policies of limited government is the logical extension of the doctrine of self-defense. But when proactive policies and polices of inefficient provision are added into the mix, a limited government is transformed into a state. And states themselves are predators that become the proper object of Christian resistance.

Fifth, while states will seek to redefine the identity of believers, Christians must be careful to maintain proper allegiance to their only legitimate nationality. They must be loyal to Jesus Christ first, to His church second, and to those who love the principles of liberty and God's Word a distant third. All other allegiances are relatively worthless and fleeting, including a Christian's political citizenship in this world. Self-defense against predators and tyrants begins with a Christian's family, then pertains to his brethren, and finally extends to others who support the same cause.

Summary of policies to be promoted or opposed

How can self-defense be applied in a practical sense today? In what way can Christians be faithful to their calling in this world? What is the specific practical outworking of Christian civic duty in America? Based on the Christian theology of public policy presented in this book, the following public policies should be promoted or opposed by Christians who live under a constitutional republic or any other participatory form of government.

Policies that should be promoted

- The establishment of fundamental rights of life, liberty and property
- Self-defense against domestic and foreign predators: human, animal, microorganism, or chemical
- Just wars of self-defense
- Criminal justice at a local level

- Death penalty for premeditated murder carried out by local government
- Jails for short term holding of prisoners
- Restitution or temporary enslavement for crimes or failure to pay debts, directly benefiting the victims or creditors
- Voluntary or indentured servitude
- Allodial or absolute real property rights in land and buildings
- Excise taxes or lotteries and other voluntary taxes
- Open immigration for any honest person, especially Christians or people fleeing persecution, provided that they are willing to assimilate into American culture and language over the long run
- Border protection provided by private contractors and overseen by the defense department to ensure that predators or terrorists do not cross the border
- Privatization of all (or at least most) civil procedure
- Right to the possession and use of all firearms and weapons systems, excepting only weapons of mass destruction which, if used, would *unavoidably* lead to the deaths of innocent people
- Bureaus to ensure orderly and peaceful commerce: mining claims, real property transfers and deeds, legal structures, etc. (privatizing whenever possible)
- Privatization of public works projects for roadways, bridges, dams, tunnels, etc.
- Privatization of facilities for the mentally ill, elderly-and-abandoned, etc.

Policies that should be opposed

- Abortion rights (in *all* cases other than tubal pregnancy)

264

- Aggressive wars (i.e., wars not initiated as an act of collective self-defense)
- Any kind of regulation of business: oversight, approval, licensing, permits, medallions
- Public enterprises and state-run businesses and so-called "natural monopolies" like electricity generation
- Any sort of environmental regulation
- Regulation of food and pharmaceuticals
- Death penalty for any reason carried out by the state (death penalty for murder carried out by a local government is a different matter)
- Prisons and penitentiaries
- Involuntary servitude, including part time slavery through taxation, military conscription, and regulation
- Socialism and interventionism in general
- Educational, agricultural, food stamps, and other subsidies and grants
- Low-income housing
- Medicare, Medicaid, and Social Security
- Monopoly licensing techniques: patents, copyright, trademarks, tariffs
- Fiat money scheme through a monopoly note issuer like the Federal Reserve System
- Standards testing for occupational licensing and product safety
- Involvement in or support of globalist organizations and pacts like the United Nations and so-called "free trade" agreements
- Zoning and land use planning
- Public education
- Truancy and compulsory attendance rules
- Public universities

- Income and real property taxes
- Urban development projects for highways, dams, bridges, clearing urban blight, etc.
- Space exploration and other promotions of science
- Control of transportation and energy
- Control of gold and other precious metals
- Control of securities and commodities markets
- Public charity for natural disasters and tragedies
- Public media broadcasts (TV/radio)
- Hate crimes and hate speech regulation
- Marriage licensing
- Regulation of churches
- Homeland security, BATF, DEA, and similar special-purpose domestic law enforcement agencies that tend to denigrate the Bill or Rights
- Driver licensing
- Family court, tax court, and other social structure courts not dealing with criminal justice
- Federal or state land ownership in city parks, national or state parks or beaches, campgrounds, etc.
- Eminent domain
- Censorship and other infringements of the Bill of Rights

The Christian worldview differs markedly from the materialist or secular humanist worldview.[163] Serious Christians must be ready to foment and carry the principles of God's Word into their economic, social, and political interactions. Doing so will put them in conflict with the opposing forces of the kingdom of Satan.

Yet the ensuing battle is one that must be fought. The Christian's coddling of vain divine right notions or abandoning his post in the world is tantamount to commit-

---

[163] See Steven Yates (2005), *Worldviews: Christian Theism versus Modern Materialism*, Greenville, South Carolina: The Worldviews Project.

ting treason against his Lord and to disobey His call for him to stand up and fight for the cause of the Truth. Therefore, let us who name the name of Christ prepare to do battle, to occupy till He comes, pulling down strongholds and everything that exalts itself against the knowledge of God.[164] We know that our victory is certain in the long run (at least in eternity), no matter how poor the odds of victory appear to our finite minds. We have firm principles to stand for and a fierce foe that we must oppose, whether there is full victory in our lifetimes or not. Let us then become informed about the theology of public policy and prepare ourselves to take appropriate action given the circumstances ascribed by Providence in our lives.

The need for toleration among differing Evangelicals

One principle acclaimed in both this book and *Bible and Government* that should be reiterated is *toleration*. Romans 14:4 says: "Who are you to judge another's servant? To his own master he stands or falls. Indeed, he will be made to stand, for God is able to make him stand." Sadly, Christians have often found themselves in opposing armies, killing one another, with each side believing that he is holding the principled viewpoint while his wayward brother abides in sin. In American history, this tragedy has played itself out in between Patriots and Tories, Lincolnites and "rebels", and so forth.

Nonetheless, Christians should respect the liberty of thought regarding public policy theology of other sincere

---

[164] Alternative (internet) news source provider Michael Rivero has keenly summed up the key social problem Americans face: "Most people prefer to believe their leaders are just and fair even in the face of evidence to the contrary, because once a citizen acknowledges that the government under which they live is lying and corrupt, the citizen has to choose what he or she will do about it. To take action- in the face of a corrupt government entails risks of harm to life and loved ones. To choose to do nothing is to surrender one's self-image of standing for principles. Most people do not have the courage to face that choice. Hence, most propaganda is not designed to fool the critical thinker but only to give moral cowards an excuse not to think at all."

believers, and should be careful not to despise other scholars on account of their relative positions. Even if one holds his view and rejects others, he should still be able to fellowship with those who differ with him. Moreover, in America, there are also other, perhaps less scholarly, positions—such as those found within the "patriot movement"—that could be added to the list of positions to tolerate. Maybe one side calls the modern state and all its licenses and taxes "Babylon" and the other does not. Maybe one side is pacifist, and the other is not. Rather than vituperating one another over the convictions each one holds from the Bible (and science), it is surely better to disagree without being disagreeable, and continue to advance the common goal of proclaiming the gospel and edifying the saints.

For the time being, the kingdoms of this world are against the Lord. The devil is about his business, even knowing that he has a short time. Surely the states of the ages do their (often foul) deeds under God's permissive will. But there is a day coming in which there will be:

> ...loud voices in heaven, saying, "The kingdoms of this world have become the kingdoms of our Lord and of His Christ, and He shall reign forever and ever!" And the twenty-four elders who sat before God on their thrones fell on their faces and worshiped God, saying: "We give You thanks, O Lord God Almighty, The One who is and who was and who is to come, Because You have taken Your great power and reigned. The nations were angry, and Your wrath has come, And the time of the dead, that they should be judged, And that You should reward Your servants the prophets and the saints, And those who fear Your name, small and great, And should destroy those who destroy the earth" (Revelation 11:15b-18).

Appendix 1: Responses to Aberrant Notions Regarding Submission to Civil Authorities

> *The state is a divine institution. Without it we have anarchy, and the lawlessness of anarchy is counter to the natural law: so we abjure all political theories which view the state as inherently and necessarily evil. But it is the state which has been in history the principal instrument of abuse of the people, and so it is central to the conservatives' program to keep the state from accumulating any but the most necessary powers.*
> —neoconservative William F. Buckley Jr. (1925-)

Even though theonomy provides an incorrect theology of public policy (from a liberty of conscience point of view), it is at least internally consistent and tractable; true to its presuppositions. Indeed, the consistent Christian thinker will naturally tend to either theonomy or liberty of conscience once he has framed his understanding about the nature of the state, the hermeneutic for interpreting Romans 13:1-7, Titus 3:1, and 1 Peter 2:13-17, and perhaps his view of covenant theology and the millennium. In the same way that the person will naturally come to hold a Calvinistic soteriology once he is convinced of the doctrine of the total inability (or depravity) of man, one's presuppositions about civil government and the apostolic doctrine regarding submission to it will lead him, logically, to embrace theonomy or liberty of conscience.

Alternatively, the divine right and Anabaptist views are left as largely ineffectual and shallow, inconsistent or incomplete viewpoints. Yet because divine right is the most prominent of these ineffectual views, this chapter will focus on it.[165] Part of the problem divine righters have with the liberty of conscience view, at least those outside of academia, comes from their unwillingness to read the idea completely. For instance, some pastors read sections of books or articles in favor of a liberty of conscience perspective without understanding the complete argument. They may even make public remarks about the idea and do little more, in the long run, than demonstrate their own ignorance, making retraction of an inconsistent position more difficult. Of course, Proverbs 18:13 offers some warning to those who answer an argument before they hear it: "He who answers a matter before he hears it, It is folly and shame to him."

The divine right paradigm proposes that nearly all civil disobedience is sin because the civil authority is a special authority sphere in life (akin to the family and the church), and the believer must submit to what it decrees as if God Himself were speaking. While they do not hold that the state's word is on par with God's Word, they do see public policy as directed by Providence, and thus a manifestation of His will for believers. Consequently, violating a public policy is said to be generally sinful *in and of itself.* But this view must be mistaken.[166] Only God Himself can decree whether a thing is right or wrong. And He has done

---

[165] Divine right is surely the most prominent Evangelical view (usually being the *default* view), making it an natural target for those who hold to a more consistent public policy perspective such as theonomy or liberty of conscience.

[166] Theonomists who hold some degree of this notion are too—even though their system is more analytically rigorous. Like a house of cards, the paradigm will fall down unless they can establish the tenuous presuppositions of postmillennialism, thoroughgoing covenant theology, and the integrated authority idea that the state is a special sphere of authority along with the family and the church (which elements form its base).

so in His completed Word the Bible. Public policy can add nothing to the Word of God by trying to create new moralities that matter.

Along with the theonomists, liberty of conscience advocates criticize the divine right perspective on account of its biblical, historical, and analytical shortcomings. The main criticism has to do with the very foundation of biblical analysis in Romans 13:1. The divine righter *reads into* the text (a practice known as eisegesis) that the state is a divine institution ordained by God to look after civil society for Him. The assumption that the state has a godly character at its root simply because it is ordained or appointed by God is thrust upon the passage. But all things are ordained or appointed by God, including authorities like Satan (the "god of this world"), false religion, and slave-traders. (The text itself of Romans 13:1 says that "there is no authority except from God" and thus all "the authorities that exist are appointed by God".) Yet the divine righter does not assume that Satan, Buddhism, or slave pirates have godly characters or purposes. They arbitrarily single out the state as a good institution for society.

Furthermore, the divine righter is willfully ignorant of history which manifests the evil actions of the state. Rulers and public policies are not generally good hitters that occasionally send off a foul ball or fail by striking out. On the contrary, good state rulers and public policies are the exception rather than the rule. America has enjoyed a disproportionate amount of exceptional policies which serves to blur the vision of the divine righter and to obscure what state-sponsored atrocities have happened in most parts of the world for millennia. The divine righter thus forces his biblical interpretation to fit the mold of Western civilization—the anomalies of societies in Britain and America in particular.

The Bible does not indicate that the state is a special sphere of authority to care for society and keep criminals in check—at least not since the Old Testament era theocracy. The divine righter brings his ideal notion about what the state is to the text and forces an interpretation that is not there. Being *ordained* (or *appointed*) in and of itself simply could not make the Roman regime (or any other state) an *institution*—a term which is neither included nor implied in the text—and certainly by no means guarantees that any resulting institution would be godly since other things ordained by God are purely evil. Consequently, divine righters err by making the logical leap that divine ordination means that a divine institution is created.

They also hold up the fact that Paul and Peter spoke so highly of Nero as proof that even the most ruthless states can be God's agents to care for civil society. The Apostles did not view Nero and his cronies as flawed men who were doing their best to care for civil society. Those rulers hated God and his ways and any sane man could plainly see it. They did not care for civil society but rather undermined it by burning Rome, killing infants in Bethlehem, etc. The Apostles recognized those rulers as evildoers but took comfort in the fact that God had appointed them to provide for further sanctification of His church ("for good") and warned believers to tread lightly around them. The good that Nero and his cronies did for society (if any) pales in comparison to the evil they inflicted upon it. To contend (as divine righters do) that the decrees of such rulers are part of "general revelation" is dubious at best, if not spurious.

The Roman state simply did not have the characteristics of a divine institution. The imperfect institutions of God in this world (i.e., the family and the church) at least resemble God's ways—even though they are guided by sinful men and prone to mischief. When considering the history of states, one cannot see the godly resemblance in general in either rulers or public policies, whereas one may see such a resemblance in the church and family. Thus, the divine right view is toppled by biblical and historical analysis, as well as simple analytics.

Response to some representative divine right criticisms

It is not surprising that divine righters, above any of the three non-liberty of conscience views, would express a strong reaction to the liberty of conscience perspective since the publication of *Bible and Government*. Knee-jerk reaction from pastors, Christian talk show hosts, and laymen have illustrated common divine right thinking.

The divine right critique of liberty of conscience may be summed up in the following ten points. The liberty of conscience view has charged by divine righters with:

1. inappropriately using an apocalyptic portion of Scripture (Revelation 13:1-8) to develop a key doctrine about civil government, arguing for the superiority of Romans 13:1-7 instead;
2. misrepresenting the Apostle Paul by stating that he declares something about the nature or character of government when in fact he does not, and that even if the Apostle John does in fact suggest that the Roman government was empowered by Satan (in Revelation 13:1-8) that fact would not imply that *all* civil government is necessarily so empowered;
3. wrongly questioning the judgment or motives of the godly but state-sponsored scholars who translated the King James Version of the Bible;
4. practicing eisegesis instead of exegesis when dealing with Romans 13:1-7 (and other passages), resulting in conclusions that are "conjecture," "unproven," "unfounded", and "errant," or based on "extremely poor logic;"
5. erring greatly in its understanding that the words *good* and *evil* in Romans 13:1-7 and 1 Peter 2:13-17

actually refer to the civil government's definition of what is good and evil rather than God's definition;

6. utilizing unproven and fallacious reasoning in general;
7. not being objective, or perhaps prejudiced and biased by philosophical or free market economic reasoning (i.e., forcing a bias on to the Scriptures);
8. using straw man arguments regarding those who hold to a divine right perspective, viz. that divine right adherents believe that Christians must obey nearly every whim of public policy;
9. inappropriately extending the rightness of rebelling against public policies which are not policies that entail "a direct command to disobey God", incorrectly stating that there was no welfare state in Rome and speculation that Paul might have qualified his obligation to believers to submit to the state it had existed during that time;
10. wrongly interpreting Paul's message to the Romans, suggesting that submission is pragmatic (practical) or expedient is unjustified (especially as it was for that era—although not exclusively).

To these charges, the following replies can be made.

First, although liberty of conscience does use an apocalyptic portion of Scripture (Revelation 13:1-8) to develop a key doctrine about civil government, it does not do so inappropriately. Divine righters go beyond proper hermeneutics in making their criticism of the use of apocalyptic literature. Christian doctrine is and should be based on the clear teaching of didactic passages—from the epistles and the gospels particularly. However, that does not preclude us from using other passages of Scripture to form doctrine. After all, Paul tells us that, "*all Scripture* is given by inspiration of God and is profitable for doctrine" (2 Timothy 3:16a).

This fact is especially true when there is no clear teaching on a subject in didactic sections of the Bible; such is the case when considering the nature of the state. Of course, caution should be exercised when undertaking the use of apocalyptic passages, and one should perhaps be careful to not conclude too much from non-didactic passages or formulate fundamental doctrine from them. In this book, as well as in *Bible and Government*, great care is taken to point out this aspect of hermeneutical principles before expounding the liberty of conscience view of Revelation 13:1-8.

Romans 13:1-7 does not deal with the *nature* of the state; neither does 1 Peter 2:13-17. These passages mainly discuss what the believer's response to public policy should be under the divinely-appointed state. All that is known about the nature of the state is inferred in other passages, and that is why Revelation 13:1-8 is used to show (in part) that the nature of the state is evil. Hence, this first criticism is invalid.

Furthermore, the related divine right contention that liberty of conscience holds a superiority of Romans 13:1-7 at one point but Revelation 13:1-8 at another is simply not true. One passage is not exalted over another. Each one is plainly utilized according to what doctrine can legitimately be gleaned from each text. In other words, when arguing for the satanic nature of the state, Revelation 13:1-8 more clearly deals with the issue. When the believer's response to public policy is discussed, Romans 13:1-7, Titus 3:1-2 and 1 Peter 2:13-17 are relied upon. These two sets of texts deal with different aspects of the doctrine or biblical perspective of the civil authority.

Some scholars claim that Romans 13:1-7 is the most significant of all the passages regarding the state or civil government, and they seem frustrated that those with other views do not broadly give it similar weight. Yet these scholars do not give any reason why Romans 13:1-7 should be given more weight. Merely stating that the liberty of conscience view handles the text wrongly is not adequate. Such a critique is shallow.

The liberty of conscience view is often *not* dogmatic when gleaning principles elsewhere in the Bible with passages that are not as clear as Revelation 13:1-8. For instance, the liberty of conscience view does not draw any strong conclusion from Luke 23:2: "And they began to accuse Him, saying, 'We found this fellow perverting the nation, and forbidding to pay taxes to Caesar, saying that He Himself is Christ, a King.'" Perhaps some could make a case for tax protesting from this verse, but the liberty of conscience view does not see sufficient evidence to do so. On the other hand, those with a divine right bias might ignore this verse entirely when creating their public policy theology on account of subordinating such texts to the "clearer" teaching in Romans 13:1-8. Yet all Christians would do well to consider more deeply the whole counsel of God regarding public policy.

Second, the charge that the liberty of conscience view has misrepresented the Apostle Paul by stating that he declares something about the nature or character of the state when in fact he does not is simply unfounded. On the contrary, Paul does not deal with the nature of the state in Romans 13:1-7. Moreover, even if one admits that the Apostle John shows that the Roman state was empowered by Satan without implying that all states are similarly empowered, the liberty of conscience viewpoint is not derailed. Is it not enough that the Bible indicates that public policy and/or states were evil or opposed to God and His kingdom about 90 percent of the time (outside of the theocracy)?

These data, when coupled with the passage from Revelation 13:1-8 and passages elsewhere in the Bible (e.g., Psalm 2:1-3), make the case for the evil nature of the state. If these other data did not exist, liberty of conscience scholars would have to conform to the view held by the divine righters, and show more caution in their judgment regarding the evil nature of the state. However, since these supportive data and principles do exist, Revelation 13:1-8 actually serves to clarify what is only hinted at or implied elsewhere: the state is empowered by Satan and shares his nature.

Third, a few divine right adherents are concerned that liberty of conscience supporters have questioned the judgment or motives of the godly scholars who translated the King James Version of the Bible. Indeed, the liberty of conscience view suggests (not dogmatically) that there might have been some motivation to translate passages like Romans 13:1-7—where there was *justifiable* scholarly reason to do so—in such a way that benefited the king who commissioned them. However, that scenario does *not* call into question the "moral character" of the translators.

Many scholars have noted that theological viewpoints can creep into translations when there is a Greek or Hebrew word or grammatical issue that can be legitimately translated more than one way. For instance, it is not surprising that the King James Version translators, being largely of paedo-baptist persuasion, chose to transliterate the Greek word βαπτίζω as "baptize" rather than employing the equally and probably more legitimate translation "immerse." The same may be said of the choice of translation for the Greek word καί as *and* instead of *even* in Galatians 6:16: "And as many as walk according to this rule, peace and mercy be upon them, *and* upon the Israel of God." Premillennialists and dispensationalists are more content with "and," but covenantalists and amillennialists prefer the equally valid translation of "even" before the phrase "Israel of God."

Translation issues are likewise apparent in other passages of Scripture. In Romans 13:1-7 and 1 Peter 2:13-17, the Greek word translated "evil" could have been translated as "bad behavior" or "misdeeds" such that the reader would be less inclined to think that evil as God defines it is being discussed. It could refer to evil as defined by Nero or Herod. Consequently, the possibility for translation bias exists in this passage, especially when the translators were commissioned to the work by the monarch King James. And the liberty of conscience concern about translation bias should not be misconstrued as an attack on the moral character of the King James Version translators.

Fourth, some charge liberty of conscience adherents with practicing eisegesis. The liberty of conscience view is accused of being built upon a radical agenda in free market economics or classical liberalism which is being inappropriately thrust upon passages like Romans 13:1-7. In other words, some philosophy is being forced into (and out of) the text that is not there for the sake of serving a free market economics agenda. Yet, this critique is rather shallow considering the thorough analysis of the Scriptures and scholarly Christian frameworks that has been undertaken by liberty of conscience supporters (such as Yates, Optiz, Schansberg, Vance, et al, not to mention the many historical figures, cited in this book).

Indeed, as outlined earlier, it is the divine righter that practices eisegesis rather than exegesis with respect to the public policy relevant texts. He forces texts like Romans 13:1 to mean that divine ordination of the state must create a divine institution that is established to care for civil society. The text contains neither the word nor the concept of godly institution with respect to the state. Neither history nor biblical records of public policy outside of the theocracy provide support for the divine right thesis. The divine righter simply interprets Romans 13:1-7 and 1 Peter 2:13-17 with an ideological bias based on preconceived notions about the nature and purpose of the state.

Moreover, the divine righter's charge of eisegesis against the liberty of conscience view is false. No Christian should have anything to fear from applying principles of economics or the sciences in helping to hone doctrinal understanding, so long as it does not become dominant. For example, chapter 1 helps hone the theologian's understanding of what public policy is, how economic incentives can become perverse, and how to identify state evils like legalized plunder. Far from moving the Bible to second fiddle, books like this one, as well as *Bible and Government* and Dr. Eric Schansberg's *Turn Neither to the Right nor to the Left* (not to mention the aforementioned work of Dr. Steven Yates, Dr. Laurence Vance, Rev. Edmund Opitz, and others) vivify Christian understanding about public policy causing Christians to use their Bible better, and to think deeper about biblical principles for public policy.

Moreover, considerably more dogmatic paradigms (like divine right) are not immune from experiencing instances of eisegesis. The divine right paradigm tends to have an aversion to looking at the Bible's teaching on public policy and the state as fragmentary, or a predilection against the idea that some passages contain pieces of relevant information or doctrine that others do not. Instead, everything is interpreted through the lens of the favored Romans 13:1-7 passage. Thus, gleaning principles from passages other than the Romans 13:1-7 backdrop is avoided. While so doing is not eisegesis *per se*, the practice is similar because it subjugates the meaning of one passage to the external paradigm extrapolated from another.

It is not uncommon for a divine right adherent to build almost an entire doctrine of civil government on Romans 13:1-7 and then take that framework and thrust it upon other passages. Nevertheless, doing so does not disprove that the biblical teaching on public policy is fragmentary. The notion that Romans 13:1-7 is the princely text is an assumption rather than an undeniable fact. Indeed, there are at least a couple dozen important passages in the Bible that constitute the body of doctrine regarding the state and public policy. Most of these passages deal with a distinct issue, and there is often no overlap on doctrinal principles between them.

Why should anyone believe that non-theological disciplines may not apply their knowledge to shed light on obscure passages of Scripture or incomplete knowledge? We use history to set a context for why the Jews (and Hebrew Christians) were suffering in AD50 to AD70, why the Corinthians were given to excess, why the Apostle John wrote about Gnosticism in his epistles, why Paul had to deal with Judaizers in the Galatian church, and why one evangelist said that Jesus died at the sixth hour and another at midday. We understand more clearly why the Sadducees and Athenians had difficulties or contentions about the resurrection from the dead based on their philosophy by consulting non-theological disciplines.

Surely divine right adherents do not question the use of other disciplines like history and philosophy to help clarify biblical truth. So why should they have a problem with bringing in light from economics, political science theory, demography, and public policy theory to bear upon the Bible? Rome had riots and social upheaval when Paul and Peter wrote to the Roman Christians. Is it merely coincidence that the key passages about the Christian's response to public policy are contained in Romans 13 and 1 Peter 2 which were primarily directed to Roman Christians? Like the Galatians and the Corinthians, the Roman Christians had a special problem that the apostles dealt with.

Fifth, in criticizing the liberty of conscience understanding of the terms *good* and *evil* in Romans 13:1-7 and 1 Peter 2:13-17, many divine right critics fail to deal with the etymological argument. They simply deny its validity without supporting their charge. But what is the alternative? Do they want to argue that the Roman government was actually upholding the law of God or God's ways? Some apparently do.[167] Do they want to argue that the Roman state rewarded Christians and others who did good things that were well pleasing in the sight of God? If so, the divine right paradigm has a lot of explaining to do. Let it prove its adherent's assertions.

Sixth, some who fall within the divine right perspective have said that liberty of conscience adherents use "completely unproven assertion" without "real proof." Whether they are referring to biblical analysis or scientific analysis, this charge is odd. On the one hand, what the Bible says is absolute truth and authoritative too. That makes biblical analysis different than scientific analysis. One need not "prove" anything about the Bible. It is accepted by faith as revelation. All scholars can hope to do is bring biblical ideas to clearer light by enhanced study and application.

On the other hand, science does not really "prove" anything, and it does not necessarily uncover absolute truth. Scientists endeavor to explain and, if possible, to predict, based on observation, repetition, and theorizing. Some theories produced may be useful but they are never absolute truth or completely proven. Even the law of gravity is not absolute. If divine right critics would refer to some logical "proof" in such criticisms, meaning that within a deductive system there are no errors in a paradigm,

---

[167] Anecdotally, the author has heard from divine right pastors and critics that believe that Rome had no abortion policy (without citing evidence for this claim). The ancient Hippocratic Oath contained a requirement that a physician should not perform an abortion: "To please no one will I prescribe a deadly drug nor give advice which may cause his death. Nor will I give a woman a pessary [a device worn in the vagina] to procure abortion. But I will preserve the purity of my life and my art." Since Hippocratus of Cos lived from about 460BC to 357BC, abortion must have been a hot issue long before Paul and Peter wrote. Why should we believe that a Roman government that had no problem with murder, gladiator events, and infanticide would have any sort of policy restricting abortion? If one were making an assumption, the other policy evidence of the era would lead us to believe that abortion would have been condoned in Rome. If so, it is doubtful that the Apostles would have sanctioned believers to submit to abortion policy.

then they need to provide some clear examples of any errors made rather than making bald assertions.[168]

Furthermore, many critics of the liberty of conscience point of view are comforted by finding many commentators who agree with their definition of "conscience" (as it is used in Romans 13:5). Even if they are right, many Christians for good reason remain unconvinced. The term *conscience* is used in the New Testament to describe the discernment we have regarding what is good or bad. It is not always bad or good as defined by God, as was also the case with the Corinthian and Roman brethren who worried about the morality of eating meat sacrificed to idols (1 Corinthians 8:7-12; 10:25-29 and Romans 14:1-23). The conscience has to do with right and wrong, but not necessarily right or wrong in a moral sense as defined by God. Heaping up well-named and respected commentaries will not help critics if all the counsel ends up being erroneous.

Seventh, some critics declare that adherents of the liberty of conscience view are biased by a philosophical or economic prejudice, bias, "glaring anti-government slant," or "skewed argumentation." To begin with, this characteristically layman's charge begs the question: Are divine right adherents purely objective when they analyze an event or a biblical passage? Is there nothing from his cultural or mental context that creeps in to "filter" how he reads something or understands the world? Without arguing determinism or deconstructionism, we may certainly

---

[168] Anecdotally, the author has heard from at least one critic with a divine right framework claims to have found such an error by showing that since there was no driving regulation when Paul wrote, Paul could not have obligated Roman Christians to comply with driving regulations, and therefore Paul does not so obligate us. This is certainly true, as many adherents of liberty of conscience, Anabaptism, and theonomy would agree. Nevertheless, the principle of Romans 13:1-7 may well in some way be applied to modern driving regulation. Christians should submit to driving rules out of pragmatic expedience, just as the Roman Christians submitted to Rome's rules and taxes. Otherwise the state will clobber them *and* will cause Christians undue worry about what the state might do to them for violating its decree. But it seems that many such critics think that the state's rules are more absolute as a rule of life.

question whether or not anyone can be truly objective in his analysis. That is not to deny that scholars should and must try to *avoid* bringing in subjective biases. All honest researchers in theology and science attempt to do so.

Alternatively, if critics could rightly accuse liberty of conscience adherents of being dishonest and intentionally bringing bias into their analysis, purposely twisting the plain teaching of the Bible, they would have a strong argument. Otherwise, how can he say that he is a better, more objective scholar than others? What would be his rationale for attacking the character and judging the motives of a liberty of conscience scholar? Perhaps he does not like the conclusions of the economic sciences? Perhaps some critics have welfarist leanings that make them smack at any ideas to the contrary? Or, is he more of a slave to his own disciplinary framework than he is willing to admit? In scholarly endeavor, anyone who operates under a pretense of objectivity will have his work called into question. All any scholar can do is utilize the gifts and skills that he has acquired under Providence, and offer the "light" that he uncovers in humility, hoping for the amelioration of all concerned. He cannot be fairly expected to do more.

Eighth, some divine right adherents accuse the liberty of conscience paradigm of using a straw man argument, namely that divine right adherents (problematically) teach that Christians should bow to virtually every whim of public policy. This denial is rather odd since the divine right paradigm clearly represents that Christians should submit to nearly any public policy. There are only a few, limited public policies that qualify for disobedience (most of which no longer occur today), like prohibiting Gospel preaching or forcing people to commit murder—surely less than 1 percent of all public policy in effect. So it is not clear why a divine right adherent would call such a statement a straw man, unless he has not thoroughly thought through his own paradigm. The vast majority of divine right adherents would resist very few current public policies, perhaps a handful of the thousands on the books. How often do divine right pastors encourage their members to break the law?

Ninth, critics who hold to a divine right framework charge that the liberty of conscience view inappropriately extends the rightness of rebelling against public policies (like paying taxes), whereas civil disobedience should be restricted to only those policies that entail "a direct command to disobey God" (e.g., to stop gospel preaching, to murder, etc.). Presumably then, those critics would say that we must obey state authorities when they obligate us to violate premises from God's Word as well, so long as there is no clear, direct command to violate.

For instance, the Bible requires Christians to be good stewards (Luke 19:15-25, Matthew 25:15-28, Proverbs 13:22) and that Christian men provide for their families (1 Timothy 5:8). Naboth was a good steward of his vineyard (1 Kings 21:1-19) and refused to obey King Ahab by giving him the vineyard. That act was active, civil disobedience. Yet, when it comes to taxation today, many of these critics are dead sure that it is *sinful* to resist taxation on account of the stewardship principle. While Christians may resist a common thief or the mafia, they may never resist the well-organized civil government over money matters. But how can they be consistent in exalting one biblical principle and ignoring others in their paradigm?

The invading Israelites (who operated under direct command of course) did not submit to any king around them that they assailed. Would Christians in the American army been able to disobey Saddam Hussein during the War in Iraq, who would have had to obey him if they were living in Iraq before the war? Why? It is not clear that the divine right submission principle could be cogently applied to such a scenario. It is simply not acceptable for divine right pastors to cop out and say "I don't know" when asked such hard questions.

Furthermore, is it just for one government to rebel against another government in war? May the American state overthrow the Iraqi regime, while the Iraqis may not do so themselves? May Iraqi Christians not rebel without sinning but still remain righteous by petitioning or praying for deliverance by the hand of the American army? Needless to say, divine right advocates have a lot of convincing to do when it comes to such issues. In short, by this reasoning, the divine right paradigm raises far more questions than it purports to answer.

Alternatively, the liberty of conscience thesis says that the state may be disobeyed any time that the Christian believes that the state is making him do something contrary to what God would have him to do. What constitutes an offense depends on personal conviction and is thus a matter of Christian liberty. The divine right view promotes a far stricter rule, but it fails to come through with a workable practical theology for many circumstances in life.

One defective area of divine right thinking is how to deal with proactive public policy. Rome had no welfare state circa AD50, and those who claim otherwise are simply mistaken. Many divine right adherents argue that liberty of conscience adherents have incorrectly stated that there was no welfare state in Rome. Further, they say it is erroneous speculation to conclude that Paul would have qualified his obligation to believers to submit to the state if welfarism had indeed existed during his day. But why should we believe the divine right thesis that Paul and Peter would have ignored the welfare state had it existed, given that its central tenets run contrary to their clear teachings elsewhere against stealing, lying, idleness, etc.? It seems more plausible that the Apostles would *not* have advocated violating biblical principles through voluntarily complying with immoral proactive public policies. If a proactive policy is wicked, then it makes no difference that states or rulers carry it out. The practice must be rejected by Christians.

Recently, Dr. John Robbins of the Trinity Foundation completed an excellent account of the Roman Civilization entitled "Christ and Civilization."[169] This paper is useful in showing the character of the Roman civilization and thus confirming why accusations about liberty of conscience adherents practice eisegesis are spurious. The fact is that the liberty of conscience view sheds new light on an area of Scripture that has not yet been adequately dealt with, especially from a non-theonomic point of view. The Puritan and Baptist scholars in the Reformed heritage have been especially lacking in formulating a doctrine of government and public policy that is consistent with baptistic principles. Books like *Bible and Government* and *Turn Neither to the Right nor to the Left* have attempted to do so. In these works, scholarly sources and reasoning are utilized, and many erudite reviewers have lauded their theses. Christians that ultimately disagree with the liberty of conscience perspective would obviously want to use sound logic in making their case.

The idea that government is a special sphere of authority that holds special sway over Christian behavior regardless of what it does is something to be demonstrated or "proven" rather than assumed. The *Westminster Confession* and *Larger Catechism* may designate the state as a special sphere of authority,[170] and divine right advocates may agree with it, but it is not clear that the Bible grants such a special designation. It is odd, to say the least, that Baptists have adopted a quintessentially Presbyterian and integrated authority notion.

---

[169] John Robbins (2003), "Christ and Civilization", *The Trinity Review* (January-March); http://www.trinityfoundation.org.

[170] Unless the Larger Catechism's term "commonwealth" is taken to mean limited government restricted to reactive public policy instead of the proactive state.

Alternatively, more in line with Baptist principles, it is more plausible that states abscond with "rights" and subsume authority under the permissive decree of God in order to carry out their judgmental purpose. Christians submit inasmuch as they possibly can in order to stay out of the state's way. This view is far different than the divine right and integrated authority idea that says God created a special office called the state to promote His kingdom in the world, and thus gave it special rights over all its subjects, obligating believers to obey it in nearly all things.

Tenth, the divine right paradigm rejects as unjustified the liberty of conscience interpretation of the practical section of Paul's message to the Romans. It is wrong to claim that submission is to be pragmatic (practical) or expedient (especially as it was for that era—although not exclusively). This thesis is a key tenet of the liberty of conscience view. On several other occasions, the Bible demands an expedient response to public policy or rulers.

While the plain meaning of the text in Romans 13:1-7 could be taken as expedient or not, when these other expedient passages are taken into account, as well as other biblical principles, the liberty of conscience interpretation is best. Plus, the liberty of conscience interpretation is congruent with culture, history and scientific principles, all of which bolster the expedience thesis. A divine right understanding fits neither the other texts in the Bible nor the reality of life and history very well.

Liberty of conscience view mingled with divine right ideas

One of the most important questions for the Christian theology of public policy is "why" Christians submit to the state (or perhaps "when" they should), rather than "if" they must. Whether Christians should submit to state rulers is always relative, depending on *if* the ruler's decree would cause a Christian to sin against God in some way. A pure liberty of conscience perspective views all submission to states and rulers (whom ultimately form part of the kingdom of Satan) as necessary *when* the state actively places demands upon the believer—so long as obedience to the state would not require disobedience to God. But the reason *why* is simply expedient: to avoid wrath and worry, as well as to not cause problems for our ministries in church and family, and certainly never to detract from the glory of God.

However, some people who otherwise like the liberty of conscience perspective are not comfortable with this idea of when and why. They still see something mystical about the authority of the state's edicts, allowing them to retain comfortable dialog on public policy issues with divine righters. There is no fear of man when one can mollify those holding to the prevailing view.

Accordingly, stemming from the divine right doctrine, a variant opinion has mutated out of the liberty of conscience view. Public policy, especially when it mimics the law of Christ, is viewed as being morally binding on believers in most cases. But in an attempt to guide believers' consciences and deal more straightforwardly with the apostolic commands to submit to the state, a formula is constructed to help determine whether or not an act of civil disobedience is *sinful*.

If a policy is *violated*	+	If a Christian is *aware* of the violation	+	If a policy is being *enforced*	=	*Unsubmissiveness* (sinful behavior)

This formula is subject to two meta-principles that can trump the equation. First, there is the guiding principle of formal versus informal process. That is, even though a public policy is active and is being enforced, the "spirit" of the policy may dominate in practice. There is often some leeway in Christian civil obedience. For instance, the posted speed limit might be 65mph (the formal aspect).

288

However, in practice (the informal aspect), only violations over 70mph are enforced. Hence, a Christian may use his liberty to drive a little bit over the speed limit and still not be sinning. So long as the probability of enforcement is zero (or very close to it), a Christian does not sin by breaking the "letter of the law" of a public policy. Whenever there is even a small possibility of enforcement, the Christian sins by knowingly breaking the law.

Second, there is the guiding principle of bringing every activity to bear under the hierarchy of biblical conventions. In other words, if there is a public policy that prohibits free medical care of poor people, or that attempts to force women to be sterilized after their second child is born, it could be disobeyed on account of a higher principle in God's Word. Christians have a positive command to care for the poor, and it is God who grants life and family—not the state. The same principle would apply in emergency situations (i.e. speeding while rushing to a hospital delivery room), since it is more important to serve one's wife's needs than to comply with stated public policy stricture. Christians are also absolved from obeying any policy that harms their neighbor, whether the policy is Hitler's Jewish extermination campaign or one that mandates reporting truant pupils to the public school authorities.

The formula also implies that any archaic public policies do *not* have to be obeyed. A Christian is *not* bound to apprise himself of all public policies of each new political jurisdiction before he enters it. A Christian does *not* sin if he violates a public policy when he is ignorant of it. He is also absolved from moral guilt if he disobeys any policy that is not enforced.

The weakness of this variant can be seen especially is these latter criteria, since the whole system and formula becomes not only subjective but also rather arbitrary and capricious. Each believer is left to decide for himself how fast he can drive without sinning, or if he should dodge the military draft. He also has wide latitude to decide whether urgent circumstances are so important that public policy stricture does not apply. Moreover, this variant view can be criticized like the divine right view, since one can avoid sinning by remaining as ignorant as possible of all public policy. Otherwise, given that there is no revealed truth to determine particulars, each believer is left to his liberty to develop his personal convictions about when he has sinned.

A pastor would hardly have recourse to reprove, rebuke or exhort a member of his flock for an act of civil disobedience with which he disagreed so long as the believer was acting out of conviction. Unless the member were doing something egregious, like driving 120mph in a posted 65mph zone, it would be hard for a pastor to make a case against the behavior. Thus, the expediency piece of the liberty of conscience view, which escapes these problems and is widely congruent with biblical principles, provides the most robust and cogent liberty of conscience view.

Another even more fundamental flaw is the implication that the state's decrees carry some moral weight or that rulers become oracles of God for a Christian. The only law that can carry moral weight is God's law. Man's law, more appropriately termed legislation,[171] does

---

[171] Regarding the important distinction between law and legislation, see Friedrich A. von Hayek (1973), *Law, Legislation and Liberty*, Chicago: University of Chicago Press. Hayek viewed the law as the embodied evolution of useful legal designs which have been adopted by society. Although Hayek was not a Christian, his understanding of law would certainly include the fact that God is the ultimate originator of all moral codes and laws. Applications of the common law of property, contract and tort have been improved by increases in social knowledge over time, undergoing a process of evolutionary improvements through marginal changes. Thus, law is not the invention of the state. Law arises from God and is modified in application spontaneously as a result of human action. Conversely, legislation represents the rules of men. It is "law" made by state edict, and should not be confused with antecedent law. As Hayek comments: "Legislation, the deliberate making of law, has justly been described as among all inventions of man the one fraught with the gravest consequences, more far-reaching in its effects even than fire and gun-powder. Unlike law itself, which has never been 'invented' in the same sense, the invention of legislation came relatively late in the history of mankind. It gave into the hands of men an instrument of great

not carry moral authority just because it carries legal authority. Legislation may be amoral or immoral but may only be moral insofar as it mimics the law of the Great Lawgiver.

power which they needed to achieve some good, but which they have not yet learned so to control that it may not produce great evil. It opened to man wholly new possibilities and gave him a new sense of power over his fate. The discussion about who should possess this power has, however, unduly overshadowed the much more fundamental question of how far this power should extend. It will certainly remain an exceedingly dangerous power so long as we believe that it will do harm only if wielded by bad men. Law in the sense of enforced rules of conduct is undoubtedly coeval with society; only the observance of common rules makes the peaceful existence of individuals in society possible" (p. 72). Thus, legislation and law have different origins.

Appendix 2:
Questions and Taxonomy of the Four Christian Views of Public Policy

Table 4: Perspectives on key issues of the four views

Issue 1	
Perspective	*Views the source or foundation of the state's rules as...*
Theonomy	►God's law when the state is a covenant-keeper; men or Satan otherwise
Divine Right	►Providence; the state speaks God's will to the church/its subjects as God's servant (or oracle)
Anabaptist	►Providence; He is doing His will in the competing realm; a few would say Satan
Liberty of Conscience	►Satan (Revelation 13:2b, 4a; cf. 12:9a), or at least the state's own cultural or moral standard

Issue 2	
Perspective	*The nature of the state is...*
Theonomy	►Evil if a covenant-breaker, good if dominated by covenant-keepers
Divine Right	►Benign: Good when good men run it and bad when bad men run it
Anabaptist	►A realm that competes with God's Kingdom (some regard as evil)
Liberty of Conscience	►Evil: the greatest source of oppression and affliction besides false religion in history

Issue 3	
Perspective	*Military service and the draft are ...*
Theonomy	▶Morally permissible under some circumstances
Divine Right	▶Morally permissible under Providence
Anabaptist	▶Not on the radar screen for a pacifist (making the draft a bad thing too)
Liberty of Conscience	▶Often morally permissible, esp. for just war (the draft is bad when it is proactive policy)

Issue 4	
Perspective	*Yes or no: "The primary role of the state is bringing terrestrial judgment upon sinners or harassing the church under God's permissive decree."*
Theonomy	▶No
Divine Right	▶No
Anabaptist	▶Yes, but also sees a role for the state in punishing criminals, etc.
Liberty of Conscience	▶Yes

Issue 5	
Perspective	*Yes or no: "The primary role of the state is promoting or upholding the kingdom of God in the world."*
Theonomy	▶Yes
Divine Right	▶Yes
Anabaptist	▶No
Liberty of Conscience	▶No

Issue 6	
Perspective	*The state is "ordained" by God just as ...*
Theonomy	▶Family and church (cf. the *Westminster Larger Catechism*)
Divine Right	▶Family and church
Anabaptist	▶Any other thing God ordains outside of His Kingdom
Liberty of Conscience	▶Satan, the "god of this age" (2 Corinthians 4:4a)

293

Issue 7	
Perspective	The church's role in political life is...
Theonomy	► The church preaches to the state and the state enforces God's Law; transforming the state (dominion mandate)
Divine Right	► Supportive and active, endeavoring to promote "better" legislation with more God-honoring rules
Anabaptist	► The church should have nothing to do with the state or politics; Christians sin by participating in it
Liberty of Conscience	► The church should not provoke the state, and must not hope that the state will help it achieve its godly ends; individual Christian involvement is left as a matter of conscience

Issue 8	
Perspective	Open rebellion, revolution or resistance to the state is...
Theonomy	► Revolution laudable and right when against a covenant-breaking state and led by a lower magistrate; resistance is morally right when resisting a covenant breaking state, otherwise wrong
Divine Right	► Revolution generally sinful; resistance ok for a few items like prohibiting preaching the gospel and forced abortion
Anabaptist	► Armed revolution wrong but rebellion unavoidable when the state intrudes into the life of the believer; resistance unavoidable but not to be sought after
Liberty of Conscience	► Revolution morally permissible so long as no other sin is committed by doing so; can be led by anyone; resistance morally right whenever it can be done without bringing public shame on Christ or wrath on the church, and when no other sin is being committed by doing so

Issue 9	
Perspective	*The godly goal of revolution would be...*
Theonomy	▶Bring down a covenant-breaking ruler
Divine Right	▶Unlikely (if ever) to be ascertained
Anabaptist	▶Unattainable since not permissible for believers
Liberty of Conscience	▶If it can be done wisely, to bring glory to God, and to benefit the church

Issue 10	
Perspective	*Lying to the state (e.g., hiding Jews from Hitler, not reporting all income on a tax return, etc.) is...*
Theonomy	▶Morally right when resisting a covenant breaking state
Divine Right	▶Generally sinful
Anabaptist	▶Unclear, but likely right or OK when it promotes God's glory; tendency to shun taxes for warfare (possibly via lying)
Liberty of Conscience	▶Morally right when it can truly be used to promote life, stewardship, and God's glory

Issue 11	
Perspective	*Yes or no: "Public policy is useful to promote good behavior (i.e., legislating morality)."*
Theonomy	▶Yes
Divine Right	▶Yes
Anabaptist	▶No, other than crime control
Liberty of Conscience	▶No

Issue 12	
Perspective	*Yes or no: "It is our duty to report 'tax protesters' or other rule breakers to the state."*
Theonomy	▶No, unless a covenant-keeping state were in power
Divine Right	▶Yes
Anabaptist	▶No
Liberty of Conscience	▶No

Bibliography

Adams, John Quincy (1837), *An Oration Delivered Before the Inhabitants of the Town of Newburyport, at Their Request, on the Sixty-First Anniversary of the Declaration of Independence*, July 4th, 1837, Newburyport: Charles Whipple.

Bahnsen, Greg L. (1991), *By This Standard: The Authority of God's Law Today*, Tyler, Texas: Institute for Christian Economics.

Bahnsen, Greg L. (1977 [2002]), *Theonomy in Christian Ethics*, third Edition, Nacogdoches, Texas: Covenant Media Press; also published in 1979 by the Craig Press, Nutley, N.J.

Bahnsen, Greg L. (1994), "What is Theonomy?", *New Horizons* (April), Covenant Media Foundation, sec. 5.

Bastiat, Frederic (1990 [1850]), *The Law*, Irvington-on-Hudson, New York: The Foundation for Economic Education.

Beeman, Richard R. (2005), "A republic, if you can keep it", National Constitution Center (online text), http://www.constitutioncenter.org/explore/ThreePerspectivesontheConstitution/ARepublic,IfYouCanKeepIt.shtml.

Bennett, Walter, ed. (1975), *Letters from the Federal Farmer to the Republican*, Tuscaloosa, Alabama: University of Alabama Press.

Bonhoeffer, Dietrich (1995 [1959]), *The Cost of Disciple-ship*, New York: Simon & Schuster (Touchstone).

Bovard, James (1991), *The Fair Trade Fraud: How Congress Pillages the Consumer and Decimates America's Competitiveness*, New York: St. Martin's Press.

Buchanan, James M. (1991), "Private Preferences to Public Philosophy: The Development of Public Choice", in James M. Buchanan, *Constitutional Economics*, Basil Blackwell: Cambridge, Massachusetts.

Buchanan, James M. (1980), "Rent Seeking and Profit Seeking", in James Buchanan, Robert Tollison, and Gordon Tullock, eds., *Toward a Theory of The Rent-Seeking Society*, Texas A&M University Pr: College Station, Texas, pp. 3-15.

Buchanan, James M. and Tullock, Gordon (1962), *The Calculus of Consent: The Logical Foundations of Constitutional Democracy*, University of Michigan Press: Ann Arbor, Michigan.

Calvin, John (1960 [1559]), *Institutes of the Christian Religion*, John T. McNeill (editor), Ford Lewis Battles (translator), Westminster: John Knox Press.

Cobin, John M. (2003), *A Primer on Modern Themes in Free Market Economics and Policy*, revised e-book ed., Greenville, South Carolina: Alertness Books.

Cobin, John M. (2003), *Bible and Government: Public Policy from a Christian Perspective*, Greenville, South Carolina: Alertness Books.

Cobin, John M. (1997), *Building Regulation, Market Alternatives, and Allodial Policy*, London: Avebury Press.

Coxe, Tench (1789), "Remarks on the First Part of the Amendments to the Federal Constitution", (writing under the pseudonym "A Pennsylvanian"), *Philadelphia Federal Gazette*, June 18, page 2, col. 1, along with Coxe's follow-up piece in the *Pennsylvania Federal Gazette*, Feb. 20, 1788).

Dabney, Robert L. (1979 [1897]), *Discussions, Secular*, Vallecito, California: Ross House Books.

DiLorenzo, Thomas J. (2004), *How Capitalism Saved America*, New York: Crown Forum.

Eidsmoe, John (1984), *God and Caesar*, Westchester, Illinois: Crossway Books.

Franklin, Benjamin (1987 [1789]), "An Address to the Public from the Pennsylvania Society for Promoting the Abolition of Slavery", in Benjamin Franklin, *Writings*, New York: Library of America.

Grenz, Stanley (1983), *Isaac Backus: Puritan and Baptist*, Macon, Georgia: Mercer University Press.

Gribben, Crawford (2003), *The Irish Puritans: James Ussher and the Reformation of the Church*, Auburn, Massachusetts: Evangelical Press.

Gruenler, Royce Gordon (1989), *Evangelical Commentary on the New Testament*, Walter A. Elwell (ed.), Grand Rapids, Michigan: Baker Book House.

Gwinn, Matthew (1997) [1603], *Nero*, Act V, Scene 4 [Act II, Scene 1], Volusius Proculus, Epicharis, Dana F. Sutton, trans.

Hall, David W. (1996), *Savior or Servant: Putting Government in its Place*, Oak Ridge, Tennessee: The Kuyper Institute (the Covenant Foundation).

Hayek, Friedrich A. von (1973), *Law, Legislation and Liberty*, University of Chicago Press: Chicago.

Hayek, Friedrich A. von (1988), *The Fatal Conceit: The Errors of Socialism*, University of Chicago Press: Chicago.

Hayek, Friedrich A. von (1944), *The Road to Serfdom*, University of Chicago Press: Chicago.

Hayek, Friedrich A. von (1945), "The Use of Knowledge in Society", *American Economic Review*, vol. 35, no. 4, September, pp. 519-530.

Heilbroner, Robert (1990), "After Communism", *The New Yorker*, September 10, p. 92.

Henry, Matthew (1721), *Commentary on the Whole Bible*, vol. VI, Grand Rapids, Michigan: Christian Classics Ethereal Library (e-book reprint).

Hoeksema, Herman (1969), *Behold He Cometh: An Exposition of the Book of Revelation*, Grand Rapids, Michigan: Reformed Free Publishing Association.

Jamieson, Robert, A. R. Fausset and David Brown (1871), *Commentary Critical and Explanatory on the Whole Bible*, Grand Rapids, Michigan: Christian Classics Ethereal Library (e-book reprint).

Jones, Alonzo T. (1891), *The Two Republics or Rome and the United States of America*, Battle Creek, Michigan: Review and Herald Publishing Company.

Josephus, Flavius (1999), *The Wars of the Jews*, William Whiston, trans., book II, 13:1, Grand Rapids, Michigan: Kregal Publications.

Knox, Vicesimus (1824 [1795]), *The Works of Vicesimus Knox*, vols. V and VI, London: J. Mawman.

Locke, John (1980 [1690]), *Second Treatise of Government*, Cambridge, Massachusetts: Hackett Publishing Company.

Luther, Martin (1972 [1545]), "Preface to the Letter of St. Paul to the Romans", Andrew Thornton (trans.), "Vorrede auff die Epistel S. Paul: an die Romer" in *D. Martin Luther: Die gantze Heilige Schrifft Deudsch 1545 aufs new zurericht*, Hans Volz and Heinz Blanke (eds.), Munich: Roger & Bernhard, vol. 2, pp. 2254-2268.

Macarthur, John (1994), *Romans 9-16* (Macarthur New Testament Commentary), Chicago: Moody Publishers.

McDowell, Stephen (2003), "The Bible, Slavery, and America's Founders", online text: http://www.wallbuilders.com/resources/search/detail.php?ResourceID=

McGarvey, J. W. and Philip Y. Pendleton (1916), *Thessalonians, Corinthians, Galatians and Romans*, vol. 3, Cincinnati, Ohio: The Standard Publishing Company.

McLoughlin, William G., ed., (1968), *Isaac Backus on Church, State, and Calvinism: Pamphlets, 1754-1789*, Cambridge: Belknap Press.

Mises, Ludwig von (1996 [1966/1949]), *Human Action: A Treatise on Economics*, fourth revised edition, Irvington-on-Hudson, New York: The Foundation for Economic Education.

Mises, Ludwig von (1985/1957), *Theory and History: An Interpretation of Social and Economic Evolution*, Auburn, Alabama: The Ludwig von Mises Institute.

Murray, Iain H. (1982), *David Martyn Lloyd-Jones: The First Forty Years*, Carlisle, Penn The Banner of Truth Trust.

Nock, Albert J. (1994 [1943]), *Memoirs of a Superfluous Man*, Tampa, Florida: Hallberg Publishing Corp

Nock, Albert J. (2001 [1935]), *Our Enemy the State*, Tampa, Florida: Hallberg Publishing Corp. (expanded edition).

Noll, Mark A. (1977), *Christians in the American Revolution*, Grand Rapids, Michigan: W. B. Eerdmans & Co.

Noll, Mark A. (1995), *The Scandal of the Evangelical Mind*, Grand Rapids, Michigan: W.B. Eerdmans & Co.

North, Gary (1973), *An Introduction to Christian Economics*, Nutley, New Jersey: Craig Press.

North, Gary (1989), *Political Polytheism: The Myth of Pluralism*, Tyler, Texas: The Institute for Christian Economics.

North, Gary (1991), *Theonomy: An Informed Response*, Tyler, Texas: The Institute for Christian Economics.

Opitz, Edmund (1999), *The Libertarian Theology of Freedom*, Tampa, Florida: Hallberg Publishing Co.

Paine, Thomas (1982 [1776]), *Common Sense*, London: Penguin Classics.

Piper, John (2003), "Wages from sin: Churches should not accept money won from gambling", *World Magazine* (January 11): vol. 18, no. 1.

Robbins, John (2003), "Christ and Civilization", *The Trinity Review* (January-March), http://www.trinityfoundation.org.

Rummel, Rudolph (1994), *Death by Government: Genocide and Mass Murder Since 1900*, New Brunswick, New Jersey: Transaction Publishers.

Rushdoony, Rousas John (1974), *By What Standard? An Analysis of the Philosophy of Cornelious Van Til*, Fairfax, Virginia: Thoburn Press.

Rushdoony, Rousas John (1984 [1977]), *God's Plan for Victory: The Meaning of Postmillennialism*, Fairfax, Virginia: Thoburn Press.

Rushdoony, Rousas John (1973), *The Institutes of Biblical Law*, Nutley, New Jersey: Craig Press.

Rushdoony, Rousas John (1995 [1963]), *The Messianic Character of American Education*, Vallecito, California: Ross House Books.

Rushdoony, Rousas John (1971), *The One and the Many: Studies in the Philosophy of Order and Ultimacy*, Nutley, New Jersey: Craig Press.

Rutherford, Samuel (1980 [1644]), *Lex, Rex, or the Law and the Prince: A Dispute for the Just Prerogative of King and People*, Harrisonburg, Virginia: Sprinkle Publications.

Schaeffer, Francis A. (1982), *A Christian Manifesto*, Westchester, Illinois: Crossway Books.

Schaeffer, Francis A. (1982), *The Complete Works of Francis Schaeffer*, vol. 1, Westchester, Illinois: Crossway Books.

Schansberg, D. Eric (1996), *Poor Policy: How Government Harms the Poor*, Boulder, Colorado: Westview Press.

Schansberg, D. Eric (2003), *Turn Neither to the Right nor to the Left*, Greenville, South Carolina: Alertness Books.

Shortt, Bruce N. (2004), *The Harsh Truth About Public Schools*, Vallecito, Calif.: Chalcedon Foundation.

Sienkiewicz, Henryk (2002), *Quo Vadis: A Narrative of the Time of Nero*, Jeremiah Curtin trans., McClean, Virginia: Indypublish.com.

Smith, Adam (1994 [1776]), *An Inquiry into the Nature and Causes of the Wealth of Nations*, New York: Modern Library.

Sowell, Thomas (1995), *The Vision of the Anointed: Self-Congratulation as the Basis for Social Policy*, New York: Basic Books.

Stout, Harry S. (1996), "How Preachers Incited Revolution", *Christianity Today*, issue 50 (May), vol. 15, no. 2, p. 10.

Tacitus, Cornelius Historiae (2003), *The Annals and the History*, 15.44.2-8, Alfred John Church and William Jackson Brodribb trans., New York: Modern Library Press.

Tollison, Robert D. (1988), "Public Choice and Legislation", *Virginia Law Review*, vol. 74, no. 2, March, pp. 339-71.

Tollison, Robert D. (1982), "Rent Seeking: a Survey", *Kyklos*, vol. 35, fasc. 4, pp. 575-602.

Tullock, Gordon (1959), "Problems of Majority Voting", *Journal of Political Economy*, vol. 67, pp. 571-579.

Tullock, Gordon (1993), *Rent Seeking*, The Shaftesbury Papers, no. 2, Edward Elgar Publishing Co.: Brookfield, Vermont.

Tullock, Gordon (1988a), "Rent Seeking and Tax Reform", *Contemporary Policy Issues*, vol. 6, October, pp. 37-47.

Tullock, Gordon (1988b), *Wealth, Poverty, and Politics*, Basil Blackwell: New York.

Vance, Laurence M. (2005), *Christianity and War and Other Essays Against the Warfare State*, Pensacola, Florida: Vance Publications.

Vance, Laurence M. (2005), "The Early Christian Attitude to War," published on www.Lewrockwell.com, 7 pages, http://www.lewrockwell.com/vance/vance60.html.

Vance, Laurence M. (2005), "Vicesimus Knox: Minister of Peace," published on www.Lewrockwell.com, 16 pages, http://www.lewrockwell.com/vance/vance59.html.

Waldron, Samuel E. (1989), *The 1689 Baptist Confession of Faith: A Modern Exposition*, Darlington, England: Evangelical Press.

Willson, James M. (1853), *Civil Government: An Exposition of Romans xiii. 1-7*, Philadelphia: William S. Young.

Yates, Steven (2005), *Worldviews: Christian Theism Versus Modern Materialism*, Greenville, South Carolina: The Worldviews Project.

Index of subjects

305

310

313

314

315

316

318

322

323

Index of Scripture references

326

327

331

Index of names

About the author

Dr. John Cobin is a financial planner in Greenville, South Carolina. He was the host of *Christian Worldview with Dr. John Cobin*, a weekday morning radio talk show (see http://www.tyrannyresponse.net for web archives). He writes a weekly column for *The Times Examiner* and *Free Market News* (see http://freemarketnews.com). He teaches MBA courses online in economics and public policy for LeTourneau University in Longview, Texas and elsewhere. In 2001-2002 he was an adjunct professor at two private universities in California along with the University of California, Santa Barbara Extension program in Ventura. Previously he was a manager of a research department in Goleta, California, as well as a public policy consultant in Cambria, California and Santiago, Chile.

Moreover, Dr. Cobin retains his status as Visiting Professor of Economics and Public Policy at Universidad Francisco Marroquín, Guatemala. In prior years (1996-2000), he taught at universities in Chile, including Universidad Católica in Santiago, Chile, the International MBA program at Universidad Adolfo Ibañez, Viña del Mar, Chile, plus the MBA program at Universidad del Desarrollo in Santiago (also in Concepción), Chile. He worked at Universidad Finis Terrae in Santiago, Chile as a full time professor for nearly 4 years.

Dr. Cobin is active in public policy research and writing. He received his ARE from Reformed Bible College, his BA in Business Economics from California State University, Long Beach (1985), his MA in Business Economics from University of California, Santa Barbara (1987), and both his MA in Economics (1995) and his PhD in Public Policy (1996) from George Mason University.

Dr. Cobin's research has focused on evaluating urban public policies such as zoning, building and fire safety regulation, and highway construction, as well as theoretical ways to reduce economic problems associated with them (e.g., his book *Building Regulation, Market Alternatives, and Allodial Policy*, 1997). He has also written about applied microeconomic topics, policy issues such as abortion, and this introductory text *A Primer on Modern Themes in Free Market Economics and Policy* (1999) covering public choice, Austrian economics, law and economics, and public policy themes—also published in Spanish as *Ensayos Sobre Temas Modernos de la Economía y Política del Mercado* (1999 and 2003). Dr. Cobin's provocative book *Bible and Government: Public Policy from a Christian Perspective* (2003) deals with the nature of the state and the interrelation between Christian action and public policy.

In addition to his academic work, Dr. Cobin has been a successful entrepreneur and consultant, having started and operated several small businesses. He is married with seven homeschooled children. His widely-visited website http://www.PolicyOfLiberty.net and http://www.PoliticaPublica.cl (English and Spanish) contains his papers and information about his books, as well as a number of popular pages for free market links, quotations for liberty, and more.

Other Books by Dr. Cobin

A Primer on Modern Themes in Free Market Economics and Policy

A Primer on Modern Themes in Free Market Economics and Policy

JOHN M. COBIN

1	Ideas and interest groups in economics and public policy
2	Capture theory and antitrust
3	Rent seeking
4	The calculus of consent, vote-seeking, and Virginia vs. Chicago political economy
5	Public policy and public choice
6	Public choice issues for regulation
7	Ludwig von Mises: a compendium of his classically liberal thought
8	Austrian methodology and the knowledge problem
9	Entrepreneurship: an Austrian perspective
10	Interventionism: an Austrian critique
11	The Austrian business cycle and free banking
12	Market failure fiction
13	The economic analysis of law
14	Cases and criticisms in law and economics with a focus on property rights
15	Allodialism as economic policy

Paperback (564 pages), Dimensions (in inches): 8.50 x 1.42 x 5.50
Publisher: Universal Publishers, Parkland, Florida, www.Upublish.Com
ISBN 1-5811279-1-X first ed. (Dec. 1999) or PDF ISBN 0-9725418-2-9
PDF revised ed. from Alertness Books Online: http://PolicyOfLiberty.net/checkout/products.php

$29.95 or $7.95 PDF—at www.PolicyOfLiberty.net & Amazon.com

A Primer on Modern Themes in Free Market Economics and Policy provides an overview of the major themes of market economics and public policy that are making inroads into the mainstream of thought.

Free market economics has made many advances during the past twenty years. These advances are due to the maturing of public choice theory and empirical studies, along with a resurgence of interest in Austrian economic themes like free banking, market process entrepreneurship, and the critique of socialism and interventionism. In addition, new avenues have opened in law and economics and regulatory studies that favor free market ideas.

The purpose of this book is to introduce and summarize some of the important advances in contemporary free market economics and policy. Many free market thinkers have been cited which will help acquaint the reader with many key contributors and their contributions.

The book is designed for a variety of uses:

- as a textbook in an economics elective course,
- as a textbook in an economics-based social science elective for advanced undergraduates in political science, public administration, legal studies, or public policy,
- for academics, free market advocates, policy analysts, or serious intellectual readers (with some knowledge of economics or political science) who want to gain a broad understanding of free market motifs,
- as a textbook to facilitate discussion in an MBA or law school elective course in regulation, and
- in some cases, the text could be the basis for an upper-division required trampoline course in economics or business programs, especially in universities which offer advanced electives in public choice, Austrian economics, law and economics, regulation, and public policy.

In the latter case, a course following this book would serve as a springboard to more in-depth studies, especially when the general focus is on regulation and policy. The book is purposefully eclectic, in that it does not favor any single branch of free market theory. There are five public choice chapters (1, 2, 3, 4 and 6), five Austrian economics chapters (7, 8, 9, 10, and 11), three chapters on public policy themes (5, 12, and 15), and two chapters on law and economics (13 and 14).

There are many long quotations in some parts of the book so that students (or even a casual reader) may have some direct exposure to the theorists behind the ideas. This format should prove to be a effective teaching device, and hopefully encourage classroom discussion of the statements by the various free market theorists. Indeed, the quotations should be exploited for their full pedagogical value given that they will likely represent the lion's share of many students' direct exposure to key free market theorists. As an additional exercise, I typically require students to memorize the definitions of rent seeking, free banking, public goods, and the Coase Theorem because I think they will be useful during other courses and their academic and professional careers.

The weights for each area of analysis in the book are (roughly):

Public choice	34%
Austrian economics	29%
Law and economics	18%
Public policy	19%

However, there is always considerable overlap between the topics and students will usually spend more time studying outside class for the relatively copious law and economics and public policy portions.

Professional praise for the book

"This is the best textbook I have seen on market economics, and I would recommend it to anyone whose main task is to teach economics or to those who want to understand how the economy works." —Dr. Alejandro A. Chafuen, President & CEO, Atlas Economic Research Foundation, Fairfax, Virginia, USA.

"I had the chance to read John Cobin's book....I believe it is an excellent work covering certain areas largely unattended by economic textbooks. His treatment of the contributions to economic science by the "Public Choice", "Austrian" and "Law & Economics" schools give readers the fundamental elements for a right understanding of the functioning of a market economy. The book, besides, successfully fulfills the goal of bringing to the Spanish reader the main concepts of these schools, which are not easy to access in that language. Finally, I must say I plan to use the book for my own classes." —Dr. Martín Krause, Rector, Escuela Superior de Economía y Administración de Empresas (ESEADE), Buenos Aires, Argentina.

"I would not be able to hold any class on Economics without having read this book." —Mario Jaramillo, Lawyer and Economist in Madrid, Spain. Winner of the Ludwig von Mises International Essay Prize in 1991 and 1992, Scholar and former Dean of Economics at Sergio Arboleda University in Bogotá, Colombia.

"Nowadays it is very difficult to recommend a textbook to undergraduate students about political economy since, strangely, many economists who produce written material for economics classes are hostile to the market economy. John Cobin's work accomplishes the huge task of providing fresh minds with a book that has a genuine understanding of the principles of free market economics and of the way(s) these principles function (with a special focus on public policy)." —Atilla Yayla, Professor of Politics and Political Economy, Hacettepe University, Ankara, Turkey; President of the Association for Liberal Thinking, Ankara, Turkey.

"John Cobin has provided us with a great service, given that the literature available in Spanish on these themes is scarce—especially at the university level. Moreover, his treatment of the topics is exhaustive and teaching-oriented (a rare combination), on account of which I predict that it will be of great use to both students and professors. 100 points!" —Julio H. Cole, Professor of Economics, Universidad Francisco Marroquín (Guatemala).

"This is a book about new ideas, or the revitalization of older ideas to which modern experience has given new force. If, as it has been often said, nothing is stronger than a timely new idea, here we find given another gigantic step in the classically liberal revolution, opening unexpected perspectives and possibilities to advance individual economic liberty, to increase productive efficiency, and to bolster individual creativity in post-modern society." —Hermógenes Pérez de Arce, editorialist for *El Mercurio* in Santiago, Chile.

"Cobin's *Primer* is a wonderful addition to the corpus of economic and public policy texts. Cobin's new text provides a useful survey and explication of free market themes and their application to public policy. Moreover, the *Primer* has an enormous advantage over most other economic texts: it is based on sound economics and an appreciation of the signal importance of property rights. The text is permeated with insights from Ludwig von Mises, the most important thinker of the 20th Century, and the Austrian School of Economics to which Mises belonged. In addition to critiquing socialist and Keynesian economic nostrums, Cobin does not shrink from subjecting even other "free-market" economic schools, such as Chicago, to criticism as it strays from the individualist and subjectivist anchors of Austrian economics.

Consistent with the Austrian economic view pervading the book, Cobin quite properly focuses on the crucial importance of property rights. He provides a fascinating introduction to his own—admirably absolutist—theory of private property ownership, which he calls allodialism. The *Primer* also introduces the reader to the revolutionary and astounding Austrian-Misesian critique of socialism. This is a great textbook on market economics without the socialist, Keynesian, and relativist flaws that permeate most other, mainstream texts. It is sure to contribute to enhanced understanding of both economics and public policy.

Of particular interest for attorneys and law professors, the *Primer* also analyzes the proper role of law and politics in economics, and of the role of economic theory in shaping law. Cobin shows how economic analysis should be used in both the study and development of law. He discusses the importance of legal certainty, the dangers of legislated law, the advantages of decentralized legal systems such as the common law, and the appropriate role of judges in the formation of law. The *Primer* would make an excellent teaching aid in law school classes focusing on law and economics or public policy.

With its incorporation of woefully neglected but cutting-edge economic theory, the *Primer* is a perfect free market text for the new millennium. Cobin has produced a work of great merit and value." —N. Stephan Kinsella, Attorney and Adjunct Law Professor at South Texas College of Law in Houston, Texas; co-author, *Protecting Foreign Investment Under International Law: Legal Aspects of Political Risk* (Oceana Publications, 1997), co-editor, *Digest of Commercial Laws of the World* (Oceana Publications 1998-present). LL.M., University of London; J.D., M.S., B.S., Louisiana State University.

Building Regulation, Market Alternatives, and Allodial Policy

with foreword by Walter Williams, Ph.D.

Introduction	
1	A case study on building fire safety (Baltimore)
2	A case study on building quality (mostly rural counties in West Virginia and Pennsylvania)
3	Market-regulatory alternatives (rare coin and gemstone industries)
4	A policy overview of American allodialism
5	Concluding implications for public policy
Appendix A	Shepardizing results of important cases
Appendix B	Chronological important case citations with topics

Paperback (252 pages), Dimensions (in inches): 0.69 x 9.10 x 6.12
Publisher iUniverse.com ISBN 0595141374 (February 2001)
PDF published by Alertness Books ISBN 0-9725418-4-5 (January 2003)
Online store: http://PolicyOfLiberty.net/checkout/products.php

$16.95 or $5.95 PDF—at www.PolicyOfLiberty.net & Amazon.com

This book provides evidence (via two case studies) of government's failure (in the USA) to regulate building safety and quality, at least insofar as the public interest is concerned. Market regulatory alternatives are suggested that could conceivably replace government regulation. In addition, allodial policy is suggested as an alternative to replace current real property policy. On the one hand, government regulation of building safety and quality does not always improve either safety or quality. On the other hand, market alternatives, which work well in other sectors, like the purely market regulated rare coin industry, could be used instead to improve effectiveness and efficiency. Moreover, allodial real property policy would be a viable alternative for alleviating many of the problems that might have led to government failure, including public choice and knowledge problems. This book will be of interest to academics and people in the architecture and building industry, or in urban planning.

Otto Scott's *Compass* (vol. 6, issue 66, February 1, 1996, reviewing an early draft of the book) says: "Mr. Cobin's dissertation makes appallingly clear by citing a long line of court decisions, property rights in a real sense have ceased to exist in this land [of the United States]. To be allowed mere possession of our homes and land only as long as we pay taxes has been to reduce us to the condition of serfs."

Pro-Life Policy: A Perspective for Liberty and Human Rights

Publisher: Gemini Books ISBN: 1929017189 (Sept. 1999). Reprinted by Alertness Books (Jan. 2003—PDF format ISBN: 0-9725418-6-1.
Online store: http://PolicyOfLiberty.net/checkout/products.php

$2.95 PDF (133 p.)—at www.PolicyOfLiberty.net & Amazon.com

This book provides a non-religious, classically liberal defense of the pro-life position derived from economic and public policy analysis, as well as moral philosophy. The debate over abortion at an academic level is quite different that what is popularly discussed. It is rare to find pro-choice academics who reject the fact that the zygote/fetus is a life and a human being, or that abortion is the taking of a life (the killing of a human being). The debate is over personhood. From a policy and legal point of view, justification for killing the unborn may be based not only on the famous Supreme Court case *Roe v. Wade*, but on an even more fundamental and ancient legal doctrine. The unborn are human beings but they are not yet persons, and thus have no right to life.

Academic abortion-rights advocates argue that some human beings, notably unborn ones, are not persons because public policy or some other social convention has not conferred rights upon them. This philosophy is not new, but it is well thought thought-out. Jews were not considered persons under Hitler, nor were enslaved negroes in the ante-bellum United States. The rationale for such policies always revolves around some genetic or development criteria, such as the ability to reason (among many others).

"The pro-life position opposes abortion (1) because abortion violates the rights of a human being, who should all share natural rights equally, (2) because it is in the public interest (a) to protect people who want to live and (b) to promote an increase in the number of human minds (the ultimate economic resource), and (3) because abortion relies on inefficient and problematic proactive public policy (a) to implement and enforce it and (b) to determine which human beings have rights and when" (from page 11).

"John Cobin persuasively illustrates that the pro-life position is essentially liberal, from both economic and philosophical perspectives. The exposition is clear and simple and the many appendices make this work suitable for use in the classroom as well. Dr. Cobin was instrumental in refining my thinking on this subject and his book is highly recommended." —Dr. Joseph Fulda

Bible and Government: Public Policy from a Christian Perspective

	Introduction
1	Public Policy
2	Modern public policy in biblical perspective
3	Public policies in the Bible and history
4	Public policy in view of Romans 13:1-7 and I Peter 2:13-17
5	The Christian's response to public policy
6	Policy analysis: the Christian and the American public school
7	Concluding remarks

Paperback (256 pages), Dimensions (in inches): 8.30 x 0.70 x 6.40
Publisher: Alertness Books, Greenville, South Carolina
Online store: http://PolicyOfLiberty.net/checkout/products.php
ISBN 0-9725418-0-2 (paperback) or 0-9725418-1-0 (e-book / PDF)
$10.95 or $5.95 PDF—at www.PolicyOfLiberty.net & Amazon.com

¡Español! Spanish version available from Alertness Books online: *Biblia y Estado: Políticas Públicas desde una Perspectiva Cristiana (2005)* ISBN 0-9725418-5-3 (e-book / PDF). Paperback edition available from Instituto de Libre Empresa in Lima, Peru: www.ileperu.org.

Quotation from the book: "...the earthly institutions of God for the expansion of His kingdom must at least resemble God's ways and serve His cause. Government, which is eminently wayward, cannot fall into this category. Moreover, since there is no unclaimed 'territory' in the spiritual world, if a government is not in God's realm then it belongs to Satan's as a matter of simple logic."

Summary *Bible and Government: Public Policy from a Christian Perspective* is a provocative book that is sure to stimulate much conversation within the Evangelical community about this complex but vital issue. Policy pundits, university professors, and pastors have already given it favorable reviews. Should Christians Obey Government? The book offers a new perspective on how Christians should view the state and think about public policy. Public policies often entail annoying, costly, and even offensive impositions for Christians. Which public policies must be obeyed and which must be disobeyed? Is it immoral for Christians break the speed limit, hire an illegal alien, or not pay taxes? The book provides both interesting answers to such questions, utilizing a new paradigm for assessing Christian behavior in a pluralistic civil society. Public policy is examined using both economic analysis and biblical exegesis to challenge received statist orthodoxy among Evangelicalism, replacing it with a better understanding for how Christians should handle their relationship to civil government. It is a great companion volume to Dr. Cobin's book *Christian Theology of Public Policy: Highlighting the American Experience*.

This book provides an analysis of the Christian's relation to government and public policy. The task is undertaken by using both economic analysis and biblical exegesis that lead to both scientific or logical conclusions as well as advocacy ones. I should warn the reader in advance that this book does conforms to neither mainstream Evangelical thought about government nor theonomy. On the contrary, it challenges received statist orthodoxy and often revered cherished state institutions. During my doctoral studies in Public Policy, I realized the necessity to have a complete basis for understanding my field, i.e., a extension to my Christian world view to better deal with public policy. This first edition of this book in 1999 was the result of that quest. The revised edition (2003) reflects far greater thought and analysis. I believe it provides the necessary basis for both doing economics and public policy work as well as providing a fundamental understanding for Christians dealing with their relationship to civil government. At times the book is polemic and advocacy-oriented. At other times it is objective and scientific. At any rate, even if it is unlike my usual written work, the book serves its purpose well and I hope you will have an interest both in reading it and thinking more about this complex but vital issue.

Scholarly, popular, and pastoral praise for the book:

"John Cobin has found in the Bible what I have been uncovering for years of research: the vast majority of non-democratic states and their public policies have been evil and have had catastrophic implications for humanity. He shows, as I have shown, that anarchy (as bad as it may be) would have been preferable to most authoritarian or totalitarian governments. He comes to a similar conclusion to mine, viz. democratic freedom is a solution to war and democide."

—**Rudy J. Rummel, Ph.D.**, Political Science Professor (Emeritus), Univ. of Hawaii; author of *Death By Government* (1994) & *Power Kills* (1997).

"Dr. Cobin is effective in explaining what the Bible says about the relationship between Christians and government. I found his distinction between reactive and proactive policy responses to be especially useful. And his prescriptions for Christians with respect to public schools are thought-provoking. Christians who are serious about public policy should read this book."

—**D. Eric Schansberg, Ph.D.**, Professor of Economics, Indiana University (New Albany) School of Business; author of *Poor Policy: How Government Harms the Poor* (1996) and *Turn Neither to the Right Nor to the Left* (2004).

"Dr. Cobin provides a valuable paradigm for analyzing public policy and understanding the state from a stridently Calvinistic worldview. Thinking Reformed Christians will greatly profit from this book. Especially noteworthy are Dr. Cobin's scathingly accurate critique of the government school and his application of standard public policy principles and methods to real world circumstances."

—**Carl Robbins**, Senior Pastor, Woodruff Road Presbyterian Church, Simpsonville, South Carolina.

"Dr. Cobin has done a commendable job of fleshing out a theme that has been lacking in the Christian Community. He provides a valuable paradigm for biblically analyzing public policy and understanding the nature and role of civil government. It is a book that every serious Christian should read. I especially liked Dr. Cobin's dismantling of the notion of Christian involvement in the public school system."

  —Franklin López, Ph.D., Professor of Economics, University of New Orleans and Adjunct Professor at Tulane University.

"Dr. Cobin has done a thorough job of outlining and analyzing critical issues related to public policy and the Christian's relationship to government. Especially helpful is his four-fold grid in regard to evaluating public policy. His assessment of government's role is both historically unassailable and biblically accurate. The Americanized Christian will be challenged at many points with Cobin's penetrating insight and thought-provoking candor. The biblical exegete will be compelled to wrestle further with Rom. 13:1ff and 1 Pet. 2:13ff among other texts. Those committed to the government school system will have to evaluate their position further. This book is a must read for those who see the value of thinking through issues, and particularly for those who understand the Christian obligation to think about all things biblically. Regardless of one's conclusions at the end of the read, Dr. Cobin has provided a valuable work that we might be reformed and always reforming."

  —Dr. Paul J. Dean, Pastor/Teacher at Providence Baptist Church in Greer, SC; Adjunct Professor at various colleges and seminaries.

"We generally agree on policy outcomes. I was also interested by your [Dr. Cobin's] incorporation of the language of public choice in a biblical context."

  —Larry Pratt, President, <u>Gun Owners of America</u>, Springfield, Virginia.

"Any Christian wanting to understand more about how the Bible relates to economics, public policy, and society in general would do well to read The Bible and Government. This is not a run-of-the-mill study that simply baptizes right- or left-wing secular policy agendas. Dr. Cobin's work is thought-provoking and draws from recent, high-quality scholarship."

"[Dr. Cobin's] argument cannot be lightly dismissed. This is a meaty book by an astute and well-read author, not a cockeyed political harangue by some unqualified hack. At the very least, the book causes the reader to re-evaluate some basic assumptions about civil government. Why does it exist? Is civil government a biblical requirement? When does the government do more harm than good? What is our Christian duty toward the civil magistrate?"

  —Dr. Timothy Terrell, Associate Professor of Economics, Wofford College, Spartanburg, South Carolina.

"*Bible And Government: Public Policy From A Christian Perspective* by John M. Cobin (a devout Evangelical Christian, father of six homeschooled children, and Visiting Professor of Economics and Public Policy, [with Ph.D. from] George Mason University) is a sharply written, critical account of the expansion of American governmental power and the threatening implication said power has for Christians and the Christian community in particular. Professor Cobin offers noteworthy and insightful evaluations on public policies ranging from speed limits to food stamps, all with an eye to what Christianity demands in terms of obeying the government. Bible And Government is a thoughtful and thought-provoking read with ideas imminently worthy of serious consideration by students of Public Policy, Political Economy, and Christian Social Issues Studies."

—*Midwest Book Review* (Taylor's Bookshelf), March 2003

"Dr. Cobin's book examines the important moral question of the morality of a citizen's relationship to his government. There is a tradition of civil disobedience that goes back to Henry Thoreau, who refused to pay taxes because of his opposition to the Mexican war. On the other hand, respect for the law is thought to be a civic virtue. Where should we draw the line? *Bible and Government* addresses this question. This makes it a rare and welcomed book, because there are few books that confront this issue in depth. Though written from a Christian, and specifically a Bible, perspective, one need not be a practicing Christian to learn and benefit from the book. In the Bible, the prophet Samuel warned the Israelites about the dangers of getting a king, as they wanted. Cobin notes that, as prophesied, government plagues the people with "conscription, involuntary servitude, confiscation or conversion of property, and taxes." Cobin distinguishes between reactive policy, for public goods such as defense, and proactive policy aimed at changing behavior, such as restricting the consumption of alcohol or to redistribute wealth. The proactive welfare state, says Cobin, supplants the role of church and family, making the state an idol. Cobin examines the text in Romans which seems at first to say that we should be subject to the governing authorities, rendering taxes to whom they are due. He points out that Paul was not saying that the Roman government was good, since it was clearly awful. Nor do these passages imply that we must obey all laws. Cobin explains that this was just pragmatic, prudential advice. Cobin concludes that "it is not immoral to resist the evil practices of the government." As to general guidance, Cobin writes that "Christians may only obey government so long as it does not command them to break God's law or His principles." As to taxes, Cobin says that each taxing situation needs to be evaluated on its own merits. However, he also says that Christians should oppose property taxation. Personally, I regard my wage income as also my property, so I don't see why taxing my wage property is not as evil or even more evil than taxing my real estate. While much of the moral guidance in the book is somewhat general, Cobin does helpfully provide some tables and examples. For the policy types of reactive, proactive, and inefficient provision, Cobin provides guidelines for employment, receiving benefits, voluntary support, and using it. He provides a table with specific policies and a Christian's proper response for pragmatic submission, voluntary participation, disobedience, and reporting violators (no to the latter on all!). Wisely, Cobin says that there must be liberty of conscience and not a hard and fast rule. Bible and Government is a thoughtful book that will get Christians and others to examine the role of government and perhaps dispel a romantic view of government as generally benevolent. Cobin strikes a good balance between subjection to the state and unrealistic rejection of anything tainted with its evil. Those seeking moral guidance will do well to consult Bible and Government."

—**Fred Foldvary, Ph.D.**, Lecturer in Economics, University of Santa Clara, California.

Bible and Government: Public Policy from a Christian Perspective is written by a Christian public policy researcher. The author John Cobin essentially espouses a Jeffersonian libertarian political philosophy while adhering to biblical norms for proper social perspective. Recognizing the tyranny of good intentions and how public policy has gone awry, Cobin looks to alternatives to more state solutions for solving social problems. John Cobin who is presently an Investment Adviser has a Ph.D. in Public Policy from George Mason University and a Masters in Economics from UC Santa Barbara. Well-versed in the Austrian and Public Choice schools of economic thought, Cobin offers an exceptional Christian perspective on law, government, authority, and public policy considerations. He esteems the vitality of the free-market, private property and constitutionally limited government to civil society. In modern times, the state has tediously concentrated a vast array of power, welding and abusing the power flamboyantly. The state has increasingly displaced and marginalized the traditional non-state institutions of family, church, neighborhood, and voluntary civil associations. Too often, both neoconservatives and statist liberals make the mistake of confusing the state with society (just like the Greeks of antiquity did.) So, Cobin offers a new paradigm to the worn-out status quo which seems posed to evolve into some sort of totalitarian democracy. One of the most prudent public policy considerations often entails not having a "public policy" on particular issue to begin with. By devolving responsibility back to the traditional institutions that have been encroached upon by the State, better solutions to social problems may be mete out. In an age of belligerent statism when more government is always posed as the solution to the various societal ills, Cobin is one of the few prudent policy gurus keen enough to pose civil society and market solutions.

Building on the Prophet Samuel's warning to the Israelites who desired their king (1 Sam. 8), Cobin methodically trumps notions of ascribing divinity to the State or seeing all State actions as inherently moral. The Scriptures warn of the consequences of unbridled power in the State, and how the power of the State itself can be an idol. For this reason, Christians should resist the concentration of power in the hands of the State. The predominantly Christian founding fathers of America desired to constrain governmental power by constitutional limitations, such as a separation of powers and checks and balances. Thus, in framing free government they sought to make "ambition counter ambition" with institutional checks and balances. Being an agent of the government never made a man saint always possessed of goodwill or free from the blemish of sin. Likewise, there is no sovereign immunity before the divine judgment throne and magistrates will be held accountable. Moreover, some of the most malevolent campaigns of mass-murder in history came as a result of the reckless concentration of power in the hands of the State. One need only peer into 1 Samuel 8 to see the prophetic warning about unfettered political power in the form of an absolute monarch. Cobin reminds the reader about the perils of rent-seeking which characterizes modern democracies. Frederic Bastiat proclaimed, "the state is the great fiction by which everybody seeks to live at the expense of everybody else." Echoing the wisdom of Bastiat, Cobin makes it clear that free government cannot endure when the law is subverted into an instrument of legal plunder, rent-seeking and spoliation. The practice of utilizing the instrumentality of the State to appropriate the wealth and property of others is immoral, un-Christian, but this has fast become the norm in the United States. In contrast to the prevailing statist philosophies of governance, Cobin advocates a minarchist philosophy of government, or the so called night watchmen state. The night watchmen state simply exists to prosecute and stifle acts of force and fraud, defend the populace, enforce contracts while upholding property rights. In sum, the government that governs the best governs the least. After securing independence from the British, America had such a form of government arguably for quite a few decades and for the most part it was minimally intrusive in the lives of Americans.

Cobin expresses discontent with public education and his concerns are just. Public education really is worldview indoctrination and usually in an amoral, relativistic environment. He recommends that alternative ventures should be pursued by Christians such as home-schooling, tutors, or private schools.

John Cobin also confronts gritty ethical questions about the Christian's duty to the state. He squarely challenges notions that the Apostle Paul gave credence to the notion of unlimited submission to the state. He makes it clear that Christians are to resist immoral edicts of the state. No Christian in good conscience could partake in the administration of concentration camps and be a party to mass-murder. Likewise, no Christian could rationalize seeking out or performing an abortion (i.e. infanticide.) Christians cannot support entrapment tactics of law enforcement to tempt someone into committing a crime in order to blackmail or prosecute them. There is no sanctifying mechanism in the eyes of God that sanctifies murder, thievery, lying and extortion merely because its perpetrators are agents of the state. There are eternal repercussions for such an abuse of power.

With regards to authority, we are to "be subject" as a matter of practical wisdom cognizant that governmental authorities are from God and ultimately under his sovereign control. Too often, Christians are erroneously led to believe that the State has some Hobbesian mandate with unfettered power or a divine right of kings. Consequently all of the state's actions are to be heeded without reservation. The early Christians who took refuge in the catacombs of Rome and elsewhere faced immense persecution from the State, and would not submit to Nero. Some Christian pastors purport a fanciful notion that the Bible demands virtually blind submission to the State and acquiescence in all of its wars. As Charles Eliot Norton surmised, "The voice of protest, of warning, of appeal is never more needed than when the clamor of fife and drum, echoed by the press and too often by the pulpit, is bidding all men fall in and keep step and obey in silence the tyrannous word of command. Then, more than ever, it is the duty of the good citizen not to be silent." Cobin reminds the reader that Anyway, Cobin does a good job at clearing the air about the Christian's relationship to the State and ethical considerations of obedience. He itinerates a theme similar to that of Dietrich Bonhoeffer, in his book Ethics.

All things considered, John Cobin has sketched together an astonishing, deeply reflective and succinct book, which should prove helpful to Christians. He offers a clever and resourceful methodology for evaluating public policy in light of Scripture. Whether in envisioning ideal public policy formulations or ascertaining the individual's relation to the State, John Cobin has put together a sensible look at public policy from a Christian perspective.

—**Ryan Setliff** (Danville, Virginia), Amazon.com "Top 500 Reviewer"

"In a clear and assessable style, Dr. Cobin elucidates on the proper G-d based origin of human rights and by doing so sheds light on the proper relationship between the Christian and the State."

—**Chuck Morse**, author and host of Boston's *Conservative Voice of Reason* (Salem Radio WROL AM 950).

Here is a succinct review of *Bible and Government: Public Policy from a Christian Perspective* by Dr. John Cobin (Ph.D. Public Policy, M.A. Economics, George Mason University). Dr. Cobin provides us a primer on the discipline of public policy and its terminology. Do you know what the terms "proactive policy", "reactive policy", "negative rights", "positive rights", "government" and "state" mean? Agree with the book or not, it's a valuable tool that defines these terms that are thrown around in newscasts, political speeches and general conversation.

If for no other reason, one should have the book to learn terminology. One of the definitions of terms that I found instructive was "anarchy" which is usually thought of as a synonym for "chaos"—not so! When speaking in technical terms, anarchy simply means, "no state". What may or may not happen in that situation is not necessarily "chaos". In fact, history evinces the fact that the state, rather than its absence, has been the greatest creator of chaos. Indeed, foggy thinking and imprecision is rife amongst Evangelicals and the general citizenry today, leading to a chaotic morass of inconsistent thought.

Every so often a book like this comes along that at the very least, if it doesn't win one over, it should cause one to reevaluate his current position. If one were to hear the term Divine Right of Kings, perhaps he would associate it with proclamations of kings or churchmen of long ago—King James for example. He was actually an apologist for that doctrine. His son, Charles I of England used this doctrine in his defense against the charges of Parliament. This doctrine said that because the King was put on the throne by God. He was to be obeyed in all matters just as the oracles of God.

Dr. Cobin discusses what he calls the "revitalized" or "reshaped" divine right doctrine of today and its influence on modern society and the church. Because there are differing views on this subject, this work has value in that it divides up the four different views that Christians espouse concerning public policy and the Christian's relationship to the state. Dr. Cobin divides them into two schools:

1.) *The Integrated authority school*: espoused by Reconstructionists (sometimes known as Theonmoists) and those he calls divine righters ("revitalized").

2.) *The Competing Kingdom school*, which is espoused by Anabaptists and their pacifistic view as well as a view called (and adopted by Dr. Cobin) the "Liberty of Conscience".

Dr. Cobin is confessional (1689 London Baptist) when it comes to the use of biblical law, however he rejects the Reconstructionist view that government can be reformed to a point where it is consistently good. In fact he says that government is inherently evil. It may be restrained for a time, but it lies in the power of the Evil One who is under God's control of course.

He is not without an argument for making this claim and proves his case. For instance, Dr. Cobin is not surprised by the emergence of wayward state leaders since he *expects* nothing different from the state as it is part of the kingdom of Satan. The shameful behavior of political agents merely confirms his view. God said that He empowers the "basest" of men to rule (Daniel 4:17) and that the "throne of iniquity...devises evil by law" (Psalm 94:20). Scripture indicates that the kings of the earth have been (and will be) arrayed against the Lord and His Christ (Psalm 2:2, Revelation 19:19). Revelation 13:1-7 is also important for Dr. Cobin in that it indicates something about what he deems to be the state's nexus with Satan.

It soon becomes obvious that he would seem to come in conflict with what are the almost exclusively favored classical passages for a Christian paradigm of government: Romans 13:1-7 and 1 Peter 2:13-17.

Strange as it seems, to most citizens of the United States today, when we look at history and in the Bible itself we see that government has very seldom been a boon or a blessing to those under its control. In fact, throughout history states have been responsible for the death, destruction and misery of multitudes in the vast majority of cases. (For support, Dr. Cobin refers the work of Professor Rudolph J. Rummel in his 1997 book *Death by Government*, Transaction Publishers: Somerset, NJ.) The Bible itself gives account after account of horrifying situations brought on by states.

This seems to fly in the face of the Apostles in the above references. A question we must then ask here is "Are these texts the definitive references for a Christian view of public policy?" Dr. Cobin demonstrates that there are other passages that we must consider throughout Scripture. (Perhaps Romans 13:1-7 is not an unequivocal statement that should be utilized as a princely text in isolation.) He also points out that Paul, in particular uses two different Greek words for evil in Romans 12 and 13: one that can be identified as "evil" (as God views it) and the other one is a more general term, possibly being as benign as something unpleasant or a misdeed. This, he says, is significant.

In short, Dr. Cobin is saying that the apostles are giving practical wisdom in commanding submission to the state. At that particular time, the Roman state could be dangerous to Christians if it perceived them to be a threat, factious, or even outright rebels—just as it had judged the Jews of that time period to be. Christians were closely identified with the Jews; many Christians being of Jewish stock themselves. The apostles gave the Christians practical advice for how to seek a quiet and peaceful existence under a wicked state that puts its *own* definition (rather than God's) on what is an "evildoer" and who should be rewarded for "doing good".

One of the problems with a book like *Bible and Government* is that readers and reviewers alike will make assumptions as to what a statement or argument the author makes would likely lead to. Accordingly, Dr. Cobin is careful to caution his readers by way of qualifying some bold statements that could embolden one with, shall we say a short fuse, to jump to conclusions or foolish actions.

Dr. Cobin recently came under fire for a statement he made at a local public meeting where the press was present. He said words to the effect that the Second Amendment is for the citizen's protection against a hostile government and that if a government agent broke into your house, you have the right to shoot him. Part of submission to the civil government for Americans is to obey the Constitution, the highest law of the land and the corollary to the idea of "ruler" or "governing authorities" as used by the Apostles. Yet the local paper absurdly reported that Dr. Cobin advocated cavalierly shooting government agents. And careless readers too will jump to errant conclusions.

This book reminds me of excavation. It's like walking through some old overgrown field or woods and finding an old foundation or a tool, or what's left of an old barn and you say, "Hey! People used to live and work here and use this old tool. What happened?" But when you read Dr. Cobin's book you will say, "Hey! People used to think and act this way? What happened?"

Some of the key benefits of this work are that it challenges commonly help presuppositions about the nature of the state, whether or not the state is transformable under the "dominion mandate", and how far Christians should be bound by public policies. Or even how far they should expect the state to morally benefit society.

Our forefathers had to deal with state problems head on. Some resisted the state and others let it roll over them. Who was right? Others resisted the state and it rolled over them anyway. Dr. Cobin's work adds the public policy aspect missing in the otherwise excellent historical work of Dr. Mark Noll's *Christians and the American Revolution*.

Dr. Cobin gives practical answers to questions like, "Should Christians resist government? When?" "How should we deal with taxes?" "What about the Welfare state?" "Should Christians participate in the public (government) school?" "Were the thirteen Colonies right when they rebelled against the Crown?" Should the United States be involved in "empire" or "country rebuilding"? "How about the Confederates in the secession of the South: were their actions warranted?"

These and other issues (historical and contemporary) are right in front of us today. Dr. Cobin's work is a remedy for—and a challenge to—the anemic public policy teaching put out by so many Christian teachers of our time. Some day I would like to hear some repartee between Dr. Cobin and some of the advocates of The Christian Reconstruction School. I would put the question, "Of what use is the Moral Law in society today?" to both of them. Knowing that there is mutual admiration and agreement between Dr. Cobin and some Theonomists (Reconstructionists) I dare say that much clarity would be brought forth. Dr. Cobin has a web site that invites comment, and the book can be purchased there: http://www.Policyofliberty.net.

    —**Gregg J. Farrier**, Christian activist, homeschooling veteran of 20 years, founding member of the Creation Study Group (Greenville, SC), special contributor to *The Times Examiner*, and occasional radio talk show co-host.

Alertness Books
▽▲▽

Christian Life and Public Policy Series

Bible and Government: Public Policy from a Christian Perspective—
$10.95 paperback (2003)
by John M. Cobin, Ph.D.

Turn Neither to the Right Nor to the Left: A Thinking Christian's Guide to Politics & Public Policy—$20.00 paperback (2003)
by D. Eric Schansberg, Ph.D.

Worldviews: Christian Theism versus Modern Materialism—$5.95
PDF e-book (2005)
by Steven Yates, Ph.D.

Christian Theology of Public Policy: Highlighting the American Experience—$34.95 hardcover (2006)
by John M. Cobin, Ph.D.

The Declaration of Independence

IN CONGRESS, July 4, 1776.

The unanimous Declaration of the thirteen united States of America,

When in the Course of human events, it becomes necessary for one people to dissolve the political bands which have connected them with another, and to assume among the powers of the earth, the separate and equal station to which the Laws of Nature and of Nature's God entitle them, a decent respect to the opinions of mankind requires that they should declare the causes which impel them to the separation.

We hold these truths to be self-evident, that all men are created equal, that they are endowed by their Creator with certain unalienable Rights, that among these are Life, Liberty and the pursuit of Happiness.—That to secure these rights, Governments are instituted among Men, deriving their just powers from the consent of the governed,—That whenever any Form of Government becomes destructive of these ends, it is the Right of the People to alter or to abolish it, and to institute new Government, laying its foundation on such principles and organizing its powers in such form, as to them shall seem most likely to effect their Safety and Happiness. Prudence, indeed, will dictate that Governments long established should not be changed for light and transient causes; and accordingly all experience hath shewn, that mankind are more disposed to suffer, while evils are sufferable, than to right themselves by abolishing the forms to which they are accustomed. But when a long train of abuses and usurpations, pursuing invariably the same Object evinces a design to reduce them under absolute Despotism, it is their right, it is their duty, to throw off such Government, and to provide new Guards for their future security. —Such has been the patient sufferance of these Colonies; and such is now the necessity which constrains them to alter their former Systems of Government. The history of the present King of Great Britain is a history of repeated injuries and usurpations, all having in direct object the establishment of an absolute Tyranny over these States. To prove this, let Facts be submitted to a candid world.

He has refused his Assent to Laws, the most wholesome and necessary for the public good.

He has forbidden his Governors to pass Laws of immediate and pressing importance, unless suspended in their operation till his Assent should be obtained; and when so suspended, he has utterly neglected to attend to them.

He has refused to pass other Laws for the accommodation of large districts of people, unless those people would relinquish the right of Representation in the Legislature, a right inestimable to them and formidable to tyrants only.

He has called together legislative bodies at places unusual, uncomfortable, and distant from the depository of their public Records, for the sole purpose of fatiguing them into compliance with his measures.

He has dissolved Representative Houses repeatedly, for opposing with manly firmness his invasions on the rights of the people.

He has refused for a long time, after such dissolutions, to cause others to be elected; whereby the Legislative powers, incapable of Annihilation, have returned to the People at large for their exercise; the State remaining in the mean time exposed to all the dangers of invasion from without, and convulsions within.

He has endeavoured to prevent the population of these States; for that purpose obstructing the Laws for Naturalization of Foreigners; refusing to pass others to encourage their migrations hither, and raising the conditions of new Appropriations of Lands.

He has obstructed the Administration of Justice, by refusing his Assent to Laws for establishing Judiciary powers.

He has made Judges dependent on his Will alone, for the tenure of their offices, and the amount and payment of their salaries.

He has erected a multitude of New Offices, and sent hither swarms of Officers to harrass our people, and eat out their substance.

He has kept among us, in times of peace, Standing Armies without the Consent of our legislatures. He has affected to render the Military independent of and superior to the Civil power.

He has combined with others to subject us to a jurisdiction foreign to our constitution, and unacknowledged by our laws; giving his Assent to their Acts of pretended Legislation:

For Quartering large bodies of armed troops among us:

For protecting them, by a mock Trial, from punishment for any Murders which they should commit on the Inhabitants of these States:

For cutting off our Trade with all parts of the world:

For imposing Taxes on us without our Consent:

For depriving us in many cases, of the benefits of Trial by Jury:

For transporting us beyond Seas to be tried for pretended offences

For abolishing the free System of English Laws in a neighbouring Province, establishing therein an Arbitrary government, and enlarging its Boundaries so as to render it at once an example and fit instrument for introducing the same absolute rule into these Colonies:

For taking away our Charters, abolishing our most valuable Laws, and altering fundamentally the Forms of our Governments:

For suspending our own Legislatures, and declaring themselves invested with power to legislate for us in all cases whatsoever.

He has abdicated Government here, by declaring us out of his Protection and waging War against us. He has plundered our seas, ravaged our Coasts, burnt our towns, and destroyed the lives of our people.

He is at this time transporting large Armies of foreign Mercenaries to compleat the works of death, desolation and tyranny, already begun with circumstances of Cruelty & perfidy scarcely paralleled in the most barbarous ages, and totally unworthy the Head of a civilized nation.

He has constrained our fellow Citizens taken Captive on the high Seas to bear Arms against their Country, to become the executioners of their friends and Brethren, or to fall themselves by their Hands.

He has excited domestic insurrections amongst us, and has endeavoured to bring on the inhabitants of our frontiers, the merciless Indian Savages, whose known rule of warfare, is an undistinguished destruction of all ages, sexes and conditions.

In every stage of these Oppressions We have Petitioned for Redress in the most humble terms: Our repeated Petitions have been answered only by repeated injury. A Prince whose character is thus marked by every act which may define a Tyrant, is unfit to be the ruler of a free people.

Nor have We been wanting in attentions to our Brittish brethren. We have warned them from time to time of attempts by their legislature to extend an unwarrantable jurisdiction over us. We have reminded them of the circumstances of our emigration and settlement here. We have appealed to their native justice and magnanimity, and we have conjured them by the ties of our common kindred to disavow these usurpations, which, would inevitably interrupt our connections and correspondence. They too have been deaf to the voice of justice and of consanguinity. We must, therefore, acquiesce in the necessity, which denounces our Separation, and hold them, as we hold the rest of mankind, Enemies in War, in Peace Friends.

We, therefore, the Representatives of the united States of America, in General Congress, Assembled, appealing to the Supreme Judge of the world for the rectitude of our intentions, do, in the Name, and by Authority of the good People of these Colonies, solemnly publish and declare, That these United Colonies are, and of Right ought to be Free and Independent States; that they are Absolved from all Allegiance to the British Crown, and that all political connection between them and the State of Great Britain, is and ought to be totally dissolved; and that as Free and Independent States, they have full Power to levy War, conclude Peace, contract Alliances, establish Commerce, and to do all other Acts and Things which Independent States may of right do. And for the support of this Declaration, with a firm reliance on the protection of divine Providence, we mutually pledge to each other our Lives, our Fortunes and our sacred Honor.

Georgia:
Button Gwinnett
Lyman Hall
George Walton

North Carolina:
William Hooper
Joseph Hewes
John Penn
South Carolina:
Edward Rutledge
Thomas Heyward, Jr.
Thomas Lynch, Jr.
Arthur Middleton

Massachusetts:
John Hancock
Maryland:
Samuel Chase
Thomas Stone
Charles Carroll of
Carrollton
Virginia:
George Wythe
Richard Henry Lee
Thomas Jefferson
Benjamin Harrison
Thomas Nelson, Jr.
Francis Lightfoot Lee
Carter Braxton

Pennsylvania:
Robert Morris
Benjamin Rush
Benjamin Franklin
John Morton
George Clymer
James Smith
George Taylor
James Wilson
George Ross
Delaware:
Caesar Rodney
George Read
Thomas McKean

New York:
William Floyd
Philip Livingston
Francis Lewis
Lewis Morris
New Jersey:
Richard Stockton
John Witherspoon
Francis Hopkinson
John Hart
Abraham Clark

New Hampshire:
Josiah Bartlett
William Whipple
Massachusetts:
Samuel Adams
John Adams
Robert Treat Paine
Elbridge Gerry
Rhode Island:
Stephen Hopkins
William Ellery
Connecticut:
Roger Sherman
Samuel Huntington
William Williams
Oliver Wolcott
New Hampshire:
Matthew Thornton

The Bill of Rights

The first ten Amendments to the Constitution, ratified December 15, 1791.

Amendment I

Congress shall make no law respecting an establishment of religion, or prohibiting the free exercise thereof; or abridging the freedom of speech, or of the press; or the right of the people peaceably to assemble, and to petition the Government for a redress of grievances.

Amendment II

A well regulated Militia, being necessary to the security of a free State, the right of the people to keep and bear Arms, shall not be infringed.

Amendment III

No Soldier shall, in time of peace be quartered in any house, without the consent of the Owner, nor in time of war, but in a manner to be prescribed by law.

Amendment IV

The right of the people to be secure in their persons, houses, papers, and effects, against unreasonable searches and seizures, shall not be violated, and no Warrants shall issue, but upon probable cause, supported by Oath or affirmation, and particularly describing the place to be searched, and the persons or things to be seized.

Amendment V

No person shall be held to answer for a capital, or otherwise infamous crime, unless on a presentment or indictment of a Grand Jury, except in cases arising in the land or naval forces, or in the Militia, when in actual service in time of War or public danger; nor shall any person be subject for the same offence to be twice put in jeopardy of life or limb; nor shall be compelled in any criminal case to be a witness against himself, nor be deprived of life, liberty, or property, without due process of law; nor shall private property be taken for public use, without just compensation.

Amendment VI

In all criminal prosecutions, the accused shall enjoy the right to a speedy and public trial, by an impartial jury of the State and district wherein the crime shall have been committed, which district shall have been previously ascertained by law, and to be informed of the nature and cause of the accusation; to be confronted with the witnesses against him; to have compulsory process for obtaining witnesses in his favor, and to have the Assistance of Counsel for his defence.

Amendment VII

In Suits at common law, where the value in controversy shall exceed twenty dollars, the right of trial by jury shall be preserved, and no fact tried by a jury, shall be otherwise re-examined in any Court of the United States, than according to the rules of the common law.

Amendment VIII

Excessive bail shall not be required, nor excessive fines imposed, nor cruel and unusual punishments inflicted.

Amendment IX

The enumeration in the Constitution, of certain rights, shall not be construed to deny or disparage others retained by the people.

Amendment X

The powers not delegated to the United States by the Constitution, nor prohibited by it to the States, are reserved to the States respectively, or to the people.

Quick Order Form

📠 **Fax orders:** 413-622-9441. Send a copy of this form.

☎ **Phone orders** (credit card): 866-492-2137 toll-free or 864-505-1386.

🖥 **Online orders:** visit http://www.policyofliberty.net (Alertness Books)

✉ **Email orders:** alertness@policyofliberty.net

📬 **Postal orders:** Alertness Books, P.O. Box 25686, Greenville, SC 29616, U.S.A., telephone 866-492-2137. Send a copy of this form.

I understand that I may return any printed books in resalable condition for a full refund, excluding shipping costs—for any reason, no questions asked.

Please send me:

Quantity

☐ *Christian Theology of Public Policy* (Hardback $34.95 each) ISBN 0-9729754-9-7 _____

☐ *Bible and Government* (Paperback $10.95 each) ISBN 0-9725418-0-2 _____

☐ *Biblia y Gobierno* (PDF $5.95 each) ISBN 0-9725418-1-0 _____

☐ *A Primer on Modern Themes* (PDF $7.95 each) ISBN 0-9725418-2-9 _____

☐ *Ensayos Sobre Temas Modernos* (PDF $7.95 each) ISBN 0-9725418-3-7 _____

☐ *Building Regulation, Market... Allodial* (PDF $5.95 each) ISBN 0-9725418-4-5 _____

Please send more FREE information on:

☐Other Books ☐Speaking/Seminars ☐Consulting on living in Chile
☐Financial Planning ☐Asset Protection ☐Investments & Insurance

Name: _____

Address: _____

City: _____State: _____Zip: _____

Telephone: ( ) _____

Email address: _____

> ➤ **Sales tax:** Add 5% for shipments to South Carolina.
> ➤ **Quantity discount:** 25% on orders of 10 or more identical books or 5 or more e-books (diskettes).
> ➤ **Shipping** (1) **America:** $5.00 for first book or CD, $3.00 for each additional. (2) **International:** US$11.00 for the first book or CD and $4.00 for each additional one (estimate).

Payment: ☐ Check (payable to "Alertness Ltd") ☐ Credit Card:
☐ Visa ☐ MasterCard ☐ Amex ☐ Discover

Card Number: _____

Name on card: _____ Exp. Date: _____